Andrew Grantham

Sustainable Business Strategy

Andrew Grantham

Sustainable Business Strategy

Analysis, Choice and Implementation

DE GRUYTER

ISBN 978-3-11-071818-8
e-ISBN (PDF) 978-3-11-071843-0
e-ISBN (EPUB) 978-3-11-071853-9

Library of Congress Control Number: 2021952253

Bibliographic information published by the Deutsche Nationalbibliothek
The Deutsche Nationalbibliothek lists this publication in the Deutsche Nationalbibliografie;
detailed bibliographic data are available on the Internet at http://dnb.dnb.de.

© 2022 Walter de Gruyter GmbH, Berlin/Boston
Cover image: Photograph by Wai Choi Wong
Typesetting: Integra Software Services Pvt. Ltd.
Printing and binding: CPI books GmbH, Leck

www.degruyter.com

Advance Praise for *Sustainable Business Strategy*

This book that rethinks strategy for challenges of sustainability and responsible business in the 21st century is very important and desperately needed. We have to develop business strategies that truly create value for society. This book does this job very well and therefore it is a must-read for responsible business managers, but indeed also for business students and future leaders of global companies, firms and corporations.

–Professor Jacob Dahl Rendtorff, Roskilde University, Denmark

This is a very timely and relevant contribution to the wider debate on the role of strategy to business organisations. Its positioning and niche are well thought-through and clearly articulated. A textbook of this sort would be of great value in its intended market(s). The sustainability angle is a clear selling point.

–Professor Stephen Flowers, Emeritus Professor of Kent Business School, University of Kent, UK

The main strength of this book is exactly this pluralistic perspective that provides different ways of resolving business strategy dilemmas vis-à-vis challenges such as climate change, global economic sustainability and pandemics. In this sense the book is timely and will help students of business and management to develop their holistic approaches to change in the 21st century.

–Professor Theo Papaioannou, Open University, UK

https://doi.org/10.1515/9783110718430-202

To Ilonka, my partner, soulmate and wife

Acknowledgements

Thank you to my readers, Dr Jenny Knight, Rosie Mulgrue and Emma Shukie; and to my reviewers whose feedback enabled the development of the book and the core ideas. I am grateful to Dr Erika Wong for designing the cover and Wai Choi Wong, whose magical photograph of the Yellow Mountain, China, adorns it. Thank you to librarians everywhere – but particularly at my institution, the University of Brighton – for "effortlessly" managing the essential knowledge resource. As a lecturer and researcher, I have privileged access to libraries and librarians globally. I am also indebted to colleagues at the Centre for Research in Innovation Management (CENTRIM) with whom I have worked on diverse and applied projects. Also, to Professor Lew Perren and Graham Clifford who helped me transition from researcher to teacher. Thanks also to Lee Humphries of Printed Matter Bookshop, who recommended and sourced many books for me through waves of the pandemic, and delivered them to my door in person! He is a member of a band of independent booksellers that keep value local and diffuse knowledge globally.

https://doi.org/10.1515/9783110718430-203

Contents

Chapter 1
Strategy, context and history

The opportunity to teach strategy in a dynamic business school is one of life's great privileges. The subject draws on all of the disciplines of business management, primarily economics, finance, marketing, human resource management and law. It captures aspects of the humanities through business and social history, culture and language. It draws on the creative arts through design, visualization, problem-solving and even architecture. It is creative, playful as well as analytical. These are the foundations of transformation, and these are times of rapid and urgent transformation. Strategy enables everyone, from all disciplines, to apply their skills, ideas and enthusiasm to bring about change in the way businesses and economies work. Change that is sustainable. Change that enables firms to operate within planetary boundaries. Change that works for all global stakeholders.

Learning the craft of strategy is challenging. It is grounded in practice. Textbooks have an important role in bridging theory and practice; they fuse them together through case studies and exercises derived from research and the experience of practitioners. An exemplar of this with regard to understanding business and the environment, by which he means "nonmarket factors", is Baron (2013). The process of teaching and learning is best expressed as the co-production of knowledge. Student projects generate new knowledge for teachers and students alike. There is a wide demographic and background and these are reflected in findings from student work. In seminars we co-reveal what we know about challenges and opportunities, solutions and the mechanics of the tools of strategy. The process of revealing ideally becomes normalized through these interactions. This is why we still share space in lecture halls and seminar rooms, invite guest speakers, and not just put everything online. We learn together.

This is particularly true and necessary in the context of climate change where the teachers, authors and publishers are complicit in the reproduction and reinforcement of harmful economic activities. Students of strategy are not well served by this. The planet is finite and to continue to teach strategy as though it is infinite in its bounty is at best irresponsible. Students and practitioners need space to explore alternatives to traditional growth and managerialism, two of the driving forces of modern strategic analysis, choice and implementation.

Some of the tools of strategy are premised on the assumption that the environment in which businesses operate and strategists inhabit, can be controlled. This premise is open for debate and to be tested empirically in firms or in the business laboratory. The forces of nature are not controllable, and the more carbon that humanity puts into the atmosphere, the more is that uncontrollability observable, observed and experienced. Business managers can deploy resources to mitigate climate change and to adapt their companies to what is currently known about impacts. In

https://doi.org/10.1515/9783110718430-001

combination, mitigation and adaptation may mean changes to products, the creation of new market opportunities, and changes to the way products are designed, manufactured, distributed, re-used and disposed of. What is known is that the climate is changing whether humanity meets so-called net-zero by 2050, or not. There is no business-as-usual. It is time for clean technologies to be deployed. That is exciting, surely?

What is strategy?

So, what do we understand by strategy? The meaning of strategy in this text is different to that of most available texts. That is the reason for writing it. A working definition and composite definition, drawing on the work of Michael Porter (1980), Henry Mintzberg et al. (2009), Alfred Chandler (1962), Henry Mintzberg and James A. Waters (1985) suggests that:

> strategy is something to do with setting and meeting organizational goals, courses of action (long- medium- and short-term), and the allocation of sufficient and correctly configured resources appropriate for those courses of action. There is usually some element of competition involved, and winning is about offerings being different and creating value. It is always about change and the tools of change derived from analysis, choice and implementation. It can be prescribed and deliberate composed by those in positions of power, or it can emerge from below, rise to the top, gain legitimacy and diffuse as though it was deliberate.

This question of emergent and deliberate refers to a distinction made by Mintzberg and Waters (1985). Deliberate is intended, often directed from above and conforms to a formal plan leading to a realized strategy (achieved as intended) or unrealized (if not successfully implemented as intended). To be realized does not mean that the strategy is successful in its consequences, only in its execution. Emergent strategy, by contrast, results from a combination of actions from people usually not in executive positions, but often with a deep operational knowledge within firms. Over time, these actions cohere as "a pattern in a stream of decisions". They find currency and advocates such that they become strategies in their own right. They are realized despite the absence of intention. This definition will be revisited at the end of the journey in Chapter 14.

Strategy is about change. That change should ultimately have the purpose of making the future better. What is generally taught in strategy modules does not lead to a better world. Rutger Bregman (2020), in his optimistic book, *Humankind*, hints at why this might be:

> Robert Frank wondered how viewing humans as ultimately egotistical might affect his students. He gave them a range of assignments designed to gauge their generosity. The outcome? The longer they'd studied economics, the more selfish they'd become. "We become what we teach", he concluded. (p. 17)

Strategy in the context of climate change

In strategy the macro context is very important to understand. In Chapter 2 the tools of macro analysis are introduced, discussed and applied. Traditionally, the macro environment is analyzed based on assumptions about the way in which the world economy functions. The economy is global, complex and inter-connected. Good business strategy decisions rely on strategists having a keen understanding of this complexity and embracing it. The complexity is what makes it interesting. Strategists are generalists; consequently, the tools of strategy and evaluation require users to be well read. An understanding of economics and business history is important, not just historic data being projected into the future.

Arguably, if businesses are to deal with climate change, it is important to know its origins and the realization that it did not need to be so. Andreas Malm, in his book *Fossil Capital* (2016), shows how humanity can often take directions – so-called trajectories – that do not embrace the best technologies, but rather serve the interests of powerful minorities. Strategists need to read history. In the case of energy, water was a far more efficient means of generating motive power than coal. Steam engines, using coal as fuel, served capital against labour in the Industrial Revolution. However, it did not need to be so. The same is true of climate change. The carbon economy is not inevitable. It is a political choice.

Regarding climate change, business strategists may need to think in terms of worst cases. Wallace-Wells (2019) is a good source for this. He presents a series of climate change scenarios and their impacts, including extreme weather, drought, sea-level rises, wildfires, mass extinctions, disease, and migration. His scenarios cover temperature rises of between 1.5 degrees Celsius and 6 degrees Celsius. Even at 1.5 degrees Celsius, it will be necessary to adapt. The BBC's *Climate Change – The facts* (Davies 2017) translated the narrative for prime-time UK TV audiences, fronted by David Attenborough. Versions of this programme have been shown in many countries. Berners-Lee (2019) provides an alternative handbook-style source for the scenarios.

Bruno Latour, in his book *Down to Earth: Politics in the new climatic regime* (2018), presents some hard truths, primary among which is the emergence of a post-truth. In a post-truth world, reason and evidence-based policy-making are in retreat. In the context of climate change, the scientific evidence that might once have brought about major shifts in policy is systematically undermined and the scientists behind it, discredited. For example, in 2009 the email server at the Climatic Research Unit of the University of East Anglia was hacked. The release of personal emails that suggested the scientists were misreporting their findings were exploited by prominent climate sceptics. This contributed to the failure of the United Nations' Conference of the Parties (COP15) in Copenhagen that year. The case is popularly known as Climategate (BBC 2019). There was no misrepresentation of data. It was wilful climate-change misinformation.

By contrast, a hole in the ozone layer was discovered in 1985; it is now under repair after scientists identified the cause – chlorofluorocarbons (CFCs) – and governments acted, globally, initially by agreeing a binding international treaty (UNEP 1987). One of those scientists, Joe Farman, has been profiled on the Open University (OU)/British Broadcasting Corporation (BBC) radio series, *Green Originals* (BBC 2020).

More recently, humanity has witnessed the possibility of significant change in the rapid response to the Covid-19 pandemic. Particularly with respect to vaccine development and diffusion. The state has re-emerged as a significant economic actor, contrary to what is frequently argued, that major change is unaffordable. There is now an opportunity for climate entrepreneurs to re-image the world economy into one that is sustainable. Where nature is part of the investment calculus, not because to do so is a good thing, but rather because without nature, there is no economy. Nature has its limits.

That is why government treasuries rather than environment ministries are commissioning reports on the value of biodiversity. The preface to the 600-page UK Treasury's biodiversity report is clear about why national treasuries need to incorporate nature (Dasgupta 2021):

> Biodiversity is the diversity of life. We will find that the economics of biodiversity is the economics of the entire biosphere. So, when developing the subject, we will keep in mind that we are embedded in Nature. The Review shows (Chapter 4) that although the difference in conception is analytically slight, it has profound implications for what we can legitimately expect of the human enterprise. The former viewpoint encourages the thought that human ingenuity, when it is directed at advancing the common good, can raise global output indefinitely without affecting the biosphere so adversely that it is tipped into a state far-removed from where it has been since long before human societies began to form; the latter is an expression of the thought that because the biosphere is bounded, the global economy is bounded.   (p. 4)

Kate Raworth in her book *Doughnut Economics* (2017) made the case for incorporating climate change into all business strategy. Raworth is an economist who has worked extensively in the third sector, in particular for Oxfam. The doughnut (Figure 1.1) maps out nine planetary boundaries that economies need to stay within. The causes of planetary boundary violations – social foundations – need to be addressed by all economic stakeholders. These are macro-level factors.

Where citizens of countries lack those social foundations, the boundaries are likely to come under pressure. Forests are felled where key societal prerequisites are absent, for example, education, political voice and income and work. Researchers at the University of Leeds in the UK (O'Neill et al. 2018) have taken Raworth's model and generated a tool to compare countries with one another, both rich and poor. The doughnut has also now been adapted and adopted by the City of Amsterdam in its recovery from Covid-19 (Boffey 2020).

Business management and strategy are relevant when firms look to address these prerequisites. All firms use energy, have employees who need housing and should be able to express opinions without fear and be represented by a trade union;

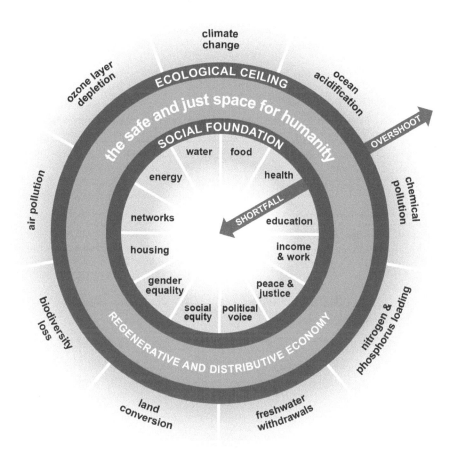

Figure 1.1: The doughnut of social and planetary boundaries.
Source: Doughnut Economics Action Lab (DEAL 2021).

employees also should be remunerated fairly and work in an environment that does not damage their health. Raworth has expectations of firms with respect to their products. The dominant business model is what Raworth calls the *caterpillar economy of degenerative industrial design*. The caterpillar economy is linear: Take–Make–Use–Lose. Firms *take* resources and materials. They *make* things out of them. They get *used* and we then *lose* them, generating waste in their disposal.

Much of this process creates externalities, often waste such as air pollution and noise, the cost of which is borne by all people. To illustrate the extent to which the planet subsidizes human consumption, in 2009, Raj Patel, a World Bank economist, calculated the true cost of a fast-food burger to be $200 when factoring in carbon, water use, soil degradation and the healthcare costs of diet-related illnesses (Gleeson-White 2020).

Raworth's alternative model is the *butterfly economy: regenerative by design*. In contrast to the caterpillar economy, all starting materials are renewable, whether they are biological or technological. In this model (Table 1.1) there are two cycles (Raworth 2017, pp. 221–223):

Table 1.1: The butterfly economy: regenerative by design.

Wing	Lifecycle	Example
Left	Take–Make–Consume–Regenerate (biological nutrients)	Coffee grounds are full of valuable nutrients such as cellulose, lignin, nitrogen and sugars. They make an ideal medium for growing mushrooms (Bessant 2015a). The grounds can also be fed to animals whose organic waste can be returned to the land as fertilizer.
Right	Take–Make–Use– Restore (technical nutrients)	Consider how many unused and/or unusable mobile phones there are in the world packed with valuable and increasingly rare materials. The devices are repaired, refurbished, reused, resold or, as a last resort, recycled. Losses are minimal and minimized.

Source: Author, derived from Raworth (2017).

The butterfly is a metaphor. The future economy – one that stays within the planetary boundaries – is a butterfly economy. This model is also known as the circular economy with its implications for product design, ownership and new business models.

That is where the business opportunities lie, and that is why the planetary boundaries are at the centre of business and corporate strategy development for the twenty-first century.

While the global picture is perhaps daunting, firms can be guided by two very simple policies:
1. Mitigate the effects of climate change.
2. Adapt to the known and predicted changes in temperatures, weather, sea-level rises and other factors.

Mitigation and adaptation

Klein et al. (2005) see mitigation as referring "to all human activities to reduce or stabilize greenhouse gas (GHG) emissions to prevent (further) climate change" (p. 580).

What does mitigation look like vis-à-vis adaptation? Mitigation is a long-run, global intervention. Mitigators adopt and implement policies that contribute to maintaining global temperatures below 1.5 degrees Celsius. This is dependent on other actors, such as businesses and institutions, doing the same with a clear understanding of carbon budgets, mitigating technologies and the implications of exceeding limits. Under the mitigation regime, mitigation encompasses carbon accounting and trading. Airlines do this when they "offset" carbon emissions. Offsetting is potentially sub-optimal (Clark 2011) as a mitigation option because some of the projects supported as mitigation are insufficiently audited and are unlikely to match the declared emissions (Pinkse and Kolk 2012). Taking the example of the railway industry, mitigation involves operators phasing out diesel trains and replacing them with new units or locomotives powered by electricity generated by renewables. However, the carbon accounting here will need to include the carbon associated with disposal of existing plant and the manufacture of new equipment. There are other technology-based mitigation interventions available such as bioenergy with carbon capture and storage (BECCS) (Obersteiner et al. 2001).

By contrast for Klein et al. (2005): "[A]daptation in the context of climate change refers to any adjustment that takes place in natural or human systems in response to actual or expected impacts of climate change, aimed at moderating harm or exploiting beneficial opportunities" (p. 580).

Adaptation has a shorter timeframe than mitigation, is more local and has a firm-level focus. Again, taking the example of the rail industry, adaptation involves ensuring that the infrastructure is resilient against extreme weather, heat and flooding, etc. As recent as the summer of 2019, the UK rail system demonstrated insufficient resilience to extreme heat. The rails are single welded, meaning that if the metal expands in extreme heat then the rails will buckle. Rails are pre-stressed to withstand up to 40 degrees Celsius; but, in direct sunlight, rail temperatures have been recorded much higher. The same is true of winter where the rails contract and crack. The stressing, therefore, is a trade-off based on the average UK summer air temperature of 27 degrees Celsius. For the time being, rail temperatures of 40 degrees Celsius and above are unusual and hence not deemed cost-effective to stress to a greater extent. In the future, this may be a trade-off in which parameters may change (Davies 2019).

The city of Arnhem in the Netherlands is also adapting. The authorities are replacing asphalt with plants to enable rain to be absorbed rather than flow into sewers; the plants are also providing shade for the anticipated heatwaves (Boffey 2020). More recently, the former Secretary-General of the United Nations (UN), Ban Ki-moon, convened a climate adaptation summit of international leaders, arguing that

> [we] must remember there is no vaccine to fix our changing climate. As climate change impacts continue to intensify, we must put adaptation on an equal footing with [cutting emissions]. Building resilience to climate change impacts is not a nice-to-have, it is a must, if we are to live in a sustainable and secure world.   (Harvey 2021)

Recent examples of failure to adapt can be seen in the case of the Texas snowstorm in February 2021 (Salam 2021) and the northwestern USA heatwave in June 2021 (Pulkkinen 2021).

There are arguments being made that mitigation is now a waste of time; the prospects of keeping to 1.5 degrees Celsius increased warming is now low. However, the Intergovernmental Panel on Climate Change (IPCC) scientific report (IPCC 2021) notes that 1.5 degrees remains feasible, but even if it is not achieved, every fraction of a degree increase matters in terms of life on the planet. Humans must never give up on warming.

Scopes – reporting requirements

An increasing requirement for firms is to report on greenhouse gas (GHG) emissions. The six main greenhouse gases are carbon dioxide (CO_2), methane (CH_4), nitrous oxide (N_2O), hydrofluorocarbons (HFCs), perfluorocarbons (PFCs) and sulphur hexafluoride (SF_6). The World Resources Institute classifies three corporate reporting scopes. Under the GHG Protocol Corporate Standard, firms and organizations must report scope 1 and scope 2. Scopes 1, 2 and 3 are required under the broader GHG Protocol Corporate Standard and the GHG Protocol scope 3 Standard. Table 1.2 summarizes scopes and application.

While scope 1 and scope 2 are relatively simple to execute with neatly defined organizational boundaries (scope 1) and easily recorded and calculated emission rates (scope 2), accounting for the whole of the value chain is a significant task. Firms should see it as a short-term aspiration and prepare ahead of being mandated by law. It is, in effect, a climate change adaptation.

International organizations

Firms do not operate in a vacuum; they are part of an international and sometimes global system. This system will be discussed in Chapter 7. The so-called post-war consensus brought into existence a number of international organizations, established primarily to facilitate world trade and to support economic stability. This text and companion website discuss the important role of the World Trade Organization (WTO), the World Bank (see also the International Finance Corporation (IFC) – its commercial lending arm), the International Monetary Fund (IMF), the Organisation for Economic Co-operation and Development (OECD) and, notably, the European Union (EU) (European Bank for Reconstruction and Development) where the makeup of strict laws can be subject to real lobbying efforts (Massiot 2020). Investments are made by these bodies that accelerate climate change (Wasley and Heal 2020). There are a number of other important international organizations that affect the way economies and businesses operate. The World Economic Forum (WEF) with its annual congress in Davos, Switzerland, is an example. The large consultancy firms are also key players, for example, McKinsey.

Table 1.2: World Resources Institute GHG scopes.

	Classification	Examples
Scope		
1	Direct emissions from owned or controlled sources.	Office/Factory heating systems; vehicles using carbon fuels; manufacturing/ processing; leaks from sealed units or landfill.
2	Emissions from the third-party generation of acquired/purchased and consumed electricity, steam, heat or cooling (collectively referred to as "electricity").	All grid electricity consumption.
3	Indirect emissions from activities in the value chain (not included in scope 2) – both upstream and downstream emissions.	GHG emissions inventory that includes indirect emissions resulting from value chain activities, both upstream and downstream. Upstream: capital goods; fuel and energy related activities; transportation and distribution; waste management; business travel; employee commuting; leased assets. Downstream: transportation and distribution; processing of sold products; use of sold products; end-of-life treatment of sold products; leased assets, franchises, investments.

Source: Derived from World Business Council for Sustainable Development and World Resources Institute (2004), World Resources Institute and World Business Council for Sustainable Development (2011) and World Resources Institute (2015).

It is the United Nations (UN), however, that has been at the forefront of efforts to change the way economies function. The cited books and audio-visual resources above are based on the work of the United Nations' Intergovernmental Panel on Climate Change (IPCC). This panel was established by the United Nations Environment Programme (UNEP) and the World Meteorological Organization (WMO) in 1988. Since then, there have been five assessment cycles and reports. These reports are the most comprehensive scientific reports about climate change produced worldwide. The numbers are complex; a grasp of scientific method, probability and statistics more generally is needed. Three numbers in particular are useful: 0.85, 95 per cent and 1 trillion (Freeman 2015), where:

- 0.85 referred to degrees Celsius, the state of global warming at the time.
- 95 per cent was the statistical certainty that it is caused by humans.
- 1 trillion (10^{12}/1000 billion) was the tonnage of carbon dioxide left in the global "spending" budget.

Since 2015, the 2021 warming is calculated to be 1.1 degrees and the remaining carbon budget, 465 Giga/billion tonnes – 10^9 (IPCC 2021).

Every year UN members meet as a Conference of the Parties (COP). COP21 in 2015 was a turning point. The world agreed to a "legally-binding international treaty to limit global warming to well below 2, preferably to 1.5 degrees Celsius, compared to pre-industrial levels", under the auspices of the *United Nations Framework Convention on Climate Change* (UN 2015). At the signing ceremony in Paris on 22 April 2016, there were 175 signatories including the UK, USA, Brazil, China, India and the Russian Federation. It is to this agreement – commonly known as the Paris Agreement – that references to carbon budgets, emissions, and warming are given legal status.

The United Nations (UN) is also the architect of the Sustainable Development Goals (SDGs). The 17 Sustainable Development Goals were adopted by member states in 2015 with a view to achieving them by 2030. The objective is to end poverty, improve life prospects for all people while also protecting the planet.

Central banks, while not strictly international organizations, are increasingly co-operating on matters of financial services supervision. The European Central Bank (ECB) is a supra-national supervisory body responsible for monetary policy in the Eurozone. Together with member- and non-member-states' central banks, they are pushing forward on the climate change agenda (Bailey et al. 2020). The Network for Greening the Financial System (NGFS) has more than sixty central-bank members, and supervisors working to change the financial system to reduce the costly financial risks that climate change presents. One of the key players, former governor of the Bank of England, Mark Carney, has established another forum for banks to de-carbonize their portfolios. The GFANZ alliance's members include CitiBank, HSBC, Lloyds, Barclays, Morgan Stanley, and Bank of America. There is a limitation whereby banks are able to offset the carbon from their investments. This involves buying carbon credits in a regulated market.

Strategy as biography and chapter breakdown

Corporate and business strategy can be seen as the product of the lives of some of the twentieth century's most recognizable and influential men. The discipline owes much to historian Alfred D. Chandler, Jr.; economist Michael Porter (five-forces, generic strategies, value chain) discussed in Chapters 2, 3 and 5; sociologist Jay Barney (the Resource-based view of the firm, RBV) discussed in Chapter 3; and mechanical engineer Henry Mintzberg (emergent/deliberate strategy; strategy in 5s) discussed in Chapters 4 and 11.

However, female economists are leading the thinking about business in the age of climate change. In addition to Raworth (2017), the work of Gleeson-White (2020), Kemfert (2017) and Mazzucato (2018b) are significant. Equally, the former round-the-world sailor Ellen MacArthur established an eponymous foundation to promote the circular economy. Fridays for Future's leading figures are largely women – Adenike Oladosu, Hilda Flavia Nakabuye, Vanessa Nakate, Luisa Neubauer and Greta Thunberg are the best known.

The curriculum vitae of business managers and strategists should demonstrate a multi-disciplinary skill set. A knowledge of science – climate change or otherwise – is a useful skill for strategists. Equally, strategists are embedded in current affairs. A good strategist picks up signals from the wider world and uses that knowledge to inform decisions and policy. The PESTEL – Political, Economic, Social, Technological, Environmental and Legal – framework provides a classification for processing these signals. PESTEL is also the basis of scenario building. These will be discussed further in Chapter 2.

The text is split into three parts: *Analysis*, *Choice* and *Implementation*. In Part 1 the macro- and micro-environments are introduced. The text presents, as in many strategy texts, the tools of analysis, for example, Porter's five-forces and Barney's RBV (Chapters 2 and 3). Where necessary and possible, the text provides a climate/ SDG critique coupled with alternative approaches, measures or options. In the age of climate change and the UN SDGs, stakeholder analysis becomes the primary tool of policy-making by firms, sectors and governments. Freeman (2010) is the lead advocate of this approach. This is the focus of Chapter 4.

Data and analysis enable strategic choice, the subject of Part 2. There are many models and frameworks that facilitate choice. Chapter 5 introduces these, such as Porter's generic competitive strategies (Porter 1980) and the customer matrix (Faulkner and Bowman 1995). In both cases, redefinition is appropriate for the new context where co-operative strategy has an equal status with competitive strategy.

Chapter 6 discusses the motives for diversification, mergers, acquisitions and strategic alliances. In a sustainable world these motives shift from achieving optimal profit and competitor advantage to one of access and sharing resources, markets and knowledge. While Chapter 7 discusses portfolio management for diversified firms and corporate governance. There is room here for playfulness with some of the tools. Play is an essential part of adapting the tools of strategy in an age of climate change.

International strategies need to be evaluated very carefully, as, for all cases, expanding beyond a defined geographic territory will attract significant environmental externalities, not least in logistics, which tend not to be counted as they happen either in international waters or in other jurisdictions such as China; these are the scope 3 emissions. Scope 3 emissions need to be a component of any decision about internationalization or participation in global value chains. Territories chosen should also benefit environmentally and socially from a firm's presence.

Chapter 9 considers entrepreneurship and innovation where product and process innovation are optimized around the use of less material, generating less waste and travelling less often and less far. Entrepreneurial start-ups begin from a position of carbon neutrality. Five generations of innovation models are augmented with a sixth, sustainability model. Examples of mergers and acquisitions, strategic alliances and so forth are, by this thinking, undertaken to gain and develop resources and capabilities *for* sustainability rather than exclusively for profit.

Finally, in Part 2, Chapter 10 considers the importance of financial evaluation of strategy in decision-making. Many financial ratios and formulas fail environmental innovation tests badly as they are designed to maximize growth usually beyond planetary boundaries. The literature, however, has many examples of sustainability equivalents, for example, Net Present Sustainable Value and Social Return on Investment.

Chapter 11 opens Part 3 with a discussion on structural forms classified as functional, divisional and matrix/networked. Against the backdrop of climate change, firms will need to organize in such a way that it becomes possible to share resources and capabilities with external stakeholders, sometimes located on different continents. These shifting imperatives for firms will also require different leadership forms.

Leadership and change are discussed in Chapter 12. Strategy texts naturally discuss leadership styles and broader personnel roles. For firms committed to sustainability, these styles will have a profound effect on outcomes. The text looks to authentic leadership as an appropriate style adapting to climate change and fostering the suitable behaviours inside organizations.

Chapter 13 considers change management in the context of turnaround, a process that firms undertake when performance declines and the firm may be in danger of failing. This chapter also introduces students to the balanced scorecard (Kaplan and Norton 1992). The scorecard is a staple of performance monitoring; it balances the financial, business process, customer appearance and learning and growth with leading and lagging indicators associated with operations and activities. The scorecard can be used to measure corporate or business unit targets infused with sustainability objectives.

Chapter 14 returns to the question of defining strategy. Do existing definitions retain their meaning and do they lead to strategic decision-making that impedes planetary survival? This chapter draws on two scenarios – *Our Now* and *Another Now* (Varoufakis 2020). With carbon-emission deadlines fast approaching, the chapter considers the extent of the change needed, and the role of firms in meeting them. In the end, there is no choice but willingly to *embrace* change. There is no climate vaccine.

How to use this resource

This book is written to be used as a core text for students studying business or corporate strategy at undergraduate and master's levels. There is an accompanying website (www.strategyteaching.net) with additional and topical resources for each chapter, including cases, lecture slides and indicative solutions to questions posed in the text. Many of the cases in the text are expanded on the website. It is also a text that anticipates students keeping abreast of current affairs and searching the

Internet to collect freely-available economic and scientific data. A sustainable future is data driven. It is also important to find more out about the people behind the science, the politics, the institutions, the firms and analytical frameworks. The book works as a cue card rather than a verbatim script.

Generations of businesspeople, entrepreneurs and students understand business strategy through the lens of competition and markets. The tools of competitive strategy are not redundant, but they can be worked differently and harder. There remains an important role for markets in meeting sustainability targets, captured in the SDGs. The book is structured in a way that is similar to many existing strategy texts. There are sections on strategic analysis, choice and implementation. What is different in this text is the extent to which each of the dominant models – whether it be Porter's five-forces (Chapter 2) or Barney's RBV (Chapter 3) – are subject to critique and adaptation against the backdrop of sustainability. Because change is happening fast in light of new evidence, laws, standards, science and customer expectations, those critiques and adaptations will themselves change. They will change by the actions of readers, practitioners, academics and learners alike.

What is also different is that against the trend, the text does not seek to over-simplify the craft of strategic analysis, choice and implementation. To some extent the constant simplification of all disciplines has brought humanity to where it is now: crisis. Countless 2x2 matrices convince students and practitioners that strategy can be reduced to generic analysis and easily applied methods. However, the planet demonstrates to humanity as its climate changes, that complexity rules. Rather than be fearful of complexity, it can be a source of wonder, challenge and expansiveness of mind and society more generally. While the text presents and demonstrates the discipline's most well-known models and frameworks, those students who want to engage with complexity are invited to do so. For example, Chapter 4 provides a guide to identifying stakeholders that goes beyond mere generic categorization. The more practitioners put in, the more practitioners get out, resulting in better decisions. However, firms need to make money and strategic analysis can be resource heavy. Trade-offs have to be made, but the trading may need to value input factors differently.

A note on sources. Most university students should have access to the cited academic papers through their libraries. Similarly, with books, though these are subject to targeted buying decisions by institutions. There is no reason why students should not request important texts from libraries. However, students with an interest may have other lending options and should ultimately seek the advice of librarians.

The visual resources are often universal, such as YouTube channels. Some are UK-specific provided by the BBC and/or streamed through *Box of Broadcasts*. Equivalents are available in other countries; for example, Germany's public broadcasters make their content available through Mediathek. Where free-to-view sources are cited in the text, a direct link is provided in the companion website.

Numerous reports cited, such as those produced by the IPCC, are readily accessible. With regard to newspapers, *The Economist* and the *Financial Times* are cited, though access may only be possible through university library portals. Where possible, *The Guardian* newspaper in the UK is used as a primary source. In recent years the editors have elevated climate in its news values. It is not behind a paywall, but the usual *critical caution* is needed.

This is a text for critical readers and practitioners. It is also a text for optimists. Business is part of the solution and firms have the capabilities and networks to transform themselves and the global economy.

Questions

1. What is the difference between mitigation and adaptation? Can firms do one without the other?
2. To a stranger, describe each scope (1–3) in five words or fewer.
3. The butterfly economy has two wings: (left) Take–Make–Consume–Regenerate and (right) Take–Make–Use–Restore. What is the difference between consuming and using? What is the difference between regenerating and restoring?
4. Why should strategists pay attention to international organizations such as the UN?
5. Why was strategy largely written by men? What difference could a feminized strategy make to businesses and sustainability? Why?
6. What is deliberate strategy? What is emergent strategy? Can emergent strategy be deliberate?

Part 1: **Analysis**

Chapter 2
Macro-level analysis – world economy and industries

Chapter 1 introduced the structural elements of world governance and international organizations that are key actors and regulators of the global economy. To bring some order to the system, firms and strategists have a series of tools available to them that can be applied to generate data and insights relating to their specific sectors.

This chapter presents and discusses the generic tools of:
- PESTEL
- scenarios building
- five-forces
- industry structure and life cycles

PESTEL analysis

PESTEL is a tool with high utility, though often insufficiently leveraged. For strategists wanting to identify the factors affecting business strategy, it is invaluable. For strategists looking to create scenarios, it identifies the variables whose configurations help strategists compose scenarios.

PESTEL stands for Political, Economic, Social, Technological, Environmental and Legal. There is overlap between these elements. Some variables can occupy one or more of the headings. There are some guidelines, however. *Legal* will refer to law. Law is written down, maybe as a formal regulation. So, this may be a good place to start (LEPEST, perhaps?). What are the laws and regulations affecting the industry? Some industries are highly regulated, such as pharmaceuticals and medical equipment. The banking industry works under the umbrella of the Bank of International Settlements.

Political (P) generally refers to the state defined in terms of nation/country, which is the guardian of the law and justice system as well as a customer, supplier and regulator and so forth. Lobby groups and non-governmental organizations (NGOs) may well also be key players. International organizations also affect the macro environment, such as the Bretton Woods institutions – the World Bank and the International Monetary Fund. Regional supra-national bodies such as the European Union are also policy-makers affecting the political. States remain key players in the world's economic system, despite boundaries being eroded and blurred due to globalization. OPEC, the Organization of the Petroleum Exporting Countries, is a non-state actor that impacts the price of oil, which remains fundamental to most economies.

https://doi.org/10.1515/9783110718430-002

The first E captures normal *economic* (E^1) factors and concepts, such as business/industry cycles, performance, economic policy of host- or home-country, finance and investment, cost structures, and supply and demand of inputs.

Social factors (S) are grouped around demographics, for example, age, gender, location and other demographic indicators. The S will also capture income, wealth distribution and concentration, equity, social biases, discrimination, ethics, digital literacy, trade union membership and other forms of social organization, including interaction on social media platforms.

Technological (T) should supply a discrete listing of technologies that may affect future business activities – technologies that may be disruptive in that they challenge so-called incumbent technologies and are possibly cheaper. For example, the MP3 file challenged the incumbent technology/music format, the CD, and also the music companies whose intellectual property was protected by the CD format. In trying to list technologies, analysts may consider patent data, industry research and development budgets and citations in scientific journals. On the explicit side, technologies that manage supply chains (enterprise resource planning systems), stock market transactions and increasingly accessing public services should be factored into the T of a PESTEL analysis. Renewable energy generation is included. It is also important to factor in risk. Poorly managed systems are increasingly open to hacking and ransomware attacks, shutting down firms and vital infrastructure (Naughton 2021b). Climate change risks include damage to infrastructure from heat and flood, among others.

There will be factors relating to the second E (E^2) for environment that overlap with political and legal. In terms of climate change specifically, pollution, biodiversity and sustainability more widely are listed here. This is also the place to record global disease, certainly Covid-19 and human immunodeficiency virus (HIV), antibiotic resistance, as well as genetic modification of organisms.

Listing the factors is only the start. How do these variables affect decision-making? Note that all of the variables are external to the firm. The firm has very little direct power over them. There are exceptions, such as large oil companies, automobile manufacturers, banks and, increasingly, big tech, including social media platforms and cloud services (we all notice if their services are interrupted). One way of making full use of the variables identified through PESTEL is to create scenarios.

Scenarios

Scenarios are plausible futures. They are *not* predictions or forecasts. The most famous group of scenario researchers are those from Royal Dutch Shell, *the* oil company. The scenario team's report for 2050 generated two scenarios – Scramble and Blueprint. They are narratives derived from hugely detailed datasets, analysis and testing. The video summary of Scramble and Blueprint (good naming is crucial), translates scientific complexity into compelling story or narrative (Shell 2010). They use colour, music with urgency and a persuasive and authoritative voiceover to reveal the preferred scenario, Blueprint. What is notable for a company like Royal Dutch Shell is that it can play a significant role in delivering the narrative of Blueprint, owing to the fact that it is a very large firm that controls a strategic resource, namely oil. Royal Dutch Shell's past and present strategies matter. It is not the only industry player, but it has clout when it comes to policy-making. Governments listen to these large firms, normally as a result of lobbying to protect its legal and resource interests. When it comes to Blueprint, however, any voluntary move away from fossil fuel extraction, distribution, refining and sale would affect other stakeholders' choices and decisions.

Royal Dutch Shell's scenarios are resource intensive. This is not a trivial enterprise. Teams of highly skilled analysts collect and crunch data over many years. Oil companies use scenarios because their business involves long-lived assets. Investments now are significant, and decision-makers need reliable insights into a future from where the returns will be earned. It is not possible to forecast fifty years into the future, but it is possible to present plausible futures. Airlines use scenarios, for example, Moyer's airline scenarios produced for British Airways (Moyer 1996).

In the early 2000s, a consortium of academic and business colleagues across Europe were engaged by the European Commission (EC) to generate a series of scenarios for the 3G wireless networks then being rolled out. The project was called MobiCom. This was before the iPhone, a significant product introduction and innovation in the history of wireless telecommunications. 3G created huge new capacity that far outstripped what could be consumed by existing voice and text applications. The team used scenarios to consider plausible futures (Mylonopoulos and Doukidis 2003). Walsh (2005) offers a straightforward and applied method. There are six steps (pp. 116–117):

1. Identification of future actionable issues or drivers of change
2. Creation of framework for conceptualizing data pertaining to issues or drivers
3. Development and testing of a number of scenarios (between seven and nine)
4. Reduction of initial scenarios to smaller number of ultimate scenarios (two to four)
5. Composition of the narrative of scenarios
6. Examination of scenarios and identification of issues arising from them

Step 1 identifies issues, drivers and variables appropriate to the sector or industry. PESTEL is a starting point and was the tool used in MobiCom. In any business and sector analyses, when data are collected, a data management system is required (step 2). A common approach is clustering – or bunching – around themes. The PESTEL framework does this to a certain extent – environment, legal and so on. However, this may be a little too rigid and predetermined. More fluid approaches can facilitate the formation of clusters around alternative, non-obvious concepts and ideas. These are best revealed by group work and iteration. These can also be tested with experts in the field, so-called stakeholder groups. In the case of Mobi-Com, the research team convened special interest groups to scrutinize the clustering and to test the robustness of the emerging scenarios. Participants were drawn from telecoms, advertising, content providers, app developers, public sector service providers, etc.

Once the key drivers have been identified, it is possible to start building narratives around them. In MobiCom, the team started building a narrative around concepts such as changing regulatory frameworks (liberalization), copyright/intellectual property, technology standards, privacy, the development of ecosystems of handset manufacturers, mobile operators and content providers. The market growth would also depend on how the technology was embraced by public-sector organizations, such as local government in the delivery of services like housing, highways, payments and parking. Having constructed nine scenarios, these were again tested within and between experts in the special interest group before four composite scenarios were agreed and developed (steps 3–5). Finally, the consortium examined the social implications for each scenario, such as access to networks (largely about price), digital literacy and privacy (step 6).

With hindsight, constructing mobile commerce scenarios, albeit with a complex, labour-intensive method and validation process, was relatively simple. Climate change scenarios, by contrast, have a complexity all of their own. They are multi-disciplinary, fluid and based on outputs from evolving research and processing techniques run by powerful information technology (Teske 2019). There are many research groups involved in building climate change scenarios. They use scenario methods that are analogous to those of Walsh. The need for strategists to develop skills and knowledge beyond the world of business is critical.

Industry analysis

When starting out on a macro-level analysis, it is important to define the industry or sector in which the firm operates, or intends to. In most instances relating to strategy, it has been done before. With the exception of new and upcoming sectors, all industries have been classified by economists. This is because industry analysis is an industry in itself. To be a good industry analyst, it is necessary to be quite precise in knowing *what is the industry*. Ask, which industry is being analysed? If it is too broadly defined, and there are too many factors incorporated, this leads to non-core activities being drawn into the analysis. The results become general and of marginal use. The most common classification system used is called Standard Industrial Classification (SIC). Originally an American system, that classifies industries into 4- or 5-digit codes, it is near-universal as an approach; for example, in the UK, it is used by Companies House. The European Union has its own classification, Statistical Classification of Economic Activities in the European Community (NACE). The United Nations also has a classification, the International Standard Industrial Classification of All Economic Activities (ISIC). Before starting the analysis, strategists need to know the industry, its classifications and what is already known about the dynamics of the industry under analysis.

Five-forces

The titan of strategy is Michael Porter. His five-competitive-forces model, commonly known as the five-forces, is often used in both strategy and strategic management. Porter's model (Porter 1980, 2008) is an industry model; when applied with rigour it alerts practitioners to an industry's attractiveness.

The forces are:
– rivalry among existing competitors
– threat of new entrants
– bargaining power of suppliers
– bargaining power of buyers
– threat of substitute products or services

Attractive industries are often growth industries and offer potential for revenues and profit. If a firm is outside that industry, a positive five-forces analysis would indicate that entry into the industry would be a good strategic move. If a firm is already in that industry, it would indicate that business development in that industry could be a good strategic option. Indeed, firms in a sector work to make the industry less attractive to outsiders by affecting some of the forces, for example, by raising entry barriers, preventing suppliers from working with new entrants and keeping substitutes unattractive.

However, should the analysis demonstrate an industry to be unattractive, then firms might choose to exit the industry, consolidate through merger, takeover, alliance or not entering at all.

The five-forces model appears simple, but is deceptively complex. Application requires care and rigour. The first task is to define the industry. Then to establish whether a force is high, medium or low for which data are required, as well as a deep understanding of the structure of the industry. Each power has its indicators. Misapply them, and the analysis will be incorrect.

Porter provides a comprehensive list of measures for each force. These involve detailed research to establish. They are listed in Table 2.1.

There is a sixth force, not derived from Porter initially, but now partially endorsed by him. This force is complementary products and services. It is not strictly a force as it does not impact on the *profitability* of the industry, which is a major component of attractiveness. However, complementary products can affect the demand in an industry. For example, in a climate change context, demand for electric

Table 2.1: Five-forces and indicators.

Force	Indicators
Rivalry among existing competitors	industry growth; fixed (or storage) costs/value added; intermittent overcapacity; product differences; brand identity; switching costs; concentration and balance; informational complexity; diversity of competitors; corporate stakes; exit barriers
Threat of new entrants	economies of scale; proprietary product differences; brand identity; switching costs; capital requirements; access to distribution; absolute cost advantages – proprietary learning curve and access to necessary inputs; government policy; expected retaliation
Bargaining power of suppliers	differentiation of inputs; switching costs of suppliers and firms in the industry; presence of substitute inputs; supplier concentration; importance of volume to supplier; cost relative to total purchases in the industry; impact of inputs on cost differentiation; threat of forward integration relative to threat of backward integration by firms in the industry
Bargaining power of buyers	bargaining leverage: buyer concentration versus firm concentration; buyer volume; buyer switching costs relative to firm switching costs; buyer information; ability to backward integrate; substitute products; pull through price sensitivity: price total purchases; product differences; brand identity; impact on quality/performance; buyer profits; decision-makers' incentives
Threat of substitute products or services	relative price/performance of substitutes; switching costs; buyer propensity to substitute

Source: Author's table, derived from Porter (1980).

cars is affected by the availability of charging points. Without charging points either at the home base or en route, the car's range is limited. Charging points, therefore, become complementary products and services, something that customers will evaluate prior to purchase of the primary industry product. In the automobile industry, the manufacturers themselves will at least contribute to the provision of charging points, but other stakeholders are clearly important and, indeed, decisive. Local governments control many of the streets in towns and cities. Charging points require dedicated space in car parks or even pavement space. Critically, there needs to be a source of electricity. Here local authorities have that capability, not least through their street lighting.

Five-forces and crisis

We might ask how could this work in a crisis? Covid-19 is just such a crisis. In the UK during the first wave of infection, there were some essentials in very short supply. The British government, for example, looked to engineering firms rapidly to design, test and manufacture medical-standard ventilators. There were incumbents in this niche industry. Because of the nature of the industry, the incumbents may have struggled to scale up production as demand was not anticipated. The call from government coupled with the potential profit opportunity drew in new entrants, notably Dyson, GKN and Airbus. In the end supply was sufficient and the new entrants did not achieve regulatory approval. However, there were no viable substitutes. Firms presented with an opportunity to enter a new industry can reconfigure their resources and capabilities to produce new products. Those capabilities need also to manage discrete regulatory frameworks. Each industry is different, even when the technology is similar.

The model needs to be applied in totality; analysts cannot just pick and choose forces to emphasize. For example, high-growth industries are not necessarily attractive in and of themselves, as the overall profitability can be very low. If there are high barriers to entry, then attractiveness is enhanced from the inside. Equally, high growth can work in favour of suppliers, especially if they are concentrated. This would affect profitability. Other factors to consider are labour and bankruptcy laws; in fact, many factors that can be drawn from a PESTEL analysis are relevant here. Caution is also needed when considering industry structure as changes occur, sometimes subtly. Digitalization has changed industry structures, from retail to music publishing. Analysts need to be able to read the changes and factor them into the model and its application.

Weaknesses and limitations of the five-forces model

In applying models, strategists achieve the best results when they apply them with a full appreciation of their weaknesses. The critique by Coyne and Subramaniam (1996) is useful in this respect. They argue that there are three core assumptions in Porter's work that bear some scrutiny:
- that industries are made up of a set of unrelated buyers, sellers, competitors and substitutes that interact at arm's length (transactional)
- erecting a barrier to entry is a source of value determined by the structure of the industry
- that uncertainty is sufficiently low to predict firm behaviour within the industry

These assumptions are challenged by Coyne and Subramaniam (1996) as follows:

– Industries are not as transactional as Porter makes them out to be. Increasingly, industries are networks, or webs of firms, in Coyne and Subramaniam's terms. They are often complementary, such as the symbiotic relationship between Microsoft and Intel. Microsoft co-develops with Intel to ensure that chips are optimized for the operating system, and vice versa. There is no "chip industry" in the Porter sense. An extension of this is "privileged access", which might be a preference for subsidiaries of multinational companies and culturally based structures such as Korean chaebol and Japanese keiretsu. In other words, the market does not determine the supply.
– The state is an actor in industry; for example, the transition to zero carbon and digitalization is one that moves from a dependence on oil to rare earth metals. These metals are essential in the manufacture of electronics and batteries. In this example, there is a geo-political dimension to the sub-sector of the mining industry that controls rare earth metals and lithium, in particular. Left to the market, Chinese mining enterprises would trade "rare earths" and price would match demand. However, these commodities are becoming strategic for states (much as oil used to be). Supply is increasingly controlled by states. China, for example, has 80 per cent of rare earth deposits on its territory; however, it imposed export quotas. This prompted action from the USA to re-open a previously uneconomic mine in Southern California (Mountain Pass) to secure supply for the domestic economy. The Japanese government, by contrast, invested in an Australian mining company in return for a secured supply of rare earth metals, amounting to approximately 30 per cent of Japan's consumption/need (*The Economist* 2021c).
– Value can be created in ways other than through structural advantage. For example, firms can simply do what they do better than others, often based on superior knowledge and/or foresight. This is an additional reason why some firms generate scenarios.

The five-forces model seeks to provide a means to control *for* uncertainty. In other words, while the world is economically and politically uncertain, it is possible to manage it with a rigorous application of the model.

With these three challenges to the five-forces as a catch-all model, Coyne and Subramaniam (1996) highlight four degrees of uncertainty for strategists (Table 2.2).

There are other challenges; for example, Teece (2019) offers an additional query of note. Rather than a concentrated market structure being the cause of superior profitability, that is, a strategic objective to achieve such concentration, perhaps it is the consequence of a concentrated market structure? If such an inversion of current wisdom is true, there are implications for strategic decision-making.

These challenges do not render Porter's model invalid. There clearly remain structural factors that generate competitive advantage and profit for firms in industries. Coyne and Subramaniam (1996) only indicate that the collection of firms delivering

Table 2.2: Levels of uncertainty for firms in an industry.

Level	Name	Description
1	Single useful prediction	Uncertainty can be mitigated by further research – including sensitivity analysis – to generate probabilities sufficient for management- and strategic- decision-making.
2	Discrete scenarios	Uncertainty can better be understood through a scenario narrative, enabling decision-making in line with a plausible future. For example, in the MobiCom case, if app developers were given source code, apps could be developed at a predictable rate and be compatible with platforms; game theory and options pricing frameworks are also deployed here.
	Continuous uncertainty	Cannot be reduced to discrete scenarios particularly in cases where the performance or acceptance of new technologies and products in the market is unknown. Acceptance is not just high or low; it can be on a continuum.
	True ambiguity	Investing in Russia in 1992 after the collapse of the Soviet Union. There were investment opportunities but with real uncertainty about property laws, taxation and oligarchs. Supply can also be subject to true ambiguity – access to rare earth metals, for example.

Source: Author's table, derived from Coyne and Subramaniam (1996).

into a market that make up the world economy and its industries are more causally ambiguous than Porter's model allows for. This was further developed by Werner-felt (1984) as the precursor to the development of the resource-based view (RBV) of the firm discussed in the next chapter.

Five-forces in the context of climate change

Without action by governments and firms, climate change, in the longer term, presents "true ambiguity" for industries. The climate change scenarios are clear only to the extent that temperatures will rise and the old certainties will disappear. The climate models are being updated continuously as inputs of new data affect the outputs of the models. It may be that competitive advantage is itself not meaningful in the future. It is not clear what will be the role of the state in regulating and allo-cating resources where and when those resources become scarce. Further, external forces to the firm will be brought to bear, such as technology, changes in economic systems and customer preferences. The assumption that liberal economics will pre-vail is open to challenge; however, depending on the economic system, preferences could be determined by availability, that is, what states or corporations determine a preference to be, or become much more collaborative and sharing. Under these cir-cumstances, the utility of the five-forces model is affected because profitability is not determined by the structure of an industry and liberal economic competitive forces.

Taking the example of the "fast fashion" industry, presently it is structured with some large, global retail/manufacturers at its heart. The industry is predicated on creating and maintaining demand for cheap, low-priced clothes. More generally, and prior to the Covid-19 outbreak in 2020, the global fashion industry was producing some 150 billion items per year (Koperniak 2015); in the UK that translates to 1,130,000 tonnes of clothing purchased (WRAP 2012). This makes the global fashion industry second only to the fossil-fuel industry in terms of carbon emissions generated by its operations. No amount of entry barriers will prevent this industry being highly regulated in the future. Under the butterfly or circular economy, new approaches to raw material sourcing, quality, manufacture, re-use and sharing, recycling and so forth will supplant it. Industries do disappear and Porter's model can embrace that. The industry life cycle charts this process of growth and decline. But what might the new textile industry look like? There are templates created by reputable business consultancies and academics, for example, the Boston Consulting Group and Earth Logic. Regarding the latter, the authors call for localized production, repairing and sharing: "[it] means moving from globalized, tangled and unsafe supply chains to small production centres based around the needs and desires of local communities" (Blanchard 2020). Care is needed however, not to confuse sharing and renting of clothes; renting can involve extended and damaging logistics and dry-cleaning using harmful chemicals (Elan 2021).

Applying Coyne and Subramaniam (1996), this might be an ecosystem/web rather than a competitive arena occupied by behemoths carving out sectors for themselves, for example, fast fashion, mid-range, branded and luxury. Moreover, under this industry model, value would be created not by structural advantage, but rather by resource use-intensity. This, itself, may be regulated by the state or industry. Substitutes, such as clothes sharing, would be normalized, even becoming part of the retailer's business model. Clothes retain their value as long as people still want to wear them either themselves or by sharing. Once their value is exhausted, they are returned to the industry for re-purposing or recycling of fibres, where suppliers and buyers become the same actors. Too few garments are currently recycled. Crucially, future business models will monetize waste and textiles will no longer be dumped in landfill. The nature of demand and industry structure change fundamentally.

The sharing economy, more generally, challenges existing resource allocation economic/transactional models. Consumers become less acquisitive. Ownership matters less. Products are used more intensively and do not extract economic rents in the form of payment for use, in the Porter sense; rather, payments are in kind. Social networks become mechanisms for the distribution of products and services. Technology, equally, facilitates bespoke manufacture. Buyers become their own assemblers with complementary components being selected remotely and integrated with the finished product prior to dispatch.

There are other challenges to the structural advantage model. Firms within industries may well not behave in a rational profit-maximizing way. Parker (2018) draws our attention to a soft-drinks firm called Premium Cola in Germany. As an extreme but useful example of non-standard/unpredictable behaviour, Premium Cola – a player in the soft-drinks industry in Germany – was asked by a distributor for a "volume discount". The company's response to the request was to provide what might be regarded as a perverse industry incentive for smaller distributors to enter by means of offering an "anti-volume discount". Therefore, where industries are under pressure to cut carbon emissions, and firms within those industries behaving against expectation, predictability might be challenged and disrupted.

Porter was writing forty years ago and his model has dominated strategy thinking since then. It has been resilient and defended at each turn. However, climate change as a decisive macro factor, or force even, may well change this.

Types of industries

There are four types of industry: monopoly, oligopoly, perfectly competitive and hyper-competitive. Their properties are captured in Table 2.3.

Table 2.3: Types of industry.

Type	Properties
Monopoly	There is one dominant player. They can be public or private. In the UK, water companies have monopoly status because it is difficult to get competitors' water into houses and businesses. Network Rail, the provider of railway infrastructure, whose customers are rail operating companies, is also a monopoly. As a public sector monopoly, it is regulated to ensure fair pricing and that it does not exploit its monopoly position. Water companies are private monopolies, also regulated and operating under licence. There are some private-sector monopolies that are not regulated, such as Google Search and Microsoft Office.
Oligopoly	Industries with just a few firms operating in them. They limit the rivalry while exerting considerable control over suppliers and buyers. An example of this is the chicken processing industry in the United States (Sainato 2020). Mining corporations also tend to operate in such industries.
Perfect competition	Populated by many firms arising from low barriers to entry. Rivalry is high and firms have little power over either suppliers or buyers. Substitute products may also be available. The perfect nature of the competition comes from the notion of perfect knowledge and limited differentiation between products in the market. But even here, differentiation is possible. Hipster coffee houses, for example, do successfully compete against high-street coffee chains with slight variations in coffee blends and roasts and the café environment they offer.

Table 2.3 (continued)

Type	Properties
Hyper-competition	Industries that are hyper-competitive tend to be technological in nature and in which change occurs fast. Consumer electronics such as smartphones is a good example. Advertising is important, along with constant incremental improvements, often pushing the limits of the technologies in question.

Source: Author's table.

Industry life cycle

All industries have phases. These are: development, growth, shakeout, maturity and decline (see Figure 2.1). The curve climbs steeply through growth and shakeout phases, levelling out at maturity before going into decline. This may be arrested if the industry innovates; the mobile handset industry did so in the transition from feature phones to smartphones.

Consider the evolving electric automobile industry. It is currently in the development phase with uncertain technology and diffusing supporting infrastructure, for example, charging stations. The firms in the industry are a combination of start-up/disruptors such as Tesla and automobile incumbents, including Nissan, BMW and Volkswagen. Analysts anticipate a growth phase as demand for electric cars increases due to climate change and government incentives to buy and convert.

The traditional, liquid-fuel-based automobile industry, by contrast, will enter a decline phase as its products are no longer required, or indeed become illegal. Where the resources are redeployed remains to be seen. The shakeout phase saw assemblers sell, merge and consolidate. For example, General Motors ended production in Europe after selling its Opel and Vauxhall brands to PSA (*The Economist* 2017; Ruddick 2017). The industry had been in shakeout for many years prior to that.

Industries plateau or level out over time. The automobile industry has been long-lived, partly achieved by the globalization of production and markets and the relationship between product, modernity, increasing wealth and lifestyle.

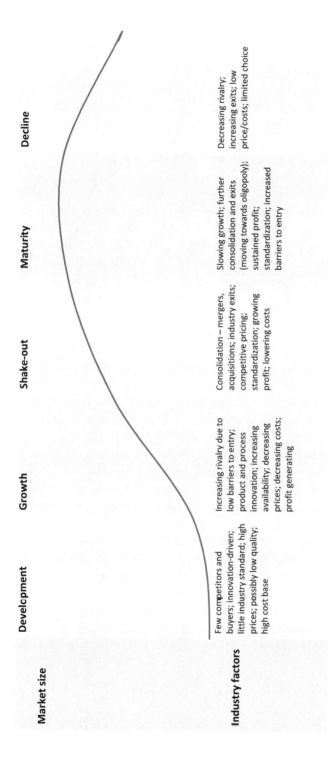

Figure 2.1: Industry life cycle.
Source: Author's figure.

Strategic groups

All firms in an industry are unique. They have different products, markets and territories. The concept of strategic groups enables us to map out an industry with firms as the key unit of analysis. In the traditional automobile industry, for example, firms cluster around:
- general auto assembly – assemblers make all classes of cars
- performance auto assembly – fast, sporty, high value/price
- luxury auto assembly – fast, elegant, comfortable, high value/price

These groups are not mutually exclusive. Luxury and performance may well overlap. In the era of electric vehicles, where does Tesla fit? Is it performance car assembly, or a group of its own? If non-traditional electric vehicle manufacturers emerge such as Google and Apple, are they auto assemblers at all? If they are, would they sit in the same group as Tesla? The answer is probably not. What is important, however, with strategic groups, is to consider mobility between them, and indeed, the barriers to move between them. How feasible is it for a general car assembler to move into one of the other groups? Tesla has done this with its Model S luxury model vis-à-vis the more utilitarian Model 3 in both performance and, crucially, price. The traditional assemblers both in the general and performance groups have struggled to move into the electric vehicle group, which require quite distinct resources and capabilities to compete in this market. The traditional assemblers have also tried very hard to protect their core engine technologies against new entrants and regulators alike. This may be an industry where the incumbents, usually the traditional assemblers, failed in their scanning of future mobility technologies.

Note also that Tesla is not so much a car assembler as a battery developer and manufacturer with cars being ancillary. It is always important to evaluate firms on the basis of their core competences; what is the technology that defines the firm and can be leveraged for other products? When looking at financial data, consider revenues from different sectors and research and development costs. Battery technology is also core to a wider discussion concerning climate change. As the economy makes a wholesale shift from carbon-intensive to carbon zero electricity generation, storage becomes more important. If the sun does not shine and the wind blow, electricity generation becomes more difficult and reserve electrical energy needs to be drawn upon. There is a role here for governments and states in policy and law. States do invest in these technologies, but as the Covid-19 outbreak in 2020 demonstrated, these investment funds can be diverted into other more acute activities causing investment challenges for new-industry firms.

Summary

This chapter has introduced the macro (PESTEL and scenarios) tools of strategic analysis. The macro environment is not stable and, largely, not controllable by managers (there are exceptions for managers of large companies operating in strategic industries and digital sectors). This so-called level of analysis is important for decision-makers not to overlook. Scenarios can help firms generate narratives around *plausible* futures. Ordinarily, however, it is to the industry level that analysts then turn; core to this level is the five-forces framework. This framework, when applied with rigour, guides the analyst and decision-makers with regard to the attractiveness of an industry. Decision-makers ask, should we enter the industry (if not already inside)? Should we leave (if operating in the industry)? Should we consolidate (erect barriers to entry or merge, for example)?

In the context of climate change, analysts should reflect on the weaknesses of the five-forces framework. The dynamics of industries will and do change. For example, if firms operating inside industries become less transactional and more co-operative, or the nature of supply changes through pressure on global supply chains, the utility of the framework changes. The macro environment, moreover, may actually affect the structure of industries, for example, through regulation. Crucially, however, the uncertainty that the framework seeks to manage for analysts is increased in a time of climate crisis. In Chapter 4 all stakeholders will be accounted for. One step before that, however, is for analysts to look inwards to the resources and capabilities of the firm itself.

Questions

1. What is an industry? What is the role of industries in local, regional, international and global economies?
2. What are scenarios, and what are they *not*?
3. What is the relationship between PESTEL and scenarios?
4. What does a rigorous application of the five-forces model tell analysts and decision-makers?
5. What is a substitute product, and what is it *not*? Give examples of substitute products to the following industries: fast food, low-cost airlines, fashion, pharmaceuticals, newspapers, university education?
6. Give two weaknesses of the five-forces model (see Coyne and Subramaniam 1996). Do you think they are actually weaknesses?
7. Give industry examples of: monopoly, oligopoly, perfect competition and hyper-competition.
8. Where do you place the following industries in the life cycle: fast food, low-cost airlines, fashion, pharmaceuticals, newspapers, university education? Why?

Chapter 3
Micro-level analysis – inside the firm

Macro-level analyses provide partial data for strategic analysis and choice, though the degree varies between industries. The question of exactly how significant are industries in terms of profitability was the subject of fierce debate in the 1990s (Rumelt 1991; McGahan and Porter 1997). Firm profitability on which strategic decisions can be based is only partly attributable to industry effects. Firms' own resources and capabilities become central to strategic decision-making. The ability to identify and classify these resources and capabilities is a key skill of strategists. The primary question is: are they strategic? If they are, can they be leveraged for competitive advantage; namely, are they dynamic? Moreover, does the firm have a core competence? If so, is there a core competence that can be stretched across all product offerings?

This chapter discusses the following:
– resource-based view of the firm and the analytical tool of valuable, rare, inimitable resources, and organization (VRIO)
– value chain
– strengths, weaknesses, opportunities, and threats (SWOT)/threats, opportunities, weaknesses, and strengths (TOWS)
– core competences
– dynamic capabilities

Resource-based view (RBV) of the firm

The resource-based view of the firm has its origins in the work of Penrose (1959), Andrews (1971) and Wernerfelt (1984). Wernerfelt overtly considered resources as a complement to the macro-level approach of Porter, and explicitly uses the five-forces model in his resource approach. Strategy is examined as the acquisition and defence of individual – or bundles of – resources rather than straight products. Critically, some of the strategically most valuable resources are intangible, that is, not measurable using classic economic tools, for example, knowledge (of technology). For Peteraf and Barney (2003), "RB [theory] is fundamentally a firm-level and efficiency-oriented analytical tool" (p. 320).

Barney (1991) draws on the work of Daft (1983) to define resources as:

> all assets, capabilities, organizational processes, firm attributes, information, knowledge, etc., controlled by a firm that enable the firm to conceive of and implement strategies that improve its efficiency and effectiveness. (p. 101)

Already the analyst has a significant task ahead to identify and classify a firm's resources. Critically, resources are *controlled* by the firm.

A key resource is the capability. A capability is, at its simplest, an "ability" to do something that enables a firm to operate. For example, all firms have payroll,

https://doi.org/10.1515/9783110718430-003

sales, marketing, bookkeeping, procurement, recruitment, legal (contracts/contract management) and invoicing. These capabilities are not in themselves strategic. Within the broad headings, there may be micro-capabilities, some of which are held by individuals and exercised as routines. Capabilities, equally, transform resources into something of value to the firm. In HRM, employees are a resource, while training, promotion management, health and safety and inclusivity are capabilities. It may be that a capability is needed to achieve a resource; for example, a contract is a resource that comes from a process of negotiation, which is a capability. Additionally, the management of contracts is a capability.

Resource position barriers

Wernerfelt (1984) develops the concept of the *resource position barrier* as a direct complement to Porter's entry barriers. Entry barriers, argues Wernerfelt, deal with the difference between incumbents – those already in the market/industry – and those seeking to enter. The concept of resource position barriers enables analysts to consider the advantages between incumbents derived from possession of particular resources, particularly those that are not tradeable – that is, cannot easily be acquired through the market. That is not to say, however, that possessing a resource position barrier is enough to protect a firm in a particular market from new entrants. In order to achieve competitive advantage, the resource position barrier needs to act as an entry barrier. The argument presented is that a resource position barrier in one market may be unique, but analysts need to ensure that such resource position barriers are *not* present in other markets from which they can be transferred to another industry by diversified firms. That said, transferring ideas, concepts, systems or resources from one domain/area to another can encounter often unexpected barriers, even though the transfer looks simple on paper. For example, implementation of generic software from one company to another, or even one machine to another, can reveal barriers.

Valuable, rare, inimitable, and non-substitutable (VRIN)

Usually when strategists refer to the resource-based view of the firm, they are crediting the work of Barney and his seminal paper, "Firm resources and sustained competitive advantage" (Barney 1991). In this paper, Barney argues that industry approaches assume that all incumbent firms in an industry or strategic group have identical strategic resources and capabilities to pursue their competitive strategies. He argues that strategic resources are often non-tradeable, are non-mobile and hence heterogeneous.

Barney introduces his VRIN framework as a tool that enables analysts to identify and test strategic resources and capabilities in firms and other organizations.

    V – Valuable
    R – Rare
    I – Inimitable
    N – Non-substitutable

Before discussing VRIN further, it is necessary to follow Barney in laying down some definitions and clarifying meaning.

Firm resources (Barney 1991, p. 101)

Firm resources are: all assets, capabilities, organizational processes, firm attributes, information, knowledge and so forth. Not all of these are strategic!
    They can be classified into three groups:
1. Physical capital – physical technology, plant and equipment, geographic location and access to raw materials
2. Human capital – training, experience, judgment, intelligence, relationships and insights from individuals, both managers and other workers/employees
3. Organizational capital – often seen to include financial capital/resources, including a firm's formal reporting structure, planning infrastructure, control systems, coordinating systems and networks (reclassified as human networks in 1994)

Competitive advantage (Barney 1991, p. 102)

Competitive advantage is understood to be real if a firm undertakes a "value-creating strategy not simultaneously being implemented by current or potential competitors".
    Moreover, sustained competitive advantage is achieved when a firm undertakes a "value-creating strategy not simultaneously being implemented by any current or potential competitors and when these other firms are unable to duplicate the benefits of this strategy".
    Having achieved sustainable competitive advantage, it is important to note that sustainability in this competitive sense does not last forever. It only makes the point that the advantage cannot be undermined by the efforts of other firms through attempting duplication. It is possible that the industry structure might change, making it less attractive and generating the incentive to leave.

Contrast with Porter: Resource heterogeneity and immobility

Porter's five-forces model assumes that resources are homogeneous and mobile. This means that all firms in an industry or sector enjoy access to, or can acquire, similar resources. These are physical, human and organizational in form. There is a market in resources. People move between firms. Firms themselves can be bought and sold and structures are replicable. This means that all firms can follow similar strategies with the same outcomes. In Barney's sense, sustained competitive advantage under these conditions cannot be achieved.

Consider just one of Porter's five-forces, namely, entry barriers. For entry barriers to exist, firms are implementing strategies that maintain and defend them. However, if resources are homogeneous and mobile, then entry barriers make no sense as all firms will be able to employ similar strategies to overcome them, albeit over time. And even within industries, there are deemed to be mobility barriers between strategic groups. For example, an automobile manufacturer of mass-market cars is said to experience mobility barriers to becoming a premium/performance automobile manufacturer. In reality, with pefectly homogenous and mobile resources, these barriers can be overcome and competitive advantage is only short-term.

By way of further illustration, analysts often talk about "first mover" advantage. A first mover gains a number of advantages over competitors. A first mover can build a significant customer base and lock-in those customers to protect against followers taking those same customers. First movers also learn from market entry, quickly adapt their products and processes and control distribution channels. However, if resources are homogeneous and mobile, it is not feasible for a single firm to achieve sustained competitive advantage from moving first. Only where resources are heterogeneous and imperfectly mobile is sustainable competitive advantage possible.

Testing resources and capabilities against the VRIN framework

Are resources valuable, rare, inimitable, and non-substitutable?

Valuable

Resources are valuable when they "enable a firm to conceive of or implement strategies that improve its efficiency and effectiveness" (Barney 1991, p. 106). Resources are valuable when they enable firms to take up opportunities and neutralize threats, drawing on two elements of SWOT (strengths and weaknesses). Unless they are valuable, they are not useful.

Rare

Valuable resources are not enough, however. Competitive advantage is the outcome of a firm implementing a value-creating strategy derived from bundles of valuable resources. If these valuable resources, bundled or otherwise, are not rare, they can also be configured by other firms with the same outcomes. It may be possible to achieve a temporary competitive advantage with valuable resources alone, but it is unlikely to be sustained. The rule of thumb might be that if the number of firms that possess a particularly valuable resource (or bundle of resources) is less than the number needed to generate perfect competition, the resource has the potential to offer competitive advantage.

Inimitable

Sustained competitive advantage arises from those resources, bundled or otherwise, being imperfectly imitable. In other words, competing firms cannot obtain them by replicating them internally or buying them in. All firms are unique. They have a unique configuration of resources and capabilities. The configuration of resources and capabilities become *causally ambiguous* over time. All firms have a unique history; the causal relationships between resources are independent of the industry structure that so determines macro/industry analysis.

Resources can become imitable if the causality is understood by the owning firm. By definition, competing firms can then obtain them, for example, through employing a former CEO, who is also a valuable and rare human resource. Ironically, the way to sustain competitive advantage may be for firms, knowingly or otherwise, not to understand the causal ambiguity. As soon as one firm understands the causal ambiguity, the greater the likelihood of its codification and transfer into another firm, hence no longer being a source of sustained competitive advantage. That said, the understanding of causality has to be deep for the CEO or other knowledge holders to replicate causal relations between resources (or bundles of) in a competing firm.

This may seem implausible. How can a firm with a competitive advantage not understand the source of its competitive advantage? The answer given by Barney is that resources and capabilities are complex in their interdependencies. Analysts may be able to generate hypotheses to test the strength of the relationship between variables (resources/capabilities and performance), but, in reality, firms do not have the awareness, time, energy, money and expertise to do this. For example, what effort would it take to examine all social relationships within a firm and those between customers, suppliers and so on? Firm cultures more generally are socially complex and difficult to understand with absolute clarity.

By way of further illustration, physical technology does not provide the means for sustained competitive advantage. If one firm can purchase the technology, then other firms can too. Technologies may be machine tools, robotics or an enterprise resource planning (ERP) system. However, the natural linkage of physical tools to a firm's complex social relations generates causal ambiguity. For example, take the case of easyJet. The easyJet ERP system that delivers planes, pilots, cabin crew, catering, fuel, etc., to each departure and arrival was bought off-the-shelf from Microsoft. The addition of the social relations, constant customization and experience generates causal ambiguity. Does that causal ambiguity enable sustained competitive advantage? The answer is no, not in and of itself. But it certainly helps and contributes to a resource becoming strategic.

Non-substitutable

Resources can be valuable, rare and inimitable, but still not provide sustainable competitive advantage if they are substitutable. To illustrate this, Barney takes the case of a firm's high-quality, top management. It may not be possible to replicate or imitate a firm's top management in terms of personnel, individual skills and knowledge. It might be possible, however, to substitute for such a top management team. An alternate management team can be strategically equivalent, despite being different. And even unique charismatic leaders are substitutable. While it may be impossible to find an equivalent charisma in another leader, it might be that a combination of resources and capabilities, whether human or systems, such as a formal planning system, can act as a substitute.

What exactly is the difference between inimitability and substitutability? Barney conceded that it would make sense to combine imitability and substitutability (in I). There remains a distinct difference between imitability and substitutability, but in terms of using the framework to test the strategic nature of resources and capabilities such that they conferred sustainable competitive advantage, the separation into different classes did not make absolute sense. Indeed, it made more sense to add another component, an "O" – denoting the role of the organization in supporting the exploitation of resources and capabilities. Is the organization structured appropriately? Are the formal and informal systems optimized for this task? For example, if a firm's human resource is deemed valuable, rare and inimitable, but not organizationally supported, what might that mean? It may be that the firm has few training or higher education opportunities, networking platforms such as conferences, special interest groups and so on, or simply, poor pay/remuneration relative to the perceived value of the resource.

The framework becomes VRIO:

V – Valuable

R – Rare

I – Inimitable

O – Organizationally supported

In applying the model, resources and capabilities that are valuable, rare, inimitable and organizationally supported give long-term, sustained competitive advantage. Resources and capabilities that are none of these actually give competitive disadvantage and should be dispensed with; though care is needed fully to understand why such resources and capabilities exist and have been retained. Those in-between can offer competitive parity or short-term advantage.

VRIO and climate change

There are two big policy types for firms to deploy: mitigation and adaptation.

Mitigation

The framework has utility for firms and analysts in the context of climate change. Firms will need to develop or acquire resources and capabilities that both mitigate and adapt to climate change, for example, capabilities around climate change reporting, such as carbon accounting, water consumption and energy efficiency. These will be new capabilities for many firms across sectors. They are unlikely to generate *sustained* competitive advantage, but will provide parity. Arguably without them, firms will not be able to trade. Some firms will offset carbon emissions and create another valuable capability, but not necessarily one that will provide much beyond competitive parity. In the future, offsetting may well qualify firms for competitive disadvantage as debates around the efficacy and honesty associated with offsetting develop. Consider offsetting in the context of airlines. Sustained competitive advantage, arguably, will be achieved by firms that can work towards, achieve and share zero- or below-zero carbon emissions by 2050 or earlier. Below zero is to trade a carbon surplus with firms that are carbon positive. For example, firms that generate an excess of renewable electricity can trade their excess with firms that are still dependent on carbon fuels.

Adaptation

Firms mitigate carbon to reduce emissions and to meet climate change targets set by governments/states/international treaties. Some firms seek to do better than the minimum. However, firms will also need to adapt to the realities of climate change. Even if global mitigation is successful, the climate will still change as global temperatures have already changed irreversibly and the effects have been experienced: floods, drought, fires and so forth. Firms, therefore, need to make themselves resilient. Resilience is the ability to "bounce back" after a shock, after a break in the *equilibrium* of normal business. The importance of understanding resilience and making a firm/organization resilient has been brought into sharp focus during the Covid-19 crisis in developed economies. The shock to the system/equilibrium was the sudden ending of much non-digital or networked economic activity. Manufacturing largely ceased; much of the service sector populated by restaurants, cafés, non-food retail, travel and tourism and so forth simply ceased overnight.

Resilience in this context was the ability of firms and companies in those sectors to get through the immediate "lockdown" and trade sufficiently through the incremental re-opening of the economy and to avoid insolvency. The history of business resilience in this period is yet to be written; however, there is a high likelihood that few firms, particularly at the downstream, customer end of the chain, would have a global pandemic in a risk register. An exception is the insurance industry where such risks are accounted for and either mitigated or excluded from cover.

Equally, one would expect states to be resilient to crises of this kind. The Covid-19 crisis, however, has demonstrated a lack of preparedness on the part of states to provide for citizens in crises. The reasons for this are yet to be established, not least because some states were more prepared than others, but possible explanations include the following: complacency; limited understanding of science; transactional models of state management whereby everything can be procured globally and just-in-time; populism; and electoral cycles.

In resilience terms, states have the advantage in that they can both create money through central banks, and borrow money by issuing bonds. In terms of paying back, states can tax citizens and firms and/or reduce public expenditure. These are options not open to firms, hence governments around the developed world offered immediate credit to firms and their employees through so-called *furloughing*, among other interventions.

Whole industries such as retail, travel and entertainment have been transformed by Covid-19. Resilience requires firms not only to pick up where they left off prior to the pandemic, but to have adapted to the new habits of customers, suppliers and new entrants. More broadly, as the world has become more globalized in terms of trade, firms have become less resilient because of a trust in modern logistics and supply chains.

In the context of climate change, firms need to adapt to the likelihood of breaks in the equilibrium, that is, shocks. Pandemics are one thing. In recent years supply chains have been broken due to natural disasters such as the tsunami that hit Japan in 2011. Re-establishing supply chains quickly is one example of resilience. Equally, a response might be the shortening of supply chains. Tim Lang (2020) discusses this in the context of the food industry and particularly retailers dependent on long supply chains for year-round fresh produce. In the Covid-19 crisis, resilience was observable in the speed of migration to online remote working and the ability of platform and network providers such as Microsoft, Zoom, BT, Deutsche Telekom and so on to keep networks functioning when demand suddenly and unexpectedly increased, at least in the domestic market that quickly became a business network as employees established home offices.

In VRIO terms, adaptation is likely to be a valuable resource or capability. It may not be rare, nor inimitable. One would expect it to be supported by the organization going forward. Here adaptation means: resilience in supply chains (multiple, shortened, on-shored, etc.); versatile employees (training, autonomy); agility; infrastructure (buildings, networks); top-up healthcare provision.

Limitations of VRIO/RBV

Similar to the critique of Porter's five-forces industry model, VRIO is based on the premise that firms are, and should always be, competitive. Achieving sustainable competitive advantage against the backdrop of a crisis or sustained challenge such as that posed by climate change, may be illusory and serve no social welfare. Resilience may well be systemic as it is in the food industry example. In the Covid-19 experience, the contradictions are exposed in the search for a vaccine. Firm resources in the pharmaceutical sector such as patents are valuable, rare, inimitable and supported by the organization. They are a source of sustained competitive advantage. In the search for a vaccine that serves a social welfare purpose, this is unhelpful to global society. It may not be ideal for a patent holder either. This is home territory for international organizations such as the World Health Organization (WHO) that is in a position to co-ordinate effort and manage the knowledge resources held within and between firms in the sector. Though recent criticisms of the WHO illustrate how dangerous economic nationalism can be when confronted by global challenges that are both economic and existential. Firms are resisting efforts at removing patent protection to diffuse the technology globally.

Climate mitigation and adaptation: What resources and capabilities might be VRIO?

Whether the world meets the terms of the Paris Agreement of 2015 will depend on government policies, and coordination between states, near and far, in the developed and developing world. At a firm-level, however, companies will have to deploy resources and capabilities developed organically or acquired that are centred on climate change. In order to mitigate and adapt effectively, firms will need to measure and audit carbon as well as other pollutants. They may also need to develop or procure capabilities around carbon and pollution trading. These resources and capabilities/methodologies are unlikely to be strategic in the RBV sense in that they will not be valuable, rare, inimitable *and* organizationally supported – but no less important for that. Firms will need to have these auditing resources and capabilities in order to trade, if not mitigate and adapt. Sustained competitive advantage might be achieved in possessing superior cradle-to-cradle (butterfly economy) product processes. This can be seen in examples from the fashion industry. These are likely to be valuable and rare; causal ambiguity could be crucial (inimitability) in leveraging their strategic potential.

Bansal (2005) utilized RBV as an independent variable in her study of corporate environmental sustainability, the corresponding dependent variable, in the Canadian oil, gas and timber industries. The scale and size of these industries enabled the study to consider capabilities such as internationalization, capital management and organizational slack in the form of spare/unallocated resources, in responding to climate challenges.

The value chain

Porter's strategy toolbox contains not only tools to evaluate the industry environment, but also micro, firm-level tools. Primarily among these is the value chain. Harvard Business School's *Institute for Strategy and Competitiveness* describes it thus (HBR n.d.):

> [T]he value chain is a powerful tool for disaggregating a company into its strategically relevant activities in order to focus on the sources of competitive advantage, that is, the specific activities that result in higher prices or lower costs. A company's value chain is typically part of a larger value system that includes companies either upstream (suppliers) or downstream (distribution channels), or both. This perspective about how value is created forces managers to consider and see each activity not just as a cost, but as a step that has to add some increment of value to the finished product or service.

Porter's value chain classifies activities of value inside firms as primary and support (see Table 3.1). Primary activities, largely involving making a product or delivering a service, are further broken down into five types: inbound logistics, operations, outbound logistics, marketing, and sales and service. The support activities are classified as: firm infrastructure, human resource management, technology development and procurement.

The support activities (see Table 3.2) are not just a nice-to-have. Without them the primary activities with their value-adding properties do not occur.

The value-chain framework invites an audit of primary and secondary activities. The model highlights the costs allocated to particular activities within a firm. It might be that firms are simply unaware of activities, let alone their cost. Moreover, in doing the exercise, managers can establish relative costs and indeed the extent to which each activity adds value to the final product or service. Under normal circumstances, the aggregate cost of primary and support activities leaves a margin of profit. Typically, the value chain is presented diagrammatically as a forward-facing arrow with the margin shown on the arrowhead.

Table 3.1: Value chain primary activities.

Primary activities	Examples
Inbound logistics	incoming raw materials, components and equipment; these involve warehousing/stock control, transportation (just-in-time) and so on
Operations	*manufacturing*: the assembly of a product, packaging the product, finishing of a product *service*: dealing with enquiries and processing orders in a call centre or through a website; travel, entertainment (play/movie/theatre management), restaurants (food preparation/dining), etc.
Outbound logistics	shipping the product or service to customers; warehousing and transportation
Marketing and sales	market research, advertising, campaigns, selling and administration; provision of samples, demonstrations
Service	activities that add value to the product or service, such as installation, online/telephone support and training in use

Source: Author's table, derived from Porter (1980).

Table 3.2: Value chain support activities.

Support activities	Examples
Firm infrastructure	finance, payroll, IT, planning and the structure of the organization more generally
Human resource management	recruitment, training, rewards and recognition for employees
Technology development	research and development of product and process, such as new products and materials development
Procurement	components, equipment, toilet rolls, distribution (if not in-house), advertising and so on

Source: Author's table, derived from Porter (1980).

With regard to primary activities, drawing up a list of activities invites thoughts about taking out non-value-adding steps in a process. By rationalizing activities, this margin can be expanded positively. Support activities, in particular, can be rationalized. Certain functions can be outsourced or merged, particularly if the firm is diversified. For example, a manufacturer can merge two functions on an assembly line, or even just move operators closer to one another; likewise, with inward and outward logistics, the same supplier can be used. In support activities, procurement and technology development can be advanced strategically in a procurement alliance such as the case of Nissan and Renault (Segrestin 2005).

In a more rudimentary sense, just the act of identifying steps and categorizing them can reveal and possibly challenge organizational routines, some of which hinder business development as they are culturally embedded and intangible. The value-chain framework can also be used as a benchmarking tool: "How do we compare with competitors or others who have similar activities but in a different sector?" The value-chain framework may well facilitate the identification of resources and capabilities to be tested against the VRIO framework, assessing their strategic importance and value in the process. In the logistics example, analysts may find that the inbound logistics operation is strategic, but not the outbound logistics operation or vice versa.

Equally, the value-chain framework can be used normatively; by which is meant each activity, once identified, is assessed not against its absolute cost, but rather the potential to be more carbon efficient, or less polluting in other ways. This is the approach of Ndubishi and Nair (2009).

Table 3.3 provides some examples for primary activities.

Table 3.3: Primary activities and normative activities.

Primary activities	Examples
Inbound logistics	Hauliers use alternative fuel or electric vehicles; energy-efficient warehousing; short supply chains; sustainably constructed buildings with minus carbon emissions, such that renewable energy can be exported to the grid or the local community
Operations	*Manufacturing*: assembly of a product, packaging the product, finishing of a product. Factory/assembly plant is carbon zero; components zero carbon. Catering is zero carbon. Products are 100 per cent recyclable. *Service*: call centre is zero carbon; employees travel by public transport, on foot or by bicycle
Outbound logistics	See inbound logistics plus minimal recyclable packaging
Marketing and sales	Communication of value-added associated with sustainability, non-obsolescence and/or recycling; benefits to the customer; truthful advertising and avoidance of inappropriate targeting of children; price discrimination between customers particularly against the poor
Service	Activities that add sustainability value to the product or service, such as installation, maintenance, online/telephone support and training in use and returns (life expired); disposal of obsolete products, handling of dangerous consumables (oil/ink) and customer privacy

Source: Author and Porter and Kramer (2011).

A similar exercise can be undertaken for support activities (Table 3.4).

Table 3.4: Value chain support activities.

Support activities	Examples
Firm infrastructure	Sustainable finance based on sustainability measures, sustainability culture within the organization
Human resource management	Recruitment – sustainability as a selection criterion, retention, sustainability training, rewards and recognition for employees based on sustainability targets, remote interviewing, health and safety, fair redundancy policies
Technology development	Research and development (product and process), such as new products, materials development and product safety
Procurement	Green purchasing from sustainable and ethical sources

Source: Author and Porter and Kramer (2011).

Limitations of the value-chain model

The stand-out limitation is one of scope. It was designed for a time when firms manufactured tangible products and did so in a linear way. In modern manufacturing separating out the primary activities is no trivial task, and may be of limited utility. One solution to this is to broaden the scope into a "value system" that better reflects the complexity of firms' interdependencies. Each upstream supplier, from first tier in the auto industry to contract industrial designers, architects and so on has its own value chain that feeds into that of the focal firm under audit. Likewise, each downstream customer is also connected to a value system. Part of the need for developing the model into a value system was the underlying logic of the model, which is to take costs out of the focal firm's value-adding activities. One of the most common outcomes of a value chain analysis is the decision to "make or buy"; can the component or service be sourced externally, retaining cost-effectiveness and efficiency?

A value-chain activity can lead to a strategic management decision to outsource activities, or parts of activities, that are deemed non-strategic or only marginally value-adding when delivered in-house. Obvious candidates here fall in the support services such as accountancy, some elements of infrastructure such as cloud computing, and human resource management (HRM). Deciding whether these activities are value-adding, and strategically so, is a challenge for business managers. It can lead to loss of a strategic capability; on that basis, the design and functioning of a value system needs careful consideration. For example, when a firm decides to outsource manufacturing it potentially relinquishes its knowledge over the manufacturing process and the ability to design for manufacture. A well-functioning value system should factor this in to ensure that knowledge is retained and shared. Such control over value systems, however, requires a global economic stability that is increasingly difficult to achieve and guarantee. The international structures and political consensus around open and fair-trading arrangements are being challenged by protectionist measures across the world.

The value chain versus supply chain: Climate change, security and resilience

Outsourcing

Outsourcing and the growth in value systems lead to long and globally dispersed supply chains. The value chain is made up of activities that are seen "not just as a cost, but as a step that has to add some increment of value to the finished product or service" (HBR n.d.). A supply chain is defined by Mentzer et al. (2001) as "a set of three or more entities (organizations or individuals) directly involved in the up-stream and downstream flows of products, services, finances, and/or information from a source to a customer"(p. 4). There is no reference to value, only flows. That is not to say that value is not a part of a supply chain – indeed they draw on the work of other writers who do define supply chains in value terms, for example, Christopher (1992) – only that supply chains can often be seen much more as an operational management issue, rather than a strategic management one.

Supply chains

Mentzer et al. (2001) identify three different kinds of supply chain, each of increasing complexity. The simple linear version they call the direct supply chain; more complex is the extended supply chain where suppliers have suppliers and customers have customers; and more complex still is the ultimate supply chain tracing all supply back to an ultimate supplier (upstream) and an ultimate customer (downstream). The authors illustrate the ultimate supply chain with an example: "a third party financial provider may be providing financing, assuming some of the risk, and offering financial advice; a third party logistics (3PL) provider is performing the logistics activities between two of the companies; and a market research firm is providing information about the ultimate customer to a company well back up the supply chain" (Mentzer et al. 2001, p. 4). Ultimate supply chains potentially are:
- lengthened geographically (spatial)
- temporally ambiguous (between time)
- lengthened by number of entities
- lengthened by scope of entities
- value-adding and non-value-adding

In Mentzer et al.'s (2001) terms, *extended and ultimate* supply chains come with their own consequences and implications. These are represented in Figure 3.1. While in absolute cost terms, outsourcing and extending a firm's supply chain(s) makes operational sense, it may lead to a reduction in a firm's capabilities (knowledge, know-how), unless a residual function is retained within the firm or organization. Where this occurs, the maintenance of the residual function *is* a cost. States do this; for example, in the railway industry in the UK the Department for Transport retains a capability to run and manage train operation in the event of the collapse of an operator. The history of the privatized rail industry in the UK is littered with examples of operators prematurely ending their franchises, or during a national emergency, such as a pandemic.

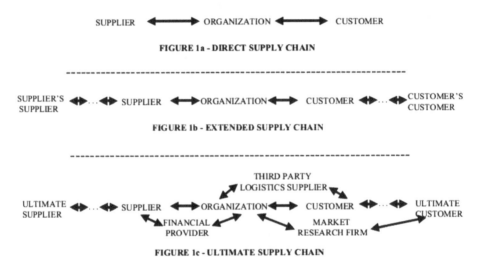

Figure 3.1: Types of channel relationships.
Source: Mentzer et al. (2001), reproduced with permission.

Current measures do not fully reflect the true costs of manufacturing, distribution, etc. For example, smartphones are largely manufactured in China. Each device is responsible for the release of a certain amount of carbon contributing to the rise in global temperatures. The price we pay for a smartphone does not reflect the *externalization* of the pollution generated in its manufacture. As Malm argues (2016), manufacturers use the concept of capital mobility to shift the carbon burden from the developed to developing economies. Until products that are consumed in developed countries are properly costed to account for the export of carbon pollution, which the value chain legitimizes, the carbon budget will continue to reduce. Put another way, developed countries have to pay the cost of the carbon that is embedded in the products that are imported.

Extended and ultimate supply chains are also risky.

Strategists seek, at industry level, to control for uncertainty. Global value chains (essentially value systems) are predicated on increasing global security of supply, trade liberalization (WTO, the EU, for example) and political stability. Political, economic and cultural globalization are not guaranteed. The current trend towards protectionism demonstrates that trade barriers are easier to erect than remove. Extended and ultimate supply chains, coupled with political uncertainty and increasing unpredictability, have significant implications for firms if they do not have a strategic contingency – in other words, local supply options.

Cultural globalization has an unsavoury history. In the UK, globalization has a colonial legacy that continues into the present and is used by politicians to retain political power, with serious implications for security. Lang (2020) amply illustrates this. The UK government and its people, he argues, believe that the world has a responsibility to feed it. With historical lows of self-sufficiency in food in the UK where less than 50 per cent of food consumed in the UK is grown within its borders, in situations of uncertainty such as in times of global political and economic change, there is market failure. States cannot assume that supply contracts will be honoured, or if they are, prices will increase to reflect supply challenges. The UK's assumption that food imports will be unaffected by political and economic change, including self-defined Brexit, is risky. It is particularly acute, argues Lang, in the UK because of its historical dependence on, and exploitation of, colonies and the developing world.

Value

Porter has a very clear view about what is value in the chain. However, Mazzucato (2018b), in posing the fundamental question of what actually constitutes value, cautions against value being merely extractive, something that much of the modern world economy suffers from. In particular, Mazzucato singles out the financial services sector pre- and post- crisis of 2008. Instead of the sector providing the means for value to be created in society by making funds available for socially useful products and services, it merely extracted more from those who were least able to protect themselves, namely new and low-wage homeowners, which is an aspiration perpetually promoted by governments for electoral advantage. Mazzucato's work is not just relevant in the context of Porter's view of the value chain where value is extracted from actors undertaking primary and support activities, but also in a wider context of social value in products, process and beyond.

Strengths, weaknesses, opportunities, and threats (SWOT)

SWOT is one of the durable concepts in strategy. The model is often credited to the work of Harvard strategy scholar Kenneth Andrews. Its origins are attributed to the Harvard Business School in the 1950s and is very much grounded in consultancy and practice.

With this framing, strategists start with an analysis of the environment. The task is to neutralize threats from the environment (to be managed internally) and to embrace the opportunities (leveraging internal strengths). These data are collected using SWOT as an audit tool. Auditing is not a trivial task as it is resource-intensive; moreover, Andrews had a bias towards large firms that possessed these resources. His book The Concept of Corporate Strategy (Andrews 1971) focuses on opportunity, internal resources, management and purpose.

Notwithstanding that, firms often use SWOT in a fairly stripped-down way. Certainly, in the context of strengths and weaknesses, it is conceivable to bring people together and ask the rudimentary questions such as, "What do we do well?", "What do we not do so well?" and "What can we learn from what we do well to improve the things we do not do so well?" In these scenarios, the opportunities and threats may already have been presented, as the same people may not be involved throughout. In which case, participants are in a privileged position to make the links, assuming that the threats and opportunities are understandable. For example, in terms of climate change, the level of understanding required to conceive of managing the threat of climate change, or alternatively embracing the opportunities, is quite high without coaching, training and a cultural affinity with, and propensity to, change.

Applying the necessary rigour to the model

Like most strategy tools, the outputs are only as good as the inputs.

With regard to climate change, without an understanding of the nature of the threat and the appropriate indicators, the alignment of a firm's strengths to the threat, or indeed opportunities, can be problematic.

Threats, opportunities, weaknesses, and threats (TOWS)

One of the dangers of SWOT is users' lack of specificity. It is easier to list strengths, weaknesses, opportunities and threats in very general terms. In so doing, it is very difficult to make meaningful recommendations. The TOWS matrix (also known as Situational Analysis), provides an additional step in the process of operationalizing findings and constructing strategic options; that is, turning findings into decisions and then policy. TOWS (Table 3.5) is conceived as a strategic planning tool by Heinz

Weihrich (1982). On reflection, it is interesting that threats (T) are identified as "inflation, energy, technological change and government actions" (p. 56). Weihrich shows the importance of evaluation and choice of strategies and highlights risk – the risk linked to either doing something such as a new product release, or the risk associated with not doing something, such as omitting to introduce an ERP system or, in the climate change scenario, not mitigating, failing to address product life cycle challenges, etc.

Building a TOWS matrix has seven steps (Weihrich 1982, pp 60–66):

Table 3.5: Operationalizing TOWS.

Step	Description	Content	Comment
1	Prepare an enterprise profile	(a) kind of business; (b) geographic domain; (c) competitive situation; (d) top management orientation	What is the purpose of the firm? What does it do? Where? What is the industry/competition? Who are the customers/stakeholders?
2	Identify and evaluate the external factors (OT)	(a) economic; (b) social; (c) political; (d) demographic; (e) product and technology; (f) market and competition	Draw on PESTEL – ensure there is an auditing capability in the firm or can be (consultancy)
3	Prepare a forecast, make predictions and undertake assessment of the future	Use evaluation from step 2. Determine the timeframes and feasibility. Forecasts based on historic data may be insufficient	Strategy is about the future – scenarios may be an option, especially in an era of climate change and economic and social uncertainty
4	Prepare an internal audit (SW)	Internal resources – physical, financial and human; within and between functions	Which are strategic? Ensure balance between internal and external factors
5	Develop alternatives	Forward/backward integration; specialization; diversification; innovation	These can be tested in a financial evaluation
6	Make strategic choices	Care needed in choices; what is the balance between SW/OTs?	Does the choice provide "real options"?; short-term gain; mitigate and/or adapt?
7	Prepare contingency plans	What if?	Things go wrong. What is to be done if X happens?

Source: Author's table, derived from Weihrich (1982).

Table 3.6 illustrates how each option has a pairing and a name.

Table 3.6: Structuring the TOWS matrix.

Options	Pairing	Name
1	strengths–opportunities (SO)	maxi–maxi
2	weaknesses–opportunities (WO)	mini–maxi
3	strengths–threats (ST)	maxi–mini
4	weaknesses–threats (WT)	mini–mini

Source: Author's table, derived from Weihrich (1982).

Having executed the process of data collection and analysis, TOWS practitioners normally introduce a scoring system for each of the listed SWOT factors in order to reveal strategic options. The temptation is to go for maxi–maxi; in many cases, the maxi–maxi option reveals the low-hanging fruit. These are strategic options that are very quickly and effectively implementable. There is an alignment between firm-level strengths and industry- or macro-level opportunities. But if the negative factors (WT) are meant to be somehow managed by the positive factors (SO), then a combination of positive and negative may be optimal. Maxi–maxi is likely to be short-term. Consider if a threat is on the horizon. Perhaps the cost of ignoring it in the short term could be high.

TOWS and climate change

There is a danger that SO options (maxi–maxi) lead to business-as-usual, namely growth, extraction and more CO_2. The elephant in the room is climate change. SWOT has the potential to be a very useful tool for business managers where climate change is the primary external threat. If strategic business managers choose to use SWOT/TOWS to reconfigure a business in the age of climate change then the threat is not primarily competition from new entrants, rising commodity prices, etc. These threats are real and are legitimately flagged up as threats. The key threat, though, is climate change and the key strategic issues are mitigation and adaptation.

The initial focus may be on (ST) maxi–mini, that is, matching firm strengths to external threats. What might this include? Firms may have many resources and capabilities that qualify: mitigation and adaptation initiatives, energy-efficient buildings and supply chains; sustainable procurement policies and practices, carbon accounting methodologies, etc. These factors make a good set of internal strengths (S) to offset the climate change threat (T). That is not to say it is comprehensive or enough. Attention then turns to (WO) mini–maxi. Depending on the firm, what if the shareholders are climate change agnostic or the manufacturing facility is in a river floodplain? What if the financial state of the firm is not so healthy due to low margins? It might be that the products are highly regulated and subject to scrutiny leading to unsustainable non-value-adding activities. These are all empirical research questions to be tested through analysis and then to be paired and neutralized by the opportunities. For example, higher margins may be feasible where sustainable technologies are deployed that are not taxed so highly. It is already the case for common consumers that polluting vehicles are charged more to enter cities and even for street parking. However, under this alternative way of thinking and using SWOT, the objective is not growth-for-growth-sake, rather growth by and with sustainability in the widest sense of the term. Businesses move away from extraction as a raison d'être, towards regeneration, re-use and social purpose. They become "responsible" (Waddock and Rasche 2012).

The (WT) mini–mini option clearly needs attention. The rigour of the analysis is important in ascertaining firm-level weaknesses. The task then is to mitigate them and ensure that they do not combine with the threat to undermine the business model. Mitigation may take the form of a turnaround strategy. It may just be insurance or risk sharing. The threats, however, being external call for contingencies (what if?) options. Where climate is concerned, business management may well be beyond contingency. It might now be that there is sufficient certainty about impacts for firm action to be taken to build resilience. The world will be warmer and wetter, and the heat and rain will come as extremes, not merely incremental heating and precipitation volumes.

There is one further factor highlighted by Weihrich (1982) and that is of consistency. Any option, whether determined by climate considerations or merely regular strategic business decisions, needs to have an internal consistency within the firm. Much depends on how firms are structured and their geographic domain. Options that are inconsistent with existing systems and structures and culture will struggle to gain legitimacy and are liable to fail at implementation.

Core competence

This chapter has identified and classified resources and capabilities, tested them for strategic potential and used them to embrace macro-level opportunities and to neutralize external threats. There is a class of capabilities that can be leveraged where diversification is a strategic option. The core competence of a firm was first presented by Prahalad and Hamel (1990). Their paper notes that diversification as practised by large firms had been unrelated. International corporations were defining themselves as a grouping of unrelated businesses, and the corporate entity with a supporting structure to match. However, they observed, particularly in the then emergent digital and network corporations, a new trend of diversification in *related* businesses – related in terms of a core product, itself based on a *core competence*. The core competence or capability is, by definition, strategic, but it requires suitable management in order to leverage it and construct the firm development around it. Traditionally, this was to foster growth; but in the present time, this can be around sustainability.

In the words of Prahalad and Hamel (1990, p. 81): "The real sources of advantage are to be found in management's ability to consolidate corporatewide technologies and production skills into competences that empower individual businesses to adapt quickly to changing opportunities." Japanese firms at the time (1990s) were particularly effective in this. Some very good examples are Honda (engines), Canon (optics) and Fujifilm (image chemistry). The Fujifilm case example (*The Economist* 2012) illustrates how a core competence can be leveraged to manage the decline of the core product, in this case, photographic roll film. In particular because the roll film industry had been an effective duopoly – Fujifilm of Japan and Kodak of the USA – the cases are culturally revealing. Essentially, Fujifilm understood its core competence, Kodak did not. The Fujifilm management saw the challenge of digital imagery and diversified on the basis of its then core competence, namely, chemistry. Understanding this led the firm's diversification towards products that could draw on existing knowledge and expertise.

The Fujifilm management saw the threat of digital photography in the 1980s. The response was threefold (*The Economist* 2012):
1. Exploit the existing products (roll-film) as much as possible for as long as possible (through marketing, pricing).
2. Prepare for digital transformation knowing that margins were going to be much smaller than for premium film.
3. Diversify around core competences. In terms of chemistry this was collagen and oxidization. The company had a library of 4000 related chemical compounds to exploit that led to a range of cosmetics (Astalift).

The firm's core competence, chemistry/collagen, was also leveraged for creating optical films for Liquid Crystal Display (LCD) flat screens. The company is now more broadly diversified with competences in medical systems, graphic systems, photofinishing products, motion-picture products, optical devices, recording media, industrial products, semiconductor materials and biomaterials. This was not a painless process. There was considerable restructuring, investment and acquisition. To some extent it was against the prevailing culture of the company and Japanese companies more widely. In business, Japanese managers and the infrastructure supporting them were conservative, and hence less prone to major change. American executives, by contrast, were culturally much more managerialist and open to major change, especially against the backdrop of a challenge to a core product. However, this is by no means universal. The US automobile industry is perhaps a contemporary example of conservatism around a core engine competence.

Kodak, however, was slow and opted for imaging as a core competence rather than chemistry. This led to Kodak-branded digital cameras. However, there was no premium price, unlike with roll-film for analogue camera. It is also similar to the premium charge for printer cartridges relative to the price of the printer in which they fit. Digital cameras were not enough to maintain revenue levels. Moreover,

Kodak did not anticipate the camera phone, an innovation of the mobile phone, that was to render most low-cost and budget digital cameras obsolete. The optics in modern smartphones, moreover, are not Kodak's. Also, while Kodak did pioneer image sharing, it did not leverage this competence into a social network. This space is dominated by Facebook.

The concept of the core competence is important in other ways. Many firms at that time, argued Prahalad and Hamel (1990), focused on brand development rather than the coherence of core technologies. While the companies discussed in their article are branded names, it was not always so. The direction of causality was in building the core competence first involving a "web of alliances" and generating causal ambiguity in the process. It is not about research and development spend; rather it is about innovation.

There are three tests for core competency (Prahalad and Hamel 1990, pp. 83–84):
1. Does it provide access to a wide variety of markets (think the engine competence of Honda in cars, outboard motors, lawn mowers, etc.)?
2. Does the competence "make a significant contribution to the perceived customer benefits of the end product"?
3. How easy is it to imitate? It is the pattern of coordination, learning and investment that provide the sustained advantage (causal ambiguity).

What might this look like in more contemporary times? Core competency is all around. Take the case of Amazon. Amazon is built on a technology and platform core competency. Assessing it from the three tests above, Amazon has a competence in retail, but it is the platform that is the core competency. Jeff Bezos, Amazon's founder, understood how important it was to leverage the platform to access an increasing number of markets. Amazon started as a book seller, which was a fairly self-contained retail space. Naive observers might have seen Amazon only through that lens, but it was from the outset a tech firm, not a book seller. The platform's capabilities were going to be leverageable in terms of scale (near global) and scope (what can we not buy through Amazon?). As a core competency, it met the first test.

The infrastructure developed by Amazon to deliver the product to customers at speed and generally cheaper than bricks-and-mortar book sellers has been demonstrated to contribute to perceived customer benefits of the end product, so called utility. The end product was not the book, but its consumption. That meets test 2. For test 3 it is necessary to ask can the model be imitated? Amazon has a number of competitors, two of which come close in terms of scale and scope, namely, eBay and Alibaba. Alibaba, moreover, operates in a market that is difficult for Amazon and eBay to enter and operate in – a factor that is often overlooked in discussions about geographical diversification.

The Amazon model has been reproduced many times with the emergence of other platform businesses such as Uber, Airbnb, and Deliveroo. One might also ask about low-cost airlines. Is their core competence flying aeroplanes, or the logistics of flying, that is, coordination of planes, crew, passengers, fuel, catering, mainte-nance, etc.? If the latter, is it a platform that is the core competence? If so, are air-lines actually tech firms? Maybe they are logistics firms? In other words, when investigating core competences, analysts should not restrict themselves to the end product; rather, the core competence may well be located in another industry. It may be what enables firms to *deliver* products and not the product itself. It may be technology-mediated process or a knowledge base. *A platform.*

There are challenges for strategists and business managers when basing policy on core competence(s). Discontinuous or disruptive forces can render a core compe-tence obsolete. For example, the music industry's business model prior to networked computers was the control of artists, copyright and publishing, and the release of music on physical formats such as vinyl and CDs. Despite the industry's best efforts at prosecuting individuals for sharing copyrighted content, the advent of small music files (such as MP3) and digital broadband networks changed consumer and con-sumption behaviour. The core competence of control over the music value chain be-came a core rigidity (Leonard-Barton 1992). The pursuit of defending a dated core competence led to a failure to evolve and lead in a world of democratized computing.

Core competences and climate change

There are implications for firms where core competences are the basis of strategic de-cision-making and firm evolution. Taking a rigidities perspective (Leonard-Barton 1992), the disruptive force of climate change is rendering core capabilities in firms obsolete – in particular, oil companies with their core competences of oil discovery, extraction and refining. Oil companies have known about climate change, and their impact as producers of carbon-intensive products, for at least fifty years. They have systematically invested in campaigns, scientific research and think tanks with the ex-press aim of undermining the science, and climate scientists themselves. They have underplayed the impacts and successfully lobbied decision-makers in governments and party politicians. It is not just in climate change, however. The tobacco industry did very much the same when the dangers of smoking became evident back in the 1950s. The promotion now of new delivery methods such as superheated tobacco burning, demonstrates continued defence of their value chain and core competence.

Dynamic capabilities

What becomes increasingly clear is that decision-makers have to consider many variables with complex interdependencies. The concept of dynamic capabilities (Teece 2018) is perhaps helpful in managing choice. In his article Teece argued that firm-level and firm-specific resources and capabilities are all well and good, but are vulnerable in environments and markets of rapid change. They are not inherently strategic. Building on the RBV, Teece et al. (1997) argue that if strategy is about acquiring and controlling scarce resources for profit, then core to strategy development and execution are skills acquisition, knowledge management and building know-how.

Competitive advantage involves not only the possession of resources and capabilities, but also the ability to reconfigure them rapidly and in a timely fashion, that is, making them strategic (Teece et al. 1997). Associated with that ability is a management capability that recognizes that very need. The rapid element is particularly important in fast-moving environments such as in technology sectors. They may well have been in evidence during the Covid-19 pandemic in 2020, where firms rapidly reconfigured their capabilities to meet demand for new or adapted products and services – from engineering firms making medical ventilators to restaurants going into the meal delivery business – or at least partnering with firms that have that capability. The management capability to see either a need to reconfigure, or that reconfiguration can be done to some profitable end, financial and in the development of new and enduring capabilities, is part of the dynamic capabilities concept. This management element is not trivial if managers are going to release funds to enable reconfiguration against a backdrop of considerable uncertainty. In the words of Teece et al. (1997, p. 515): "the key role of strategic management [is] in appropriately adapting, integrating, and reconfiguring internal and external organizational skills, and functional competences to match the requirements of a changing environment".

Strategic managers looking to foster a dynamic capabilities approach have a lot to assimilate either by themselves (CEOs or owners of small firms) or through strategic planning functions by larger firms with strategic resources available for that purpose. For example, strategic managers have to account for what Teece et al. (1997) classify as processes, positions and paths. These include:
- organizational culture, routines, coordination and learning
- asset management – financial, technological, knowledge
- path dependencies (where the organization itself comes from and how the route to the present ordinarily determines a future direction)

Dynamic capabilities and climate change

The concept of dynamic capabilities belongs very much in the RBV competitive strategy approach, optimized for fast-moving arenas where the rewards can be significant, but failure can lead to liquidation. One of the issues with climate-change policy is that the change is gradual. Until it is not. By this is meant the impacts of climate change seem gradual and manageable in a traditional reactive way. Temperatures are rising year on year, but, until recently (summer 2021), they continue to be within broad acceptable tolerances for most infrastructure. Take, for example, steel rails used in the railway industry. Historically, for rail operators, it seemed not worth making significant investments to expand the temperature tolerances of steel to cope with higher summer and colder winter temperatures. There are, however, more storms and heatwaves, and their severity more noticeable and empirically recorded. Summer 2021 saw significant and persistent forest fires across Europe, the Arctic and North America; the link to climate change has been established. Still, however, the world remains broadly recognizable and predictable. The majority are not yet impacted. That said, the question for rail operators now is, should steel that can withstand extreme environmental conditions be used and procured?

The key issue with climate change is when the climate reaches a tipping point. The tipping point occurs when temperature rises are no longer controllable because of chain reactions of severe weather, drought, flooding, ever-higher temperatures as locked-in greenhouse gases are released from melting ice, disease from locked-in pathogens being released, etc. Under these circumstances, firms with dynamic capabilities will be better positioned to cope with the extremes, uncertainty, and the fast-moving nature of change. There will be altered demand patterns, scarcity of resources, pressure on supply chains and labour, among other things.

Summary

This chapter examined the internal workings of firms on the basis that firms are a bundle of resources and capabilities that are configured and reconfigured as the environment changes whether that be technology, resource scarcity, pandemic or climate change.

At the centre of the analysis have been theories of the resource-based view of the firm and the analytical framework VRIO – valuable, rare, inimitable, and organizationally supported. Resources and capabilities that are VRIO are strategic; those that are not valuable, rare, inimitable, or organizationally supported actually give a strategic disadvantage and might be dispensed with.

Porter's value chain enables analysts to equate resources and capabilities with activities and functions – primary functions such as logistics, operations, marketing and sales and services, support services such as HRM, firm infrastructure, technology and procurement.

Finally, this chapter explored the concept of core competences and how they can be leveraged to offer sustained competitive advantage and dynamic capabilities as those that are constantly reconfigured speedily and in a timely fashion. This reconfiguration is easier said than done. Firms have many procedures and routines that are causally ambiguous. They are also path dependent, meaning that what they did in the past determines where they go in the future, even if the path leads nowhere.

Before completing strategic analysis, it is necessary to consider stakeholders in their narrow and broadest senses. How the stakeholders are determined and their influence on business and strategic managers affects choice. This is the subject of the next chapter.

Questions

1. What is the resource-based view of the firm? Why are resources and capabilities so important in strategy formulation and choice?
2. Does a resource have to be unique to be rare? Explain your answer.
3. If a resource is valuable, rare, inimitable and organizationally supported what advantage does that offer?
4. Why if a resource is *not* rare, inimitable and organizationally supported should it be disposed of? Under what circumstances might such a resource be retained?
5. Apply the value chain to one of the following businesses: auto assembler; smartphone manufacturer; fashion retailer; supermarket.
6. What is the difference between a supply chain and a value chain?
7. Why are supply chains important fully to understand with respect to carbon accounting?
8. TOWS is a prescriptive technique of strategic choice. What are its limitations?
9. What is a core competence? Should a core competence always be the basis of product and business strategies?
10. What is a dynamic capability? What makes it different from a capability?

Chapter 4
Stakeholder approaches to strategic analysis and strategy formulation

This chapter introduces the concept of the stakeholder and that strategic analysis and choice can and should be determined by meeting stakeholder needs and expectations.

This chapter:

- provides a definition of stakeholders and classifies them
- explores the complexities of forms of power
- considers the utility of the power-interest matrix for strategic management purposes
- introduces methods of stakeholder identification
- introduces the idea of managing for stakeholders
- discusses the limitations of accountancy and reporting standards in managing for stakeholders
- posits the proposition that the natural environment should be incorporated into the management for stakeholder framework

What is a stakeholder?

The concept of the stakeholder and the idea that stakeholders should be the basis of strategic management, and by definition strategy formulation, dates back to the foundational work on stakeholder theory done by Edward Freeman in his book *Strategic Management: A stakeholder approach* (1984). Freeman defined a stakeholder as an actor that "can affect or is affected by the achievement of the organization's objectives" (p. 46). From that definition, note that someone or some collective of humans set the objectives of an organization, usually firms, but also charities or civil society.

Organizations are usually hierarchical. A firm will have an executive committee and a board that also has non-executives that sit on it, so it tends to be a senior officer or group of senior officers in the organization that have a particular view of what are the interests of the organization, and therefore define the objectives. For firms, this is usually aligned more generally with the key stakeholders, particularly shareholders. However, Freeman's definition raises some questions about the boundaries of a firm.

Often, firms and organizations are viewed as legal entities, defined and regulated by law, such as the Companies Act (2006) in the UK (HMSO 2006). Firms, legally constituted, have liabilities and responsibilities, such as the health and safety of employees. In exchange for registration and the protection of a system of established law, governing property rights, for example, firms have reporting duties.

https://doi.org/10.1515/9783110718430-004

These usually require audited accounts to be presented to the ministry, in the UK to Companies House. Public listed stock companies will hold annual meetings of shareholders where the board of directors is elected, executives' remuneration agreed and policy endorsed. Charities have similar transparency and structural obligations. In England and Wales the regulator is the Charity Commission. This is known as the licence to operate. Implicitly, there is also a social licence to operate. This implicit social licence to operate is often the target of environmental interest groups (Rosenberg 2016).

However, firms and other organizations do not exist in a vacuum. The stakeholders are not confined to the executive, shareholders and employees; rather, a stakeholder is any actor that can affect the activities of the firm or is affected by them. Stepping back and thinking about the implications of such a claim, stakeholders are everywhere, and each have their own interests and objectives. Firms through their agents (executive and non-executive) need to manage stakeholders and their expectations. These agents, however, have additionally to manage for stakeholders. This is because the purpose of a firm may well change. Under stakeholder approaches, firms cease to be pure profit maximizers. They have a purpose that might include very human properties, such as generating meaning for employees and customers, learning, fulfilment, sharing, and civil rights. Though not at the expense of long-term shareholder value. Stakeholder theory does not imply that financial returns to shareholders are reduced or compromised in adopting this framework. However, they may be deferred. This is not the trade-off; indeed, quite the contrary. Freeman makes the reasons for this clear in his YouTube video (Freeman 2009).

Stakeholder management and corporate social responsibility (CSR) are categorically *not* the same.

Bearing in mind the discussions about the boundaries of the firm, and the broadness of the definition of a stakeholder, analysts need to be systematic in the process of identification (who they are), classification (how powerful/influential they are), management approach (trade-offs between stakeholders and resources needed or claimed) and corporate governance – understood as the formal rules, practices, structures and processes that determine the way a firm is managed, ideally ethically, transparently and sustainably.

There are initially two classes of stakeholder, those in the core and those in the periphery. An auditing process may well derive a classification such as that in Table 4.1.

Each identity in Table 4.1 may be broken down further. For example, employees can variously be located in a hierarchy or be of a different profession and seniority. They are not all the same. This will impact on, or determine, their relative power to affect the organization. Moreover, this simple classification of core and periphery may not be sufficient. Much will depend on the type of firm. For example, a firm designing and manufacturing medical devices is likely to work more closely with

Table 4.1: Stakeholder identity.

Type of stakeholder	Identity
Core	owners, shareholders, (shareholder activist groups), managers, employees, suppliers, trade associations, financial institutions, government (regulators)
Periphery	customers, trade unions, competitors, community groups, political groups, lobbyists, customers, universities

Source: Author's table.

government regulators than if it was a software developer or an outsourced office cleaning company. However, having undertaken an assessment of resources and capabilities – in a VRIO analysis, for example – analysts will know what the company is, what it does and what its core competences are. For many firms, consequently, government and regulators are peripheral and not core.

The same is true of customers. Using the case of airlines, most customers have a transactional relationship with a chosen carrier. A ticket is purchased either directly or through an agent (another stakeholder); on doing so a contract is entered into which is protected by consumer law. The airline should then transport customers in a timely and safe way to, and probably from, the specified destination. Some customers have a different relationship with an airline. Loyalty schemes for business and frequent fliers differentiate customers, though they remain transactional. A customer pays more to receive differentiated benefits. On that basis customers are peripheral and are managed in a transactional way.

As has been seen, when considering resources and capabilities, some relationships with customers are more trust-based or even symbiotic. In the automotive industry, suppliers have a preferred status with customers (brands/assemblers, but *not end users*). They work in tandem to supply components that are optimized for the products of the specific customer. Suppliers take on roles such as product development as well as manufacture. The customers outsource capabilities in component design, development and manufacture.

The relationship is less transactional. Even in the example of Microsoft and Intel discussed earlier, the relationship generates conflict and needs to be managed (Casadesus-Masanell and Yoffie 2007). In the medical device industry, customers have an even more integral and symbiotic relationship with suppliers where design, prototyping, testing and licensing are undertaken with real users such as surgeons, and their patients in real-time. The products are often highly specific to sub-specialisms in medicine and surgery. The customers are likely to be public health providers, though the development work is undertaken with professionals who work for those institutions. In this case, it is necessary to differentiate between the end customer and the user (Özel et al. 2016).

Managing stakeholders using a power-interest matrix

The power-interest matrix is best illustrated in Robert Newcombe's paper on the management of stakeholders in a railway construction project (Newcombe 2003). It has been adapted by many others for more general use across sectors and not exclusively for project-based management. The matrix asks, if time and effort are resources, how should managers allocate those resources consumed in the process of managing stakeholders? In the first instance, it is necessary to define our terms. What is power? What is interest?

Dimensions of power

Power has many meanings, but it is usually understood as "power over" something or someone. Essentially, where a manager or superior can make an employee do something that that person would not ordinarily do, the manager has power *over*. It is not absolute because there are ethical and legal constraints. This point alerts us to a key weakness of the concept.

This sense of power is derived from the work of Wright-Mills (1959) and Hunter (1953) and became known as the power-elite model. This model was contested by Dahl (1961). Dahl's study revealed that power is distributed and, while there are powerful actors – at that time in the United States of America largely men – their power was checked by the other actors or organizations. The elite form of power, under this thesis, did not exist. Power in a democracy is not absolute because of a plurality of forces, some of which have equal influence and some, when allied to others, can equalize the power of a dominant actor or stakeholder.

Dahl's work was itself criticized in by two sociologists, Bachrach and Baratz (1970). Bachrach and Baratz argued that Dahl's approach was too descriptive and too reliant on the observable and what is written down. They argued that power cannot always be observed, and, as such, it is difficult to measure. Additionally, there are decisions and non-decisions (Bachrach and Baratz 1963) that occur as a result of what is called a *mobilization of bias* (Schattschneider 1975). Here, those who are subject to power modify their behaviour on the grounds that they understand the forces of power ranged against them; they choose non-decision over decision. In other words, they do not exhibit behaviour indicating a contrary opinion or desire. They consciously accept what is decided. A gets B to do something that B would not ordinarily do, even without asking or instructing them to do so. This might be part of a personal strategy of choosing the fights to have, or it is a structural barrier such as a process that is beyond the individual's influence, but nonetheless, there is a non-decision arising from the exercise of power.

There is a so-called third-dimension of power (Lukes 2005). This is an important dimension in the context of business strategy and climate change. Lukes' approach is a neo-Marxist view, that posits the idea that power is hegemonic. Actors/Stakeholders subject to it are not conscious of this power being exercised over them. Nor are they conscious of, or know that, what they do in response to this power being exercised may be against their own interests.

This approach has a serious weakness. It is the same as that made by Dahl (1961), namely, what is not observable cannot be tested by investigation. The research community can hypothesize but is unable to demonstrate links or correlations because there are no indicators or reliable proxies. It is impossible to show that actors do not know what they do not know! Or that consumption may be against actors' own interests.

There remains a well-documented climate change denial lobby of corporate interests with considerable fossil capital (Malm 2016), and an interest in burning it. So-called "big oil" has been undermining the science of climate change for many years in full knowledge of the consequences (Bell 2021; McGreal 2021). Under a Lukesian analysis, this lobby has hegemonic control over a global population that would be better served by an alternative fuel and economic system, one that does not threaten future life on the planet, let alone individual and short-term welfare. Hegemonic power is exercised through consumption. Those subject to it see their welfare being served by consumption and acquisition, thus perpetuating the ongoing cycle of energy and finite resource extraction and exploitation. It is hard to see any long-term interests of the powerful or powerless being served by *not* mitigating the effects of climate change and/or adapting to its effects.

The notion of power as being able to get individuals to do things that they may not ordinarily do, even if it is achieved by a simple request, equates cleanly with our sense of "power over" and also recognizes plurality in the Dahl sense and, conceivably, non-decisions. Power is located in hierarchy, influence, control over resources, knowledge, communication (skill) and involvement; this is true for core and peripheral stakeholders. The indicators of power include status, claim on resources, representation and symbols. These change over time and are often "semiotic" in that they are revealed through communication, interactions between bosses and employees, executives and shareholders/stakeholders. Even physical artefacts such as the trappings of the corporate office are bestowed with semiotic meaning; that is, they mean different things to different people at different times (Fiol 1991). Hence, these indicators are not so easy for analysts to quantify, and where they are, the analyst will need to validate their meaning with others.

What, then, is an interest? Newcombe (2003) does not define an interest explicitly, only that is it the level of interest in the project. These levels are listed in Table 4.3. In the context of the railway construction project, the stakeholders with an interest are the general public (low level of interest), the rail company, the insurance company (low level of interest, though they have high power), local authority (high level of interest, though with low power), contractor (high level of interest, though with low power) and designer (high, though with low power). On that basis, interest can be seen as the project having an impact on the activities of a stake-holder but, in and of itself, does not elevate the stakeholder to having power, because there is little the stakeholder can do to change the status. For such stake-holders, firms will ordinarily need to do very little to manage them; certainly, it would not be worthwhile in terms of resources to do so. That said, the analyst has to be very careful.

For example, what is "the general public"? Is it a single, homogeneous or dif-ferentiated, heterogeneous entity? For a railway project, for example, some mem-bers of the general public will be living in close proximity to the project and are likely to have a higher interest than those living farther away. Those living closest may well have their own special classification, in *recognition* of their higher level of interest vis-à-vis the general public.

It is important for the analyst, when assessing how to manage stakeholders that have interest but low power, to assess whether they can ally themselves either with those who do have power, for example, the general public with a health and safety regulator, or can build a coalition of stakeholders with interest, where a critical mass makes them powerful. Rosenberg (2016) created a typology of environmental stakeholders that provides a useful guide to types and scale and scope of interests (Table 4.2).

Table 4.2: Typology of environmental interest groups.

Type	Characteristics	Examples	Activities
Conservat-ionists	Focus on the richness and beauty of nature. Their members have broad ideological and political affiliations Membership organizations	National Trust (UK); Royal Society for the Protection of Birds (UK); British Trust for Conservation Volunteers (UK); Ramblers' Association (UK); Sierra Club (US); American Bird Conservatory (US); Union of Concerned Scientists (US); Deutscher Alpenverein (DE); Die Deutsche Stiftung Denkmalschutz (DE)	Buy and manage land and buildings; lobby; protect rights of access; repair and create habitats and supporting infrastructure
Activists	Threaten companies' social licence to operate on the basis of some environmental infringement(s) or intentions. Membership organizations; networks	Greenpeace (international); Friends of the Earth (UK); Extinction Rebellion (UK); Earth First (UK/US); Global Justice Now (UK); Client Earth (UK/DE); Plan B (UK); 350.org (US); Robinwood. de (DE)	Direct action; non-violent protest; legal interventions

Table 4.2 (continued)

Type	Characteristics	Examples	Activities
Localists	Associations of neighbours, villages, towns. Loose associations funded through donations, merchandise, in-kind, etc.	Guides/Scouts associations; residents' associations; localities resisting environmentally damaging economic/ infrastructure development; for example, Frack-Free Lancashire (UK)	Direct action; lobby; legal interventions
Advocates	Consultants who exclusively promote environmental methodologies and technologies such as energy, town planning, landscape architecture and water management Fee-based/Think tank	International Energy Agency; Catapult Energy Systems (UK); TMG Research GmbH (DE); Adelphi (DE); Network for Greening the Financial System (NGFS) (international); see also ERM directory: https:// www.endsdirectory.com/	Environmental services

Source: Author's table, derived from Rosenberg (2016).

In 1995 Royal Dutch Shell planned to dump the Brent Spar oil storage buoy in the North Sea. The company unexpectedly encountered a powerful coalition: a pressure group (Greenpeace), the media (enjoying a good story of people in small boats taking on a global corporation), motorists (threatening boycotts of Shell fuel stations), and, increasingly, international governments. Prior to Brent Spar, this coalition did not exist and, indeed, the stakeholders themselves may not have featured on Shell's power-interest matrix at all. The story is well documented (Özkan and Pfanz 2010; Huber 2015).

Firms need to be aware not only of the potential for coalitions, but also the rate with which they can be formed. Firms then have the option of preventing them from forming, or engaging with the coalition to satisfy it prior to any conflict. The Greenpeace protestors created a highly dangerous situation by actually climbing on to the structure as it was being towed out into the North Atlantic. This case also demonstrates how information asymmetry can work against corporations. The story might have been different had the true nature of the threat to the marine environment been revealed by Royal Dutch Shell and shared with members of the coalition.

What do these cases reveal with respect to indicators of interest? There are a few stakeholders that analysts should seek out, though all stakeholders, by definition, have an interest:

1. *Proximity to the impact (affected by):* an employee is proximate to executive de-
    cisions. A resident is proximate to a rail project.
2. *Access to information is important:* all employees have access to information
    about a firm and its stakeholders. Firms and organizations reveal information
    all of the time. Annual reports are good examples. Other employers publish in-
    ternal newsletters and/or periodic email notifications. However, some employ-
    ees seek out additional information, and those that are members of trade
    unions leverage a third-party to gather and process information increasing
    their level of interest.
3. *Stakeholders and coalitions*: stakeholders with high interest build coalitions
    within and without of the boundaries of organizations; in the Brent Spar exam-
    ple, Greenpeace built a coalition with the media, and then with consumers.
4. *Urgency:* causes stakeholders to increase their interest and build coalitions.

The power-interest matrix has four zones:

Table 4.3: Power-interest configuration.

Level of interest	Power	Zone	Response
Low	Low	A	Minimal effort: possibly willing to join coalitions when mobilized
High	Low	B	Keep informed: able to create coalitions when mobilized
Low	High	C	Keep satisfied: often difficult to manage, critical to successful outcome
High	High	D	Key players: mechanisms exist to manage

Source: Author's table, derived from Newcombe (2003).

Under conditions of stability and predictability, strategic management would allocate
resources according to the relative importance (power/interest) of stakeholders. The
key players (zone D) – those who can directly affect the firm or organization and pay
attention, such as owners, regulators and key investors – receive careful management.
For example, the board of easyJet has devoted considerable effort (Pratley 2020a) in
managing Stelios Haji-Ioannou, the founder and whose family owns 34 per cent of the
company (high interest, high power), in a pre-pandemic dispute about investment in
new aeroplanes.

It is also clear that those in zone C are powerful, but under conditions of stability
are generally non-interventionist. These are most likely to be institutional shareholders
such as pension funds. They can, however, ally with others and move into zone
D. Some activist shareholders can mobilize players in this zone to affect outcomes,
particularly at annual general meetings. The recent activist shareholder action
at ExxonMobil is a case in point (Pratley 2021). Stakeholders in zone B such as

community groups, trade unions, most employees and transactional customers benefit from regular communication. Trends towards alliance with others in the same zone and those in other zones should be monitored. Finally, stakeholders in zone A, largely the amorphous general public who may, or may not, be customers, now or in the future, need little management, if indeed such a thing is possible. Once again, these stakeholders can change their level of interest in crisis situations, as was the case in the Brent Spar example.

Adding rigour and system to stakeholder identification

The preceding sections demonstrate that analysts can approach their understanding of stakeholder interests from many different angles. As is the case in all strategic analysis, the choices that can be made on the basis of that understanding depend on the quality of the inputs. So often, the tools of strategic analysis are under-leveraged. They are not worked hard enough. In the case of stakeholder analysis, identifying the stakeholders and categorizing them may seem a relatively straightforward task, but there is a danger in making assumptions about classes of stakeholders, their unanimity (homogeneity) and their anticipated behaviour in situations of stability and predictability. Climate change and global pandemics, with the attendant uncertainty they bring, demonstrate how the environment can change, and do so fast. Identifying stakeholders and quantifying their power and interest becomes a key task of analysis. For analysts keen to ensure high-quality and reliable inputs, more rigour is needed in the stakeholder identification phase.

Mitchell and Lee (2018) propose five sequential phases for the task of stakeholder identification: (1) stakeholder awareness work, (2) stakeholder identification work, (3) stakeholder understanding work, (4) stakeholder prioritization work and (5) stakeholder engagement work. It is important to note that Mitchell and Lee are concerned with stakeholders engaged in value-creation.

1. Stakeholder awareness work has many familiar elements for strategists, that is, those related to macro- and micro-economic forces. For the macro, Mitchell and Lee (2018, pp. 58–60) suggest managers pay attention to the socio-economic environment that surrounds the organization, the competitive landscape or ecosystem of stakeholders. Analysts need to pay attention not only to current stakeholders in this ecosystem, but also potential ones, like new customers, suppliers, competitors and communities more broadly. In the micro-environment, analysts will trawl the activities of largely internal stakeholders, those that touch the levers of the organization.

2. Stakeholder identification work builds on phase 1 and starts to quantify value creation by stakeholders in the macro- and micro-domains. This is done because in working with all stakeholders, energy and other resources would be wasted and value would be destroyed as a result. However, this does present a real challenge to the analyst. In the macro-environment, for example, does the community in which the firm is embedded add or subtract value, or is it neutral? Does a community with a school or college add value to the firm in a way that a community without a school does not? This is partially answered in the third phase.

3. Stakeholder understanding work involves "organizing activities aimed at knowing the needs and desires of stakeholders of a given organization" (Mitchell and Lee 2018, p. 59). This is where corporate social responsibility (Carroll 1979) comes in, along with corporate citizenship (Carroll 1998) and the responsible enterprise (Waddock and Rasche 2012) more generally – in Carroll's terms, "the social responsibility of businesses encompassing the economic, legal, ethical, and discretionary *expectations that society has* of organizations at a given point in time" (Carroll cited in Mitchell and Lee 2018, p. 59). The emphasis was added to highlight two things. First, society has expectations of organizations, and the responsibility to meet those expectations is discretionary, that is, voluntary. Second, society is a stakeholder, or more precisely, comprised of multiple stakeholders beyond the boundaries of the firm. Pushing this even further, corporate citizenship involves not just passive implementation of the responsibilities of the organization to its stakeholders, but active citizenship, which conceivably involves defining the responsibilities for society more generally. Again, care is needed. These responsibilities are only value-adding if managers are aware of the difference between stakeholder needs and what an organization delivers. That is a management skill in itself.

4. Stakeholder prioritization work requires the aforementioned managers to make the correct and tough calls on prioritization. What do we do next in the hierarchy of stakeholder needs? The stakeholders are not homogeneous; they have competing claims on organizations' resources. They have different levels of power, legitimacy and urgency. Some may be geographically or contractually closer than others (have proximity); some may well have a greater sense of urgency in the value-creation process, such as a customer trying to meet an onerous product delivery or, in the event of organizational tragedy/catastrophe (loss of a plane or toxic chemical leak, for example), to regulators and investigators to ascertain cause and provide support to families who suddenly have elevated needs.

5. Stakeholder engagement work is defined as "organizing activities aimed at taking action with respect to the stakeholders of a given organization" (Mitchell and Lee 2018, p. 60). This is done by building trust between the organization and stakeholders, engaging in charitable ventures and offering employee stock options, though that can seem to be rather more of a bribe than trust-building. It also involves "reputation management" and "impression management", again, potentially rather cynical, but nonetheless value-creating.

Operationalizing this by creating a method inside and outside of the firm is no trivial task, but the data collected and the understanding achieved may be worthwhile in the longer term, especially in fast-moving situations such as a pandemic or catastrophic accident. Equally, if firms use, or plan to use, scenario analysis, these data can add context to the variables and the narratives that are the outputs of scenario analysis.

Moreover, when applied to the power-interest matrix, such rigour enables a much more nuanced analysis. Stakeholders are rarely as homogeneous as they seem in rudimentary classifications. Often the focus is on managing stakeholders; but maybe this is the wrong preposition? What if firms manage for stakeholders?

Stakeholder utility

Stakeholder utility, as discussed by Harrison et al. (2010), decouples stakeholder theory and social responsibility. In line with Mitchell and Lee (2018), they position stakeholder utility as an opportunity to create value for customers and not as a simple nice-to-have. Their approach works on the following logic:
- Knowledge about stakeholders (utility function) leads to an understanding of market imperfections and the potential that knowledge presents firms to create value.
- The creation of value is the starting point for generating competitive advantage and assessment of sustainability (in a business rather than environmental sense).

Harrison et al. (2010, p. 60) specify a focus on core stakeholders, namely, "employees and managers, customers, suppliers, and the firm's owners (i.e., shareholders, partners and/or members)". They exchange "goods, services, information, technology, talent, influence, money, and other resources". The welfare of the firms is a top priority. It is a largely instrumental view; that is, it is advantageous for the firm to manage for stakeholders in this way. Relationships with stakeholders are not just transactional. Firms operating in this way allocate more value to stakeholders than the market requires. In their example, a coffee shop can offer a market rate for employees' wages, but can offer higher wages (more than a market value) on the basis that firms that do not intentionally ascribe additional value to employees or suppliers are missing an opportunity to create additional value and hence generate sustainable competitive advantage. Information about stakeholders in managing for stakeholders is everything. Poor information and judgment can lead to an over-investment in certain stakeholders that is not optimal for the firm, that is, does not create value.

What are the tangible advantages for firms associated with managing for stakeholders? These are identified as (Harrison et al. 2010, pp. 66–68):
- increased demand, often at a higher price, and efficiency of decisions about product properties
- increased innovation, usually product and process
- ability to change, rapidly if necessary, to deal with an unexpected event or technological change; it may also reduce the need for change in the first place

– being able to incorporate external knowledge, that is, absorptive capacity (Cohen and Levinthal 1990)

Stakeholder utility is a measure of the welfare of a stakeholder. Welfare is understood to mean "the well-being of an individual or group and is often conceptualized by a utility function" (Harrison et al. 2010, p. 62). In product terms, it is possible to gauge the value ascribed by customers to various aspects of the product offering, knowing that not all properties are equally valued. In the coffee shop example, a customer does not equally value the quality of the coffee, the nature of service and the comfort of the furniture in the seating area. It is helpful to know what the relative value is because, for example, a competitor or new entrant could have a different configuration of value that is better suited to a customer or customers more generally. A new entrant may have a distinct future orientation, something that firms need to evaluate consistently so as to retain relevance and align with stakeholder utility.

This raises the question about how firms can collect the information and data needed to assess stakeholder utility. Certainly, in an age of big data, customer stakeholders are revealing what they value and by how much relative to other things in the offering through most transactions. Supermarkets, for example, know customers' shopping baskets better than customers themselves and adjust their ranges accordingly. Online surveys are now common outcomes of a transaction, online or physical: "Can we send you a link to our customer survey?" More locally, the owner of a local bookshop used by the author during the Covid-19 lockdown recognized the value in prompting customers (in many cases reminding them that the business was still trading) about new books, or books of interest, *and* offering delivery by hand. In this bookshop case, transactional and non-transactional issues are revealed. The seller trusts the customer to pay after delivery (by bank transfer). The customer values the mere existence of the bookshop in the wider community, and is prepared to pay more for the service than he/she would in a straight transactional relationship with a large online retailer.

Employee stakeholders reveal their utility in terms of retention rates, productivity, absences, union membership, consultation and negotiation. Suppliers reveal their utility through reliability, trust in knowledge transfer, pricing, alignment of processes and investment in systems, optimized for a customer, among other things. The distribution of the benefits to stakeholders is not, therefore, equal and may not occur synchronously, that is, at the same time particularly where relationships are not purely transactional. All stakeholders, however, engage on the basis of an expectation that welfare is enhanced by doing so. It should also be clear that not all stakeholders are equally powerful, and that power is still wielded by the powerful in managing for stakeholders.

Dramatic imbalances of power, however, are a problem, and can lead to a breakdown of the perception of distributional justice between stakeholders. Powerful stakeholders may also betray the trust of stakeholders and leverage their knowledge against a stakeholder. This may happen, for example, if a powerful stakeholder has a change of ownership.

For Harrison et al. (2010, p. 67), competitive advantage is generated from not only sharing of value with stakeholders, but being seen to do so. In other words, managing for stakeholders generates a leverageable reputation. Moreover, managing for stakeholders and the capabilities associated with it can become a core competence. This can be used beyond a single business unit. This also provides an opportunity to "lock-in" customers by "locking-out" competitors whose knowledge of stakeholder utility is less developed. This acts as a first-mover approach and enhances the experience curve.

In order to assess whether management for stakeholders can lead to sustained competitive advantage, Harrison et al. (2010) draw on familiar firm- or corporate-level concepts introduced in Chapter 3. Both "first mover" and "locking-in" link back to the resource-based view of the firm (RBV). Resources and capabilities can be valuable, rare, inimitable, and organizationally supported. Causal ambiguity, for example, will occur in instances where competitor firms are unable to reproduce the value created because they cannot easily know the exact stakeholder relationship(s) that resulted in the benefits and additional value.

Moreover, when considering reputation, such a thing is very difficult to procure; the best way of becoming a firm with a reputation, argue Harrison et al. (2010), is already to have one built by a complex set of actions, some of which are sequential, others not. In other words, to be authentic, consistent and reliable. These are difficult firm-properties to buy.

Managing for stakeholders is not easy and requires resourcing. Harrison et al. (2010) offer the following cautions:
- Estimations of stakeholder utility can lead to an over-allocation of value to a stakeholder. This is a waste for resource.
- A wide and temporal distribution of value to stakeholders might not appear on standard bottom-line indicators. Reporting may need to utilize other indicators of value creation for the purposes of meeting the needs and expectations of some core stakeholders such as owners.
- Longer term time horizons may need to be adopted in order to realize the value created by managing for stakeholders and on which to report.
- Trust-based relationships cannot be relied on absolutely in cases where resources are shared. There is still a role for contractual and transactional stakeholder relationships.

A key factor in moving to a managing for stakeholder strategic approach is demonstrating the value and opportunities created as a result. Porter and Kramer (2011) have their own stakeholder approach, which they call "creating shared value". They define shared value as "policies and operating practices that enhance the competitiveness of a company while simultaneously advancing the economic and social conditions in the communities in which it operates" (p. 66). In particular, Porter and Kramer argue that the creation of shared value is needed to save capitalism from itself. They admit that unbounded competitive business strategies have delegitimized capitalism and that the concept of shared value can re-legitimize it, directing businesses to solving societal problems while driving profitability.

This approach was widely praised at the time, but also had its critics, notably Crane et al. (2014). While on the one hand, they argued, it elevated social goals to a strategic level, it had a number of weaknesses (p. 132):

1. It is *unoriginal* by virtue of its similarity to stakeholder theory and approaches without reference to it.
2. It *ignores the tensions between social and economic/financial goals*: the impression is given that win–win is an outcome of a shared value approach. However, for as long as profit remains the primary objective of firms, the trade-offs necessary create sub-optimal outcomes, or shift the costs on to less powerful, more peripheral stakeholders further down the value chain. Often issues are structural in nature and are reinforced by society more generally. They are not resolvable by firms, even those with social values.
3. It is *naive* about the challenges of business compliance to regulations. It is true that the government sets standards but businesses – particularly in the global context – organize themselves often to circumvent these, for example, labour practices and tax regimes. It cannot be assumed, therefore, that firms will comply.
4. It is *based on a shallow conception of the corporation's role in society*: they set as an objective the relegitimization of capitalism as an objective, without challenging any of the major tenets of capitalism such as self-interest and the operation of the financial markets.

Managing for stakeholders, or creating social value, is *not* corporate social responsibility. Bottom-line benefits are always the purpose and expected by shareholders, though in some circumstances under stakeholder management they are deferred to a later date. It is to reporting that this chapter now turns.

Stakeholder theory and accountancy

Accounting is a necessary activity of firms. In strategy terms, it is a non-strategic capability. Depending on the sector, firm type and size, it can be undertaken internally or outsourced. Even if undertaken internally, the outputs, usually the annual accounts, are externally audited before being published and/or submitted to the Ministry. Accounts serve a number of purposes.

Parker (2018) declares that accounting information is created to "produce better control systems for management . . . and useful information for manage, investors and regulators . . . which often leads to the production of different versions of the truth for different purposes" (pp. 26–27). Anglo-American accounting standards are self-regulated by the profession. The bodies that regulate the profession are subject to lobbies working on behalf of investors, and this affects the nature of the standards and skews the reporting towards meeting the needs of investors, lenders and other creditors. When it comes to sustainability reporting, there is a danger that the reports are "decoupled" from financial reporting so as not to broaden the perceived financial responsibilities of firms beyond the legal entity and the stated purpose. This means separating out the activities of firms over which it has control, from the impacts on the ecosystems that firms externalize. For example, scope 3 emissions derived from the activities of the firm beyond its borders, including distribution and sourcing, are externalized and unreported.

Drawing on Miles's (2019) work on accountancy and stakeholders, Anglo-American accountancy theory is wedded to the purpose of maximization of shareholder wealth, associated with property rights and increasing the value of the firm. Miles draws attention to the two different schools of accounting, namely, financial accounting, meeting stakeholder information needs, narrowly defined; and management accounting, which is control and performance management exercised most effectively in the balanced scorecard (Kaplan and Norton 1992; Barsky et al. 1999).

Financial accounting

The importance of stakeholder influence can be seen in the UK electricity sector, post- and pre-privatization. Miles directs readers to a study by Thomson (1993), which reports that pre-privatization the attention was on core stakeholder groups then defined as government and consumers, with a focus on minimizing profits to avoid price-capping.

Post-privatization, investor stakeholders were prioritized, leading to profit maximization strategies being adopted. Miles also reports on a study by Mattingly et al. (2009) showing that firms with effective stakeholder management processes follow more conservative accounting choices and have greater transparency in their reporting than those that have poor stakeholder management processes. Other cases and examples discussed by Miles include decisions to delay reporting to avoid bad news and the defensive reporting in the tobacco industry in response to health, state and society expectations. Alternative standards have been discussed in the academic literature, for example, *accounting for stakeholders* (Mitchell et al. 2015).

There are also many issues with regard to financial ratios used to justify investment and decisions. The financial evaluation of strategies is important when it comes to making strategic decisions. Many ratios and formulas fail environmental innovation tests as they are designed to maximize growth usually beyond planetary boundaries (Raworth 2017). The literature, however, has many examples of sustainability equivalents, for example, Ecological Value Added (Kratena 2004), Net Present Sustainable Value (Liesen et al. 2013) and SROI – Social Return on Investment (New Economics Foundation 2008). Bansal and DesJardine (2014) show how net present value (NPV) is ordinarily incorrectly framed:

> Each measure collapses data that are recorded over time into a single number, which removes the temporal dimension. Although accounting-based performance measures are historical, they aggregate revenues and costs into a single point in time. The share price also collapses income flows over time into a single figure that reflects the net present value (NPV) of discounted future cash flows. Even mixed market-based and accounting measures, such as Tobin's q (market value of the firm's asset relative to its replacement cost) or economic value added (the value that the firm creates beyond the market return demanded for its risk profile), remove time and are collapsed into a single number. In fact, market measures that look far into the future use discount rates so that future earnings are valued less than present earnings, whereas sustainability scholars aim to give equal or more value to the future. At the heart of most strategic performance measures are assumptions that might be at odds with sustainability.
>
> (p. 75)

Management accounting

Stakeholders in this branch of accounting are important only to the extent that they contribute to the performance of the firm, not in satisfying stakeholder claims and meeting their interests. For example, the balanced scorecard (Kaplan and Norton 1992) links indicators of financial, customer, internal business process, learning and growth with a company's vision and strategy. Clearly, learning and growth involves human stakeholders, many of them direct employees. But the purpose of the balanced scorecard was not to support equity among stakeholders; rather it was to achieve procedural justice, a qualitatively different idea. Sundin et al. (2010) provide a useful case study around an energy supplier that demonstrates the conflicts that can open up, particularly where environmental sustainability has real and tangible costs to the detriment of core stakeholders and the bottom line.

This leads on to the wider question about sustainability reporting and Key Performance Indicators (KPIs). The selection and deployment of sustainability KPIs raises questions about the difference between meaningful and progressive stakeholder and/ or environmental and sustainability reporting, and mere public relations. It demonstrates additionally the importance of thorough stakeholder identification and classification. There are also considerations around normative (what should be) and instrumental (what serves the organizational purpose) reporting. Organizations need to make some decisions early about where they are on this spectrum and deploy reporting protocols appropriately. In particular, should they be integrated with the financial reporting or reported on separately in a sustainability report (Laasch and Conaway 2017)?

Accountancy standards and reporting mechanisms are a feature of firms with a legal status in countries. Increasingly, firms are having to present sustainability reports as a condition of incorporation, that is, having a legal status as a firm, and a licence to operate. The accountancy standards may have some way to go if the nature of competition and the purpose of the firm changes. However, sustainability is not absent from accountancy standards. The Sustainability Accounting Standards Board (SASB) classifies Environmental, Social and Governance (ESG) material issues such as intellectual capital and social capital. These have been used by analysts to track the performance of firms and their stock value.

The Global Reporting Initiative (GRI) is another notable standard and framework that claims the most widely used sustainability disclosure standards.

Firms that have strong management of ESG material issues often perform better than those that do not (Khan et al. 2016), and could even act as a measure of the quality of management. More important is the positive change in the measures, as there comes a point where having good ESG ratings plateaux. In other words, a strong and effective management of ESG material issues gives competitive advantage when it is dynamic and constantly improving (Schoenmaker and Schramade 2018). An open question remains, is the strong management of ESG material issues enough in an age of climate change? Is something missing?

Stakeholder theory and climate change

Stakeholder theory was never conceived as a platform for strategy in the context of climate change. However, of all of the strategy paradigms, it has the most potential currency, but arguably only if the natural environment itself is a stakeholder (Hörisch and Schaltegger 2018). The case for this is:
- all firms rely on the exploitation of natural resources to function whether as raw materials for products or in the consumption of energy to convert those raw materials into products or to drive the machines, whether mechanical or electronic/digital, that add value
- all stakeholder interactions are a sub-system of the Earth's ecosystem and as such cannot sustainably go beyond the planetary boundaries
- human beings assign the natural environment intrinsic value, not just because it is monetizable, but because humans see themselves as part of the ecosystem and seek to protect it from those that deny the fact

(pp. 132–33)

The contemporary origins of this thinking can be traced back to the Brundtland Commission report (WCED 1987) also known as *Our Common Future*. Strategy theorizing is dominated by men. Strategy theory often maps on to the biographies of the people behind the theories and frameworks. Brundtland is as significant as Porter or Barney in the strategy discipline. She transformed the World Health Organization in her time as Director-General from 1998 to 2003. In the 1970s she was Minister for Environmental Affairs in the Norwegian government, and then Prime Minister. It was in her time chairing the World Commission on Environment and Development (WCED) that she developed and popularized the concept of sustainable development. She tells her own story in the United Nation History series (UN 2010).

The precursor to *Our Common Future* was the study undertaken by researchers at Massachusetts Institute of Technology (MIT) (for the Club of Rome), known as *The Limits to Growth* (Meadows et al. 197). This was a computer simulation – imagine computing power in the early 1970s – which hypothesized that exponential economic growth was not sustainable (that is, feasible), because the raw materials for that growth would either run out, they being a finite resource, or be so difficult to extract because of location (natural environments that were too deep, in deep water, too cold, etc.). The Limits to Growth model did not explicitly factor in climate change, despite being known about at that time. The study did highlight limits to global food production (decline after 2020), limits to industrial outputs (peaking in 2008), and population peaks and decline (from 2030), among other factors.

The Limits to Growth had its critics, not least by researchers at the Science Policy Research Unit (SPRU) at the University of Sussex in the UK. They produced a critical report called *Thinking about the Future: A critique of the limits to growth* (S.P.R.U. et al. 1974). Their conclusions were that the MIT models were over-sensitive to particular variables leading to an unnecessary pessimism. Researchers at SPRU are known for optimism and technological solutions, so it was not surprising that they envisaged technological solutions to problems to have a greater impact than the MIT model allowed for. Moreover, the MIT model focused on non-renewable resources, population, agriculture, capital and industrial output and pollution, which amounted to a significant challenge in terms of sufficiency: there simply was insufficient data to run the models with any degree of confidence. This is important for contemporary debates and critique of climate science. Earth's systems are so incredibly complex that data sourcing is an ongoing challenge. With each new source and application, the models improve their predictions to a point that they become highly probable. Also relevant for contemporary debates is that the assumptions that go into modelling are not objective; they come with methodological and political baggage. Surprising in this case was the pessimism coming from MIT in the USA, and the optimism from researchers at a UK university.

The philosophy of Earth as stakeholder

What would the case be for rendering Earth or the natural environment as a stakeholder? Hörisch and Schaltegger (2018) assemble the case by drawing on the work of key scholars writing in this area, in particular Driscoll and Starik (2004) and Stead and Stead Garner (1992). As discussed, all businesses whether in manufacturing or services rely on the natural environment's resources for use, and additionally to process the generated waste. Moreover, in 1886 the US Supreme Court granted the corporation equal protection in law to "persons" (Mintzberg 2015). These rights of the corporation contributed to the further exploitation of the natural world for profit.

There were times – and in some countries still are – when indigenous peoples, slaves and women were not deemed stakeholders. There is a progressive case that the non-human should be a stakeholder if it is being exploited. There is a philosophical debate here. The case has been made for the great apes to be afforded rights similar to humans (Cavalieri and Singer 1996).

What makes the natural environment possibly different to other stakeholders is voice. The natural environment does not have its own; it relies on the proxy voice of other stakeholders. These stakeholders tend to be peripheral and not powerful vis-à-vis other core stakeholders such as owners. Equally, these voices might not articulate the interests of the natural environment, only the voices of those speaking for it. Therefore, the natural environment does not have a means to say exactly what is its stake. What is more, stakeholders as defined (Freeman 1984) are exclusively individuals and groups. They cannot be resources, renewable or otherwise. There is also a fairness argument linked to John Rawls's (1999) philosophy, arguing that while the natural environment cannot be viewed as a stakeholder, its voice can be heard by stakeholders, though not in stakeholders' terms as discussed (Phillips and Reichart 2000). It is also important to note that stakeholder management is not a scheme of ethics.

The natural environment has had a voice before, however. The discovery of the hole in Earth's ozone layer in 1985 was an example of this. The biography of the discoverer of the hole and the full story of discovery to elimination of the causes is told in the BBC podcast Green Originals (BBC 2020). The hole is repairing after the world community came together and agreed an international treaty to end the use of CFCs in refrigeration and aerosols. This case demonstrates the problem with nature not having a voice. The argument has been made that had nature had its own voice in the immediate post-war period when aerosols and refrigeration started to be common features of a growing consumption, it would have told humans that a hole was developing, and it would have consequences for humanity if it was to extend farther. In the absence of nature's voice, humanity was a little behind in its discovery of the phenomenon. Some will say that at least in the end it was discovered, and the voice was heard. The difference between now and then is that ozone layer depletion had one simple solution. There was a single cause (CFCs) and there were also readily available alternatives. Ironically, however, those alternatives, so-called HCFCs, are potent greenhouse gases (BBC 2021). The need to sequestrate HCFCs in the disposal of refrigerators remains high. There is also evidence, that had CFCs not been banned, their effect would already have led to temperature rises in the region of 3.5 degrees Celsius (Young et al. 2021)

Earth's current message of climate change threatens powerful stakeholders' short-term interests. The proxy voice is being managed through international organizations such as the UN, but is slow to being heard among powerful stakeholders, or for powerful stakeholders to ally with it against other powerful stakeholders with sunk assets, such as fossil fuel extraction and refining companies. Climate change is a wicked problem (Buchanan 1992).

A recent example of Earth as actual stakeholder can be found in the case of the Mar Menor lagoon in Spain and reported in *The Guardian* newspaper (Perez-Solero 2020). The lagoon has been particularly susceptible to agricultural pollution that causes extreme algal growth. This, in turn, depletes oxygen levels in the water killing fish and other important aquatic flora and fauna. Legal experts have come together to generate a new mechanism of justice that can grant the lagoon its own rights to exist as an ecosystem. The voice element would be provided by a combination of legal guardians, a monitoring committee of "protectors" and a scientific advisory board. There would also be a right of citizens to file a lawsuit on behalf of Mar Menor. The architects of this proposal have drawn on the experience of New Zealand, Ecuador and India where water courses have been similarly protected.

The pivotal stakeholders are likely to be actors in financial services. Were they to be mobilized, they could have two very particular impacts. First, they could divest from firms whose operations are damaging to the natural environment or are unsustainable. Second, they could decline to invest in projects and/or firms whose operations will damage the environment or not have sustainability policies to deliver carbon neutrality by, at the very latest, 2050. Both of these options require careful and honest reporting, auditing and compliance. It also requires the financial services sector to move from a position of extraction where profit is an end in itself, to one of facilitator of investment in sustainable technology deployment. To do that, the financial services firms' own core stakeholders need to move away from profit maximization and risk, towards rewards (dividends) derived from sustainability-based investments. There have been many such firms engaging in public relations over this, for example, BlackRock and Goldman Sachs. In 2020, BlackRock had a 5 per cent shareholding in ExxonMobil and at the annual meeting that year exercised some influence over policy without actually divesting. Critics have cautioned against taking these firms at their word as they amount to being both poachers and gamekeepers. They effectively "decouple" their mission and vision from their activities (Furrer et al. 2012). However, things change quickly. BlackRock supported Engine No. 1, the activist shareholder hedge fund in securing the appointment of three members to the ExxonMobil board on the basis that the companys' poor environmental record and non-action were actually affecting shareholder value (Pratley 2021; *The Economist* 2021d).

Summary

This chapter has defined stakeholders and examined their heterogeneity in terms of power and interest. Practical methods for identifying stakeholders have been introduced and a detailed consideration of stakeholder utility has been presented as a means of moving from the management *of* stakeholders to management *for* stakeholders, though both within a traditional value-creation framework. The final section introduced the natural environment as a stakeholder and considered the implications for firms in terms of their functions and purpose requiring some adjustments to financial and environmental reporting.

By this stage, analysts should be clear about data, data processing and application. In Part 2, attention turns to the application of tools that enable strategists to decide on strategic options. The more rigorous and comprehensive the analysis, the more likely advantageous and sustainable options will be selected and implemented effectively.

Questions
1. What is a stakeholder? What is not a stakeholder? Why is the distinction important?
2. Take a company from one of the following sectors: oil, pharmaceuticals, social media, construction, higher education, auto manufacture, airline. Identify core and peripheral stakeholders and represent them in a table and/or a diagram. On what basis are the stakeholders selected and classified?
3. What is power? What are the indicators of power in businesses and their networks?
4. What is interest? What are the indicators of interest in businesses and their networks?
5. Does a community with a school or college add value to the firm in a way that a community without a school does not?
6. What are the tangible benefits of managing *for* stakeholders and how does that compare with management *of* stakeholders?
7. Should sustainability reports be part of the annual report and accounts, or presented in a separate document? Why?
8. Why is the natural environment important in business strategy analysis?
9. What are the philosophical and practical issues associated with making the natural environment a stakeholder?
10. Would you adopt a managing for stakeholder approach if you were a director of strategy in one of the industries in question 2? If so, why? If not, why not?

Part 2: **Choice**

Chapter 5
The Tools of prescriptive choice

This chapter returns to competitive strategy and the tools of choice in that paradigm. Principal among them is the generic strategies framework (Porter 1980). This model is contrasted with Faulkner and Bowman's customer matrix, that offers the prospect of a hybrid strategy. Staying in the competitive strategy paradigm, the chapter considers interactive strategies, namely, game theory and cooperative strategy, for competitive advantage (Faulkner and Bowman, 1995). The chapter concludes by reflecting on the implications for sustainability in the application of these frameworks and the choices they present.

This chapter discusses:
- generic strategies
- customer matrix
- competitive strategy
- interactive strategy
- cooperative strategy

Generic competitive strategies

Strategic choice is made on the basis of value. The strategists' preceding analyses (Part 1 of this text) reveal macro- and micro-level factors that affect the nature of value for customers and the ability of firms to deliver it. Readers have seen the importance of knowing in which sector the firm operates, the strategic nature of resources and capabilities, the different interests that stakeholders have and the challenges associated with reconciling those differences. Firms' decision-makers will know, therefore, what is possible and what is not; with which of the competitors to go head-to-head, and which not. In organizing these thoughts, Porter (1980) presents three generic competitive strategies to enable decision-makers to choose a position in which the firm can compete successfully. In other words, a space in which it has competitive advantage, preferably sustainably in the purely economic sense. The generic strategies are:
- overall cost leadership
- differentiation
- focus – cost or differentiation

For each of these there is a dimension of competitive scope (broad or narrow/industrywide or segment) and competitive advantage (lower cost or differentiation). Note that this is a cost model, not a price model. Low cost is often associated with low price. Low cost is an essential component of low price but firms with a low-cost

https://doi.org/10.1515/9783110718430-005

base do not always offer low prices. Much depends on the nature of the industry. In industries where competition is not so intense, the benefits of low cost can be passed on to shareholders rather than customers.

Overall cost leadership

A cost leader's competitive scope is broad and lower cost. The cost leader seeks the lowest broad industry cost base. There can by definition be only one cost leader. To choose cost leadership is a strategic choice that assumes an incumbent's cost base is higher than the sector's lowest cost base can be. In other words, decision-makers at a new entrant or existing competitor in a sector have concluded that their firm can be structured to achieve the lowest cost base in the sector and *supplant* the incumbent. The decision to opt for a cost leader position has a number of implications. Decision-makers need to have an excellent knowledge of their own firm's cost base and how, year on year, to reduce it. Other firms will, at the same time, be vying for cost leadership in a sector. Those vying for cost leadership will need to have a good knowledge of an incumbent's cost base and how that cost base reduces year on year. Though it may be the perception that the incumbent's cost base is not reducing, a fact that gradually undermines the incumbent's competitiveness. Cost leaders need to know precisely the value they create. Techniques employed by cost leaders are some of the following:
- scale economies
- outsourcing or offshoring of inputs
- efficient design of product and process
- total quality management (TQM)

Differentiation

Firms with a broad competitive scope that do not achieve, or aspire to, cost leadership are differentiators. Differentiation implies product offerings that can attract a premium price on the basis of characteristics that customers value. Competitors position themselves accordingly to highlight their differentiation and the value represented. These include:
- brand
- quality and reliability of product and service
- unique product attributes, functionality, compatibility with other products in portfolio or with other companies, customizability
- customer service, for example, loyalty schemes, returns policy
- environmental sustainability, including packaging, energy consumption and recyclability

Being a differentiator does not imply a high cost base, or indeed limited attention to, and action on, the cost base. It implies that being a cost leader would require an aggressive strategy of cost-cutting that might come at the expense of the factors of differentiation that attract a premium price. It is important also to note that firms have many customers of different types who equally pay in different ways. For example, the customers of new media platforms are *advertisers*, not users. Users are attracted to the platform by its functionality and are given access to it not by the payment of a fee, but rather by allowing the platform owner to harvest data about the user that enable targeted advertising. This is valuable to *paying* customers, namely, companies seeking to sell their own products and services knowing their own key customer demographic. This volume has a Twitter feed, @ClimateDaily1. The advertising it attracts aligns with the theme of the account, albeit imperfectly.

Cost focus (focus – cost)

Firms with a cost focus have a narrow competitive scope, that is, they operate in an industry segment, and hence cannot be cost leaders in some industries broadly defined. Broad competitive scope attracts costs that are militated by scale economies and highly efficient processes. Cost focus firms can occupy a space in a bigger or broader industry, offering value to a portion of the potential customers in that industry sector. Scale economies are again important for firms with a cost focus, and, indeed, their ability to construct unique value and chains around their narrow offering is key to their success. Cost focus firms, in common with cost leaders, do not add cost unnecessarily. Growth comes from gaining market share rather than diversifying into other products and services. They know what they do and how they do it, and the value of what they do for their customers. Aldi supermarket's competitive scope in its industry is narrow. It also changes/broadens over time. Aldi is primarily a discounter with a limited range. It has scale partly facilitated by its narrow focus and the opportunities that present for competitive sourcing.

Differentiation focus (focus – differentiation)

Some companies target markets with narrow competitive scope, but with a product that is distinct and often, but not exclusively, premium. There are many examples of this kind of focus. Tesla with its offering of high-performance electric cars could logically be seen as pursuing a differentiation focus strategy. This relies on the assumption that Tesla is in the same industry as more traditional automobile manufacturers such as Mercedes-Benz/Daimler and BMW. Tesla is now widening its competitive scope with a range of mid-price vehicles with reduced performance, while arguably remaining niche. Tesla may not in actual fact be an automobile manufacturer at all; rather its core business and competences lie in battery technologies.

Ecover, the Belgian cleaning products manufacturer, appeals to environmentally conscious consumers. That presents a narrow competitive scope, with high price acting as a compensation for limited scale. While in the supermarket sector, some retailers have limited ranges at limited locations: Waitrose in the UK. Equally, in Germany, the growth of the narrow focus "bio Supermarkt" is evident. Retailers such as Alnatura, Basic and Denns are good examples here. Moreover, niche does not need to be premium price – Convenience stores in towns and cities also have a narrow focus both in terms of product range and geography; many cater to a particular demographic in very specific neighbourhoods. Many so-called luxury brands fall into this category. Louis Vuitton Moët Hennessy (LVHM) is a family-owned conglomerate with a large portfolio of brands – seventy-five "houses" operating in six sectors in 2020 – that are notionally differentiation focus. The brands are high-end fashion, exclusive jewellery and watches, quality or regional wine/spirits and aromatic perfumes. Arguably it is better understood as seventy-five subsidiaries each with their own strategies, focus or otherwise. The governance of these houses may well require portfolio management thinking.

Application

The rigorous application of the generic strategy framework is, again, not trivial, though it appears deceptively simple. For the cost leader, what is a broad target? Cost leaders that are frequently cited include Ryanair (airline) and Aldi (supermarket), but this depends on how the industry is defined. Ryanair is arguably not a cost leader in the airline industry; it is a cost leader in a sub-sector of the airline industry determined by the flying range of its aeroplanes. It is short haul; it does not compete directly with full-service airlines such as Lufthansa, Air France or British Airways. Its competitive scope is narrow, though appeals to price-conscious consumers who are prepared to accept lower levels of service in return for access, affordability or cheapness.

A cost leader in the transport industry is likely to exhibit the following characteristics. Its fleet, whether buses, planes, cars, trains, etc., will be of one class/type, making it easier to maintain, service and clean. It also enables procurement savings to be made as a result of bulk purchase, often a whole fleet in a single order or transaction. Low-cost transport operators are unlikely to have signature head office buildings. Service will be frugal. On aeroplanes food will be extra and passenger density will be high. Fuel costs will be hedged, that is, traded in the futures market. This enables the firm to anticipate costs and price accordingly well into the future. The stowing of luggage may attract an extra charge. Ancillary services will be outsourced. Destination airports are often in secondary locations, some way away from metropolitan centres. Transactions with the firm are likely to be virtual, namely, bookings, cancellations and customer service more generally. The companies themselves will have significant behind-the-scenes investments in IT systems. Arguably their core competence may not be flying aeroplanes or maintenance, rather IT systems management and capabilities. Though perhaps counter-intuitively, the fleet is likely to be young. Newer vehicles or aeroplanes are more efficient; they reduce overall costs and are more reliable, requiring less maintenance, repair and other downtime. For a low-cost operator, safety is paramount; it is not a "frill" to be traded away. The whole reputation of the company depends on safety.

While these characteristics are to be anticipated for firms pursuing cost-leadership or cost-focus strategies, the application is tricky. For Porter, strategic choice requires decision-makers to choose a position and go with it. Be a cost leader, a differentiator, cost focus or differentiation focus firm. Pick one and one only. Not to do so is to lose strategic focus. Hence there can be only one cost leader. There is an obvious limitation with this approach. Maybe it is possible at least to straddle the types? For example, in the short-haul airline industry, could easyJet be both a cost-leader and a differentiator, assuming that the industry is defined in terms of the range of the aeroplanes flown by operators? The cost-base of easyJet is higher than that of Ryanair, but it is very low in the context of its differentiation. easyJet differentiates in terms of destinations; it does have slots at primary metropolitan airports across Europe, including Gatwick in the UK and Munich and Berlin in Germany. The airline does have a premium club for frequent fliers. The management chose not to be a cost leader in the short-haul, point-to-point, industry sector, while exhibiting a fair percentage of cost-leadership traits without being one. It is also the case that in dynamic markets and sectors cost leaders may need to start to differentiate. Size is a trait that enables economies of scale, but it can also lead to inertia. Younger, more nimble competitors do aspire to cost leadership. There may come a point where a cost leader relinquishes that position through a progressive, incremental differentiation.

Equally, is it meaningful to think of all firms with a cost-focus not to be differentiators? Is it true that the LVHM houses do not have a cost focus as well as a differentiation focus? In the sector in which they operate, they may well have the most efficient supply-side operations, namely, supply chains and control inputs like cost leaders. They have scale economies and a global reach. On the demand-side, however, their brands are differentiated. They are luxury products that are attractive to wealthy international elites, or those who aspire to be. Is it possible, therefore, to be "stuck in the middle", or better, to be hybrid?

Hybrid generic strategies

While Porter's generic strategies are determined by cost, Faulkner and Bowman (1995) use price offered to customers as their choice mechanism and their framework, expressed in Table 5.1, takes the shape of a compass. Price is something much more tangible to buyers. In making choices, however, strategists have to know what is the perceived satisfaction experienced by the customer of buying and using the product or service (Perceived Use Value, PUV) at any particular price point.

Table 5.1: Customer matrix.

Route/Direction	Perceived use value (PUV)	Price	Comment
1 – North	High	Middle	Firms often start here; cost base can be low due to experience and scale economies. Can build market share – but where quality is imitated/matched, may warrant shifting to route 7 and then 8
2 – North-east	High	Middle-high (premium)	Similar to focus-differentiation (generic strategy); danger of moving into upmarket segment that cannot be sustained
3 – East	Middle	High	Firms raise prices to maintain profitability without increasing PUV; only works if all firms in sector follow suit and avoid a price-war
4 – South-east	Low	Middle-high	Sustainable short-term only in situations of supply constraints – long-term route to decline and failure
5 – South	Low	Middle	Cost cutting or competitors increasing quality (PUV) causing a relative downward movement. Firms need constantly to monitor customer PUV
6 – South-west	Low	Low-middle	Moving into down-market segments; danger of undermining any products in a portfolio that have a high PUV – dragged down by association
7 – West	Middle	Low	Price relative to value is low. Delivers market share, scale economies and learning experience. Can enable a shift to route 8 in due course
8 – North-west	High	Low-middle	Optimal – product is higher quality than competitors and cheaper for customers – can maintain market share, but must be "lowest-cost producer" by employing new process technology. If imitable, may need to move to route 7

Source: Author's table, derived from Faulkner and Bowman (1995).

Using this framework, it may seem that low-cost airlines or low-cost automobile manufacturers take routes 6 and 7. Customers have a relatively low PUV, other than a means to travel at low price or to purchase a car with few frills. However, managers need to ask what is the PUV associated with safety. While low-cost airlines may offer only cramped cabin conditions and make extra charges for luggage and food, they do not compromise on safety, which is probably the highest quality of them all. Equally, they tend to have good punctuality, another factor that is valued by customers and the airlines themselves as turnaround time is vital to lower airport charges and full utilization of planes. This may contrast with unbranded clothing, or even branded fast-fashion where limited durability is expected: the price and quality match each other. Fashion customers look for the product to last for a season.

Differentiation strategies occur in the East (routes 2–4). Products from route 2 strategies command a price premium (brand, unique technology). Maintaining the PUV is central to the strategy. It may be also that the firm has a complementary product ecosystem that locks customers into the brand – Apple, for example.

Firms looking to adopt a route 2 strategy will need to ensure that there is a suitable infrastructure to support the products. For example, Faulkner and Bowman (1995) consider an Italian restaurant looking to move from routes 6 or 7. They have to change the menu and increase the quality of the food, the ambience of the restaurant and the quality of the service. However, do they have the know-how or even the right location? High-end restaurants are not easy to copy. This strategy can easily fail.

Routes 1, 7 and 8 are hybrid strategies and are similar to being "stuck in the middle"; many, however, will be consciously following hybrid strategies. Common to hybrid strategies is low-to-middle pricing. Counter-intuitively, for a relatively low price, the perceived benefits to the consumer may be high, much higher than the price indicates it should be. There are a host of reasons for this approach. Firms may be:
- seeking to achieve market share by under-cutting rivals that are pursuing differentiation strategies
- new entrants – seeking to gain market share
- responding to recent moves by competitors that have cut their prices – a so-called price war is developing (this may also be a game-theoretic response)
- natural low-price differentiators that have enabling scale economies

Margins, costs and prices

Not all cost leaders offer the lowest price. Depending on the competitive nature of the sector, cost leadership can enable high margins and hence high profits. For example, if a firm has a unique product, perhaps one that is patented, and a low-cost base, it can charge a premium price for the product. Many pharmaceuticals have this quality. Very few "budget" product providers, however, are *not* cost leaders or cost-focused. Non-cost leaders may adopt a pricing policy based on parity whereby a product is price-matched but at higher cost of production. These companies accept lower margins in order to compete. True cost leaders confronted with such pricing strategies by competitors can, of course, leverage their cost-leader privilege and reduce their prices further, themselves earning a lower margin, but sufficient to maintain and sustain price leadership of a particular product, family of products or service. This strategy was followed by Morrisons supermarket chain in 2014 responding to falling market share, particularly to discounters (Butler and Farrell 2014). The company admitted that price-cutting would impact on profits.

Generic competitive strategies in perspective

As with all tools employed in what are known as prescriptive schools (Mintzberg et al. 2009), data are crucial. Every aspect of the business has a cost and a value to that cost associated with it. Strategic choice correlates closely with what the data illustrate about markets, both aggregate and segmented. Common in prescriptive schools is benchmarking against competitors or exemplars in other sectors. In the public sector, this translates into league tables that are designed to offer customers measures of the relative merits and benefits of "transacting" with one provider over another. For example, universities have in recent years been benchmarked, graded and classified, in line with secondary schools before them. The danger of benchmarking, however, is that firms and institutions seek to climb into higher quartiles. Benchmarking manuals represent and display performance in these terms, leading at best to mimicry and institutional isomorphism. At worst, however, firms, products and services become uniform, indistinguishable and me-too. It is also the case that a rise in a league table comes at the expense of a competitor or partner institution, if not a firm. Elements of the prescriptive schools are often based on war analogies. Competition is a battle to be won. There are missions, manoeuvres, tactics. There is a necessary discipline, authority, leadership, troop morale, etc.

Also characteristic of these models/frameworks is the assumption that sectors and markets are stable and that data and the analysis they enable are fit for the future: what is true today should be true also tomorrow. However, in line with the theme of this text, stability is not a given. Global pandemics are no longer what Taleb (2007) calls, black swans. Climate change is happening; its impacts are knowable, though unpredictable. An over-reliance on prescriptive methods to determine strategic choice is cautioned against. *That is not to say* that analysts should not apply rigorously the models and frameworks. They tell us much about market dynamics, consumption patterns and the environment more generally. The future will incorporate some of these trends and exhibit these patterns. What will become more important in the future is resilience. Strategists will need to build resilience beyond competitive strategy. Successful strategies, therefore, may not always be competitive ones.

There is evidence also that firms operating in emerging economies (EEs) are differentiating on sustainability grounds. They are engaging in what are called voluntary environmental management (VEM) practices. In emerging economies, environmental standards can be quite lax, something that can be exploited by domestic and international firms in order to externalize environmental impact costs. Firms in these economies (India, Brazil, Turkey, China, Russia, Mexico and Indonesia, for example), may be less regulated by the state than those in developed economies. However, research shows from a leading EE, Turkey (Tatoglu et al. 2020) that firms in EEs are deploying VEMs as differentiators; that is, as a strategic choice. Such practices include applying for and implementing the global ISO 14000 series environmental accreditation and/or becoming a B-Corp. Such accreditation is interpreted by customers as a measure of quality of product and process, and it also potentially mitigates the negative impression given by governments in EEs – though not exclusively – that environmental standards and social responsibility more broadly are not important.

The discussion so far has been about competitive strategy that is, to some extent, discrete and restricted to a firm. In reality, firms interact with one another. It is to this thinking that the chapter now turns.

Interactive strategies

Game theory

There is a sub-discipline of micro-economics known as game theory. Managers make decisions relative to others within and without of the firm. The game of chicken simulates a situation between two players on a collision course. Imagine two car drivers consciously driving at each other. If they both hold their nerve, the likelihood is that both drivers will die in an awful crash. If one driver deviates, the crash is avoided; one driver is declared a victor, the other the loser. A good illustration of chicken is the British government's approach to negotiating with the EU over treaties, for example, the Northern Ireland Protocol (NIP).

The game is captured in Table 5.2.

An analysis of the situation indicates that the British government seeks not to implement all of the provisions of the Protocol because it compromises the sovereign integrity of the British state. However, the only way to negotiate a trade deal prior to departure from the EU was to agree the Protocol with the EU and implement the treaty's schedules, which included erecting an international border in the Irish Sea and building the physical and digital infrastructure for customs checks.

Table 5.2: Political chicken between the British government and the EU.

Actor 1	Actor 2	Decision	Outcome
Government – no compromise	EU – no compromise	no compromise	Crash – both lose (implications for single market integrity and return of violence to NI)
Government – no compromise	EU – compromise	one-sided compromise	Government wins temporarily; EU swerves (extends implementation period)
Government – compromise	EU – no compromise	one-sided compromise	EU wins; government swerves (implications for integrity of the UK single market)
Government – compromise	EU – compromise	shared agreement	Both win; ideally, no side is seen to back down or lose face. Maybe

Source: Author's table.

Economists can use game theory – and the game of chicken in particular – to assess the utility of options ranging from compromise on both sides to no compromise on both sides. This is a particularly interesting game of chicken because the Protocol is a ratified international agreement. Observers believe that the British government is attempting, rather unconventionally, to redefine the Protocol at implementation rather than during the preceding negotiations. Hence, in knowingly missing a deadline, the British government witnessed the EU putting back the deadlines for the implementation of the commitments. In this case, the EU swerved to avoid the crash. However, in agreeing an un-negotiated extension, the EU only turned around the car, and is again on a collision course with the British government. If they crash, both lose. Peace in Northern Ireland is at stake. The British government seeks, by executing this game, to get the EU to abandon the Protocol; the EU cannot do so because it is an international border with the EU and hence provides access to both the EU's customs area and the single market. It also complies with World Trade Organization rules. The sensible option for all, one involving co-operation, would be for both parties to make concessions.

While this is an overtly political example and application, it raises some interesting questions about economic rationality. What if one of the actors is not rational? Alternatively, what if the two actors (even that assumes that the British government and the EU are homogeneous entities, which they are not) have a different sense of rationality? Chris Grey, a leading academic observer, astutely writes (Grey 2021):

> Some in the EU may still think, as some British commentators do, that the UK will quietly become more reasonable whilst continuing to bluster for domestic purposes. I think that is unlikely and, as mentioned, the placing of the Frost-Lewis [chief negotiator–NI Minister] article in the Irish Times is one indication of that. It also underestimates the extent to which post-Brexit British politics has become detached from rational calculation or, perhaps, operates according a rationality of its own. Thus . . . it seems clear that Frost-Johnson [chief negotiator–PM] believe that their approach works, has no domestic downsides and will have few international repercussions.

How might this work in the context of a price war between supermarkets and their response to so-called discounters gaining market share at their expense? In the case of Morrisons, a large supermarket cuts its prices to customers in store at the expense of margin. The managers at the supermarket's competitors had two tangible options: either respond themselves by price-matching or ignore the competition and hold prices. What is the logic of both? The scenario was that one supermarket in particular was losing *critical* market share in the sector, albeit at a time when all other big players were losing market share. The management surveyed customers and ascertained that the most important part of the value proposition was price. The management decided that reducing prices was a strategic option and calculated that a higher market share, or retention of the existing share, would offset the effect of reduced margins. The management decided on a price-cutting policy knowing that their competitors would respond. Holding prices would have been a logical response; however, the management had the discounters (Aldi and Lidl, in particular) in sight, not the other members of the "big four" club of UK supermarkets. What the big supermarkets did mattered less.

Where the goal is to gain market share from other big supermarkets in the absence of discounters, should the competitors, or competitor, also cut prices, what would the benefit be to the original price-cutter? Actually, this might be the least good outcome, as both/all price cutters would forfeit margin and profit without increasing market share. Other aspects of the growth strategy might come in to play, such as advertising, but for the purpose of this exercise, the analyst assumes no other variables impact on decisions. So, the original decision was based on a hope or some expectation that the competition would not follow suit and cut prices. The strategy only works if market share can be gained by price-cutting. The competitors also know this. Competitors would be fearful that the gain in market share of a rival might have a long-term impact and customers might not return having experienced the competitor's product. Arguably, customer loyalty to supermarkets is not that high. The switching costs for customers are low. The prices will have to be very low and stay that way if the market share is to be maintained. Price cutting, consequently, is unlikely to be viewed positively in supermarket boardrooms.

If the product was high value and the switching costs higher, then customers might be locked-in to the product for some time. For example, bus companies purchasing a fleet from a limited number of suppliers (in the UK, Scania, Alexander Dennis, MAN, Mercedes). When purchasing vehicles, there are scale economies that can attract favourable pricing from suppliers. There are also issues about maintenance, parts availability and finance, among others. If the decision on a new fleet was based on price alone, it would need to be a significant discount to convince the buyer that the switch was worth it. However, if the switch was made, then the competitors would have lost an important customer for a number of years, if not decades. Bus fleets are renewed in cycles, not piecemeal.

Game theory frequently demonstrates that co-operation makes business sense. Winning may bring its rewards, though it may have unintended consequences. Losing can be catastrophic. Holding one's nerve may deliver an adrenalin rush, but sustainability is not measured that way.

Cooperative strategies

Cooperative strategies are not incompatible with prescriptive approaches to strategic choice. Cooperation in growth strategies through strategic alliances, or alliances that raise barriers to entry, are common. Cooperative strategy can go beyond mere competition. There are three types:

1. *Cooperative strategy to grow the customer base* – consider Bluetooth chips. Bluetooth connects devices together, for example, mobile phones and headphones, computers and printers. It is a component of the Internet of Things (IoT). Indeed, it is the intermediary technology that enabled Track-and-Trace in mobile apps during the Covid-19 pandemic. It was not developed for that purpose, but would likely be endorsed by its developers. Bluetooth transmission and receiving technology is owned by Ericsson Mobile. Bluetooth works over a shortwave, short-range, unregulated radio frequency. Ericsson originally designed it to enable hands-free mobile headsets. However, Bluetooth chips, now ubiquitous, were quite expensive in 1997. To make them cheaper, they needed to be in more devices, not just those made by Ericsson, but also competitor products. Ericsson achieved that by adopting a cooperative strategy. They created a Special Interest Group (SIG), initially with IBM, Intel, Nokia and Toshiba. The purpose of the SIG was to develop standards for the diffusion of the technology and make it available to all firms that were potential users or developers free of charge, subject to the SIG's rules for exploitation. Ultimately, the more users, the greater the utility of the technology and the cheaper the costs of the enabling chips. There are now more than 1500 members of the SIG. The technology was introduced to BBC radio listeners on an edition of Global Business in November 2000 (Day 2000).

2. *Open-source cooperative strategy* – while Bluetooth is a free resource for developers, the code is not freely revealed. Other projects, however, are what are known as open-source. The code can be downloaded, manipulated, developed and commercially exploited. The most well-known open-source project is the Linux operating system for PCs. It may seem insignificant in that context, powering less than 3 per cent of PCs globally, but the Linux kernel can be found in Google's Android and Chrome operating systems. It runs many of the world's servers and digital televisions. That kernel is freely maintained by volunteers remotely working together in user groups. Some large corporate users provide resources to the user groups to help support development that can later be commercialized further. Innovation

becomes democratized (von Hippel 2005). A business model can be generated around branding of commercial products (for example, Red Hat) and/or technical support for commercial users. The code is freely available through an open-source licence known as GNU General Public License. The user groups have their own cultures, which are the subject of their own study (Christian 2015).

3. *Cooperative strategy to improve social welfare* – free-revealing serves social welfare. Enabling borderless communication, democratization of product development, the building of *communities of practice* (Wenger 1998) and unconscious mentoring are good things. But cooperative strategy serving social welfare is not just about digital code. The growing and developing sharing economy is illustrative of this. There are now many platforms that enable people to exchange resources with cash or in-kind payments (*The Economist* 2013). Indeed, small farmers have traditionally worked cooperatively, sharing plant, labour and knowledge and leveraging collective purchasing and selling power. Photographers share idle equipment, as do car owners.

At a business-to-business (B2B) level, spare capacity in manufacturing, for example, can be exchanged. This is the business model for the sustainable clothing manufacturer Community Clothing in the UK. To keep costs down and meet a mission of providing employment and restoring economic prosperity to deprived areas in the UK, it manufactures "timeless" and quality garments using the seasonal excess capacity of clothing factories in Blackburn in the UK. The fashion industry is cyclical and there are months in the year where factories are idle as they await the next seasonal collection. By dispensing with the concept of fashion, or at the very least seasonal collections, firms like Community Clothing can buy spare manufacturing capacity when it is plentiful. That said, the fashion industry itself may well be in transition. Gucci has reduced its annual fashion shows from five to two, reflecting the new reality and aspiration of seasonless and sustainable fashion and also capsule wardrobes. Jean Paul Gaultier is a recent convert to sustainability (Nicholson 2019).

Business models

Firms employing cooperative strategies often have business models that have different notions of value, serve different industry segments and exhibit different ownership models. Table 5.3 summarizes perspectives from competitive, hybrid and cooperative approaches.

Table 5.3: Comparison of competitive, hybrid and cooperative business models.

Factor	Competitive	Hybrid	Cooperative
Purpose	Profit maximization	Profit maximization with social welfare objectives	Social welfare maximization
Ownership	Shareholders	Shareholders	Members, partners, family, shareholders, hybrid
Value	Unique proposition	Unique proposition	Timeless circular proposition
Intellectual property (IP)	Protected (copyright/patents)	Protected (copyright/patents); SIGs	Unprotected, open/freely revealed; open SIGs
Resource utilization	Peak/demand	Peak/demand	Off-peak/slack
Costs	Optimized – scale, transactional suppliers	Optimized – scale, tiered suppliers with social welfare obligations (for example, fair trade); employee engagement; remuneration	Distributed – social welfare driven
Prices	Optimized – costs, markets, volume	Optimized – core stakeholder utility	Optimized – broad stakeholder utility
Innovation	Closed and/or fast	Closed and/shared	Open, timely, appropriate, sustainable
Sources of capital	Shareholders, banks, other financial services – short to medium terms	Shareholders, banks, other financial services – medium to long terms	Shareholders, members, ethical funds, family, sponsorship, crowdfunding
Product life cycle	Degenerative/linear	Imperfect butterfly	Butterfly/circular

Source: Author's table.

These classifications are ideal types and as such do not represent reality, only a form of reality for comparative purposes.

Firms employing competitive strategies are likely to be profit maximizers and focus on core stakeholders, namely shareholders. They will have a growth imperative. The value proposition is likely to be unique or focused on a particular industry segment, satisfying a customer value preference for some configuration of valuable functionality. Intellectual property is likely to be owned. Though in technology sectors, SIGs may be evident. Firms will have or be members of efficient supply chains or value networks with costs maintained by scale or by shifting to suppliers, or indeed customers. Prices reflect the cost base and/or monopoly status in a market. Innovation occurs fast, either entering markets as "first movers" or "fast seconds". Capital is supplied internally or through existing financial services bearing responsibilities for timely returns. In life cycle terms, products are sold shifting end-of-life disposal on to buyers.

Firms employing hybrid strategies are likely to be profit maximizers with social welfare objectives. For example, Innocent Drinks, owned by a profit maximizer, The Coca-Cola Company, that facilitates its subsidiary to maximize social welfare while still returning profits to the parent. Their sustainability credentials may come through external auditing such as B-Corp standards and view profit as a force for good. Growth will be an objective. They work to scale and apply technology solutions to supply chains. Costs are optimized with clear internal stakeholder welfare measures. They often operate energy-efficient factories/warehouses. Prices reflect the premium nature of their value proposition. They are constant innovators that are protective of intellectual property. Capital is provided from shareholders or acquired on the basis of security from the parent. They are unlikely to be butterfly with respect to their product life cycles, but they may utilize recycled materials.

Firms employing cooperative approaches to strategy may have social welfare maximization at the heart of the mission and vision. Community Clothing, for example, has a clear mission, but it is not a charity. Ownership is likely to be plural and the value proposition not subject to temporal changes such as trends or leading technological shifts. Intellectual property is likely to be unprotected, shared, freely revealed or simply generic. In technology sectors, SIGs may be evident. Growth is unlikely to be the overriding objective; but it will be an objective if it serves social welfare purposes. Innovation meets sustainability and social welfare objectives and may well be around the business model rather than, or as well as, the product or service – for example, in the care sector, Buurtzorg in the Netherlands. Sources of capital are likely to be plural and the product life cycle tending towards butterfly (Raworth 2017).

Summary

Strategic choice builds on the analysis already conducted (Part 1 of this text). Decision-makers know what they are both in terms of market participants and resources and capabilities. On that basis they can optimize their product and service offerings around a series of generic cost and/or price competitive strategies. Decision-makers may also engage in game-theoretic approaches that are interactive, sometimes damagingly so. Alternatively, but equally interactive, decision-makers can opt for more cooperative approaches to strategy. This may align with broad stakeholder engagement to meet social welfare as well as profit objectives. These different approaches will have contrasting impacts on organizational structure, business partners, sourcing of finance, internationalization and innovation. Critically, these choices will impact on growth, how to achieve it and whether it is ethical to do so. It is to that question that this text now turns.

Questions

1. An overall *cost leader* serves a broad market and a firm following a *cost-focus* strategy serves a narrow market. Consider broad and narrow in the context of the following industries: supermarkets, airlines, tourism, automobile assembly, social media, fast food, fashion, wind turbines. Provide examples of firms and justify the selection.

2. A *differentiator* serves a broad market and a firm following a *differentiation focus* strategy serves a narrow market. Consider broad and narrow in the context of the following industries: supermarkets, airlines, tourism, automobile assembly, social media, fast food, fashion, wind turbines. Provide examples of firms and justify the selection.

3. Faulkner and Bowman's customer matrix differs from that of Porter's generic strategies model in what way?

4. What can a firm that is not a cost leader do to match the prices offered by cost leaders? What is the danger of doing so?

5. Why is chicken a dangerous game to play?

6. What is free-revealing and how is it functional for businesses operating in competitive environments?

Chapter 6
Growth through diversification, merger, acquisition, joint venture and strategic alliance

On the back of strategic analysis (Part 1 of this book) business growth can be achieved through strategies of organic development, mergers, acquisitions, joint ventures and strategic alliances. Firms seeking to grow take different approaches depending on their industry, resources and capabilities and ethics. In this chapter each concept is considered against a template for what makes the perfect match and the appropriate mechanisms for ascertaining the likelihood of success, itself defined in many different ways. The chapter concludes with a discussion on the implications for climate change.

This chapter considers:
- modes of growth delivery – diversification, organic, merger, acquisition, joint venture or strategic alliance
- implications for climate change

Diversification

The dominant thinker in terms of diversification as a growth strategy is Igor Ansoff. Ansoff (1957) offers a two-step process for selecting a diversification strategy (or not, as the case may be). Table 6.1 captures the first of these: product lines and product missions.

Table 6.1: Product lines and product missions.

Product line	Physical characteristics of individual products – size, weight, materials tolerances, etc.
	Performance characteristics of individual products – speed, range, fuel consumption, charging time, maintenance regime, etc.
Product mission	Detailing the job that the product *intentionally* performs

Source: Author's table, derived from Ansoff (1957).

Ansoff was writing about product lines and missions in the context of manufacturing. In particular he had the aircraft and defence systems aerospace industry in mind. However, these definitions enable strategic managers to clarify and determine the utility of products to the firm. Consider electric automobiles where the physical characteristics fit well into size, weight, tolerances, etc. In terms of performance,

https://doi.org/10.1515/9783110718430-006

high-end manufacturers designed their vehicles for speed and acceleration comparable to fossil-fuel competitor products. Range is determined by battery capacity and durability, often linked to the number of moving parts.

Detailing the product mission is somewhat more challenging and can, if not executed correctly, lead to *mission creep*, that is, doing too many things for the same input. The high-end electric automobile, therefore, has the task of enabling human or digital drivers, and their passengers, to move safely at speed and in comfort between single or multiple points on public roads within a specified range before needing to be re-charged. To add "off road" capabilities to the vehicle's specification would require a wholly different set of tolerances and technologies. This would amount to mission creep.

Many products *unintentionally* perform jobs. These are discovered in the course of use. For example, a smartphone unintentionally acts as a wallet or vaccination passport. Its underlying technologies permit this, but few manufacturers defined their product missions with those jobs in mind. Manufacturers consent to these jobs, not least because it integrates their products into the lives of users, making it increasingly difficult to function in society without it. The intentionality of manufacturers, however, is captured in the platform nature of their products allowing third-party developers to create apps that act as wallets and vaccine passports.

Product missions also provide focus such that the inevitable trade-offs are coherent. By trade-offs, it is understood that products are bundles of compromises where one property may be traded-off against another either for physical reasons, in that materials cannot tolerate multiple physical forces, for example, or because of cost implications.

Having determined the product lines and product missions, strategic managers can consider four diversification options: market penetration, market development, product development, and diversification. The attributes of these are listed in Table 6.2.

Table 6.2: Strategic options for growth.

Option	Features	Product/market combination and risk
Market penetration	Increasing volume of sales to existing customers or finding new ones – marketing, price, acquisition, alliance	existing product, existing market, low risk
Market development	Adapting existing products to a new mission, and hence new customers	existing product, new market, low to medium risk

Table 6.2 (continued)

Option	Features	Product/market combination and risk
Product development	Retaining the product mission while developing new characteristics that improve the performance of the mission	new product, existing market, medium risk
Diversification	Moving away from existing product line and present market structure	new product/new market, high risk

Source: Author's table, derived from Ansoff (1957).

Empowered with the decision to diversify, executives can draw on the Ansoff framework. Risk is lowest when corporate growth strategy decisions stay within the realms of existing products and existing markets. Decisions involving moving into new markets and new products simultaneously have the highest risk profile, though they may have the greatest financial reward.

Market penetration

The advantage of adopting a market penetration growth strategy is that it involves familiar markets and products. In other words, scope remains the same, while scale is to be increased. The selection depends on the product. If it is a consumer product, the approach will be different from that of a capital product, for example, a machine tool. Decision-makers will also need to consider the extent to which their choice of market is one that is growing.

Assume, therefore, that a firm has a 20 per cent market share in the identified growth market. Other competitors have 25, 25 and 30 per cent, respectively. There are a variety of options to increase their share:

1. *Pricing strategies* were discussed previously in relation to the customer matrix and hybrid strategies. Firms can offer more value to customers for the price in order to increase market share. This approach does have implications. Competitors will retaliate either by matching the new price, in which both lose, or not matching it. In this latter case, the firm looking to increase market penetration will need to have a superior product, one that has more value to buyers, and be clear that the customers of competitors are not locked-in to the product, either contractually, or as a result of complementary products or an ecosystem, such as in the case of Apple. If the product is superior, buyers know that firms trade-off one product property over another. There is rarely a single perfect product, and as a consequence, competitors may match the price. If it is not superior and/or customers are locked-in, market penetration by this strategy may be unsuccessful and could be costly.

2. An alternative approach is to *acquire a competitor*. This option also has traps that can sometimes prove to be costly. Acquisitions are subject to national and supranational competition law. It may not be legal to achieve a market share of greater than 30 per cent. Or a competition regulator may just consider it not in the public interest, as in the case of a recent attempt in the UK by Sainsbury's supermarket to purchase a major competitor, Asda (Wood 2019), or in the EU for Three mobile network to purchase O2 (Farrell 2016).

   Competition regulators can also have much higher societal welfare ambitions than just the price of food or mobile phone contracts. Firms operating in strategic industries may be subject to political interventions as well as regulatory ones. Takeovers in the global medical drug industry, for example, always attract attention. In 2014 AstraZeneca fought off a hostile takeover bid by US firm Pfizer amid much attention from politicians (Pratley 2020b). However, the UK has a laissez-faire approach to acquisition of even strategic firms by foreign concerns. With regards to the case of Covid-19 vaccines with both Pfizer and AstraZeneca independently developing and manufacturing alternatives, social welfare is unlikely to have been served by a merger/takeover.

   The successful takeover in the UK of Cobham by US private-equity firm Advent might not have been possible in other European countries, such as Germany (Pratley 2019). In Germany, growth strategies do not focus on full acquisition, rather on small shareholdings in other companies in partnership with banks (Mayer 2018). This has implications for the structuring and control of firms.

3. *Advertising/social media endorsement/influencing* affect particularly mass-market consumer products. Market share is increasingly won by a raised profile. Where in the past, television advertising around mass-audience programming provided the route to rising profiles, this is no longer as important. Targeted advertising made possible by the Internet and consumers' willingness to provide social media firms with consumption data enables digital marketing firms to offer access to key consumers. In the process of writing this chapter, such advertising arrives on the screen periodically. It usually reflects a past search that may, or may not, have already been acted upon. Consumers are rarely randomly targeted.

   The digital world has also created a new class of celebrity, namely, influencers. Influencers first build up a social media presence such as on Instagram or YouTube; they can then be paid to endorse brands, for example, Zoë de Pass, aka *Dress Like a Mum*. Influencers are often given considerable editorial freedom in how the endorsement is made, on the grounds that this increases authenticity. The role of influencers even stretches to cleaning – so-called Cleanfluencers (Mahdawi 2019).

Market development

The second option, market development, brings existing products to new markets. This may take a number of forms:

1. Entering a *new territory* is risky and involves strategic analysis and decision-making around internationalization.
2. A *new demographic* may well be an older population whose adoption of a technology is likely to be slower or less frequent than younger counterparts. Communication technologies and social media are good examples here. It does, equally, work the other way around. Younger people are slower to adopt healthier lifestyles and hospitality products, etc. There is also the so-called *bottom of the pyramid* demographic (Prahalad and Fruehauf 2005). Multinational firms have previously avoided certain, often poorer demographics. In recent years, however, they have seen the value of markets in the developing world and have adapted their packaging to make products affordable to people in these territories. For example, where in the developed world it is normal to buy 200 ml of shampoo, in developing countries such quantities are unaffordable. A sachet containing one or two washes may be affordable, however. It is also important to consider future generations that are not currently economically active, but will be in the future. What is more, this generation is likely to be willing to pay for products and services that contribute to meeting the UN SDGs.
3. *New applications* can be deliberate or serendipitous (chance). In the world of materials, for example, some are developed for very specific purposes and for particular demographics. Teflon is normally associated with non-stick pans. It was accidentally discovered and was first used in the war-time Manhattan Project to develop nuclear weapons to ensure that radioactive uranium hexafluoride did not break seals. It subsequently migrated to domestic equipment, waterproof clothing, grafts to bypass stenotic arteries and in the ignition of solid-fuel rocket propellants.

    Low-cost airlines *broadened the mission* of their product by adapting the offer to business travellers through membership clubs enabling flexibility in bookings and priority boarding.

Product development

The third option shifts the focus from the security of existing products and services to new products and services albeit in the same market. The scope of activities changes for this option. However, this strategy is likely to require firms to have or develop a research and development capability. All new products, even if they are based on existing technologies, will require further development and testing. They will need packaging, even if it is only a metal box for a controller or industrial instrument. It is also known that new products, no matter how good, are not guaranteed success. There are a number of options open to decision-makers, again, contingent on the product and the market.

1. *Ecosystems* are formed of individual sometimes diverse products and services that when linked together provide a higher utility for customers than the sum of the parts. A familiar ecosystem is that of Apple: iPhone, iStore, iPods, iMacs, etc. It is not unusual to see Apple users with multiple products linked and working together. It is not only Apple, however, that operates an ecosystem. Nestlé developed an ecosystem around its Nespresso coffee capsule and Google around its Nest home appliance/security platform (Jacobides 2019).

2. Not unrelated to ecosystems is *partnerships*. Where an unrelated product is involved, it could be developed by a partner firm with the expertise to develop the product for the market. Braun, for example, partnered with Oral B (a subsidiary of P&G) to develop a high-end electric toothbrush. Oral B had the brush and toothpaste technology, while Braun had both design and electrical competences. The partners bring complementary brands that arguably are greater than the sum of their parts.

3. *Performance improvement in meeting the mission* is achieved through constant technological developments, whether it be smartphones with their loading speed, battery capacity/charging time, memory, etc., or airlines deploying more efficient aircraft. It is not just about technology; it may be possible to renegotiate contracts around service delivery that enhance the mission and value proposition.

It is worth noting that these three options are not exclusive of one another. As Ansoff (1957) notes, well-run firms may be executing all three of these simultaneously. Diversification, however, is a different prospect altogether. It is high-risk strategy because it is new product and new market. Firms are bundles of resources and capabilities, namely, human, financial and physical. A diversification strategy requires these to be extended. This may involve restructuring the company around capabilities, products or regions. It may involve contemplating merger, acquisition, joint venture and/or strategic alliances.

Conglomerate diversification

A conglomerate is a firm – often a multinational – with a series of subsidiaries and products that are largely unrelated. There are many examples and forms. The Virgin Group is a diversified conglomerate, as are Associated British Foods, the owner of Primark as well as Silver Spoon sugar, Berkshire Hathaway (*The Economist* 2020a), Tata (Schumpeter 2018) and Samsung (Cain 2020). Google (*The Economist* 2015b) is a conglomerate, that is increasingly diversified in nature. Conglomerate diversification is risky with new products and new markets combined; though capital markets do look favourably upon them (Untiedt et al. 2011). Conglomerates tend to have structures that protect the kernel of the firm from subsidiaries that may fail. They tend to have a corporate parent that sets performance targets rather than intervene in the day-to-day running of the firm. An executive management is left to develop strategy, but they have to report their performance and financial results periodically. These managers act as business strategists rather than corporate strategists. Corporate strategy here is the decision to acquire a subsidiary in a new market with an unfamiliar product, to invest or to divest. Berkshire Hathaway is made up of businesses and subsidiaries/strategic business units (SBUs) in familiar industrial production industries, such as chemicals, metalwork and energy. It also has interests in investment and financial products such as insurance. It is also an asset portfolio management business. In other words, it is highly diversified.

Many Chinese tech firms are diversifying as conglomerates. Alibaba diversified away from its trading platform into financial services (Alipay/Ant/MYbank), cloud services, sport (Guangzhou Evergrande soccer team), cinema and TV (Alibaba pictures) and newspapers (*South China Morning Post*) as well as managing an investment portfolio. Baidu, China's biggest search engine business, is diversifying into cloud services, live streaming (YY Live); and so-called "intelligent driving" – robotaxis, electric vehicle production and mobility data services – maps, parking (*The Economist* 2021a).

Decisions about which type of diversification to embrace can additionally be informed by direction:

1. *Vertical diversification* – all firms have suppliers, of which some are strategic in that they sell components or provide services that are essential for the delivery of the end product. For example, the automobile industry has many strategic suppliers of components ranging from seats and engines to tyres and windscreens. These suppliers undertake their own research and development, often to meet exacting standards stipulated by the focal firm, usually the assembler. It is this function that makes them strategic as the focal firm surrenders this capability in-house. A decision to buy a strategic supplier in order to bring the capability in-house, enhance efficiency and secure supply where the supply chain is global in reach and subject to disruption, would constitute upstream/ backward, vertical diversification. Insecurity of supply was observed during the Covid-19 pandemic and arising from extreme climate-change-related weather events and other natural disasters.

2. The downstream equivalent is a decision to enter retail markets where automobile manufacturers would own and manage their own showrooms, which is a distinct capability. Apple moved into retail with its Apple Stores in order to improve and control the presentation of the company's products to consumers. Now with more than 500 stores, the retail business unit is profitable in its own right. The stores have been fundamental to the success of product launches and in maintaining brand loyalty. Downstream activities often take the lion's share of the value of a product. Coffee retail, for example, adds 15 per cent of value to the end product,

merely by adding water, milk and armchairs! Though the value-adding activity with the greatest share of the overall value – 30 per cent – is achieved by roasting coffee beans (Byrnes et al. 2016). It is not surprising, therefore, that some of the most familiar coffee names in the world's cities are roasters as well as retailers.

3. *Horizontal diversification* occurs where firms expand often by acquiring competitors or others in the same business. Firms may stretch their core competence to enter related markets. Honda is well-known as a manufacturer of cars and motorcycles. Its competence in engine technologies was extended into other markets, such as outboard motors for boats and lawn mowers. Canon, best known for cameras, leverages its optics core competence to develop lenses for photocopiers, printers and sight adjustment (spectacles). Truck manufacturers can further diversify horizontally by moving into buses.

It may be that firms diversify horizontally by leveraging existing marketing capabilities or logistics such as warehousing and enterprise resource planning, rather than a core technology such as optics. Amazon, for example, has diversified on the back of its platform. It started with books and subsequently leveraged its research and development capability to offer digital book readers, tablets and voice activated/operated digital assistants. Celebrities use the brand to diversify horizontally into physical products – perfumes (Beyoncé, Jenifer Lopez, Ariana Grande) clothes (Victoria Beckham, Reese Witherspoon, Beyoncé), headphones (Dr Dre). Firms that approach growth by market penetration take an aggressive stance to their existing market subject to any regulatory controls. It is attractive because managers know their products and the markets in which they operate. However, there may be a point where the market is saturated and an alternative strategy is required. This may involve vertical or horizontal diversification as captured in Figure 6.1.

Firms are also diversifying inadvertently. Firms that are mitigating for climate change by generating electricity with photovoltaic cells on buildings become de facto generators, selling excess into the grid. Some firms are becoming generators by design as part of an explicit strategy and business model. These tend to be firms that are huge users of electricity, such as those providing digital cloud services (servers are major consumers of electricity). They have built the infrastructure to become carbon negative, meaning that they sell excess electricity for general consumption.

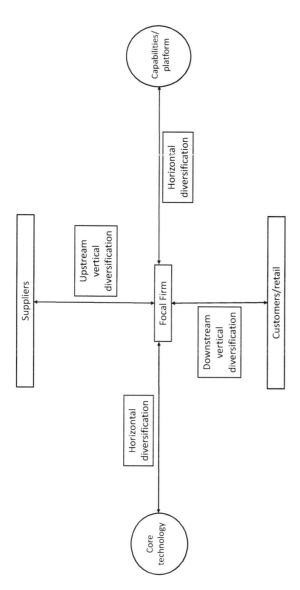

Figure 6.1: Vertical and horizontal diversification.
Source: Author's figure.

Implications for structure and climate

Chandler's (1962) dictum that structure follows strategy means that the selection of any of the growth strategies has implications for the way firms are structured and constituted. The main structural implications are the following:

1. Market penetration
   - acquisition of competitors raises challenges associated with assimilation of entities and their cultures; for purposes of regulation, it may be necessary to keep the business entities as separate SBUs or subsidiaries
   - if the role of marketing is elevated, the marketing function may need to be expanded and organizationally accommodated

2. Market development
   - entering new geographical markets may need a new territory-specific subsidiary depending on product and jurisdiction

3. Product development
   - if the new product becomes part of an existing ecosystem, then a new SBU may be the outcome
   - partnerships may need the support of an alliance-management function and/or the establishment of a new entity if the partnership is formalized

4. Conglomerate diversification
   - diversified businesses establish SBUs/subsidiaries as separate legal entities so that they can easily be divested and have little or no impact on the conglomerate should it fail
   - parent companies will be configured centrally dependent on their purpose; where synergy is an objective, the central operation is likely to be larger and itself functionally diverse, and where the parent is simply a holding company, the central operation can be smaller

Before considering other modes of growth, it is worth revisiting Ansoff's concepts of product lines and product missions. A slight adaptation can transform the product offered and developed by a firm. It remains necessary to retain the intentionality of the job to be performed by the product. In pursuit of sustainability, it can be augmented, adding the need not to harm the natural environment or extract excess human capital (Table 6.3).

Table 6.3: Product lines and product missions revisited.

Product line	Physical characteristics of individual products – size, weight, recycled materials, tolerances, etc.
	Performance characteristics of individual products – speed, range, durability, recyclability, etc.
Product mission	Detailing the job that the product *intentionally* performs without harming the natural environment or exploiting unprotected labour

Source: Author's table.

Organic growth, merger, acquisition, joint ventures and strategic alliances

Diversification can be delivered in a number of ways. In order to achieve the objective of determining the ideal conditions for strategic managers in selecting the growth strategy and executing it, some options are captured in Table 6.4.

Table 6.4: Modes for growth delivery.

Mode	Definition
Organic	Growth by leveraging internal resources and capabilities, including finance generation; normally avoiding acquisition, that is, "non-acquisitive"
Merger	A merger is the coming together of two legal entities (firms), usually of similar size to achieve synergies of operation (sharing of functions) to build/achieve critical mass, market share and/or erect barriers to entry for new entrants into an industry
Acquisition	Acquisitions involve the legal transfer of the equity of one firm to another in return for payment – cash, equity, board membership, assets, etc. They can be consensual or hostile
Joint venture	Geringer (1991) defines joint ventures (JVs) as the involvement of "two or more legally distinct organizations (the parents), each of which actively participates, beyond a mere investment role, in the decisionmaking activities of the jointly-owned entity" (p. 41). For the purposes of business/corporate strategy, the decision-making is strategic for both firms
Strategic alliance	Albers et al. (2016) define strategic alliances as "purposive relationships between firms that share compatible goals and strive for mutual benefits" (p. 583)

Source: Author's table.

There are a number of factors each has in common:
- all have strategic intent – even if that is only to maintain revenues
- they can be international in their make-up

- governance is a necessary condition for success, but is not sufficient
- power informs governance

Organic growth

Organic growth is difficult. It is potentially slow, but it *does* allow firms and their managers to control resources and capabilities, intellectual property and their deployment. Other approaches trade control for growth. Meer (2005) surveyed 107 "non-acquisitive" firms and attributed their success to three key factors. Strategic managers following largely organic growth strategies:
- employ longer-term thinking and are not overly conscious of shareholders (if they have them) and focus on research and development, customer insight (market research) and innovation skills training
- develop and nurture internal resources and capabilities – crucially marketing and innovation – in that they are dynamic and (re)configurable; they also retain talent
- build a supporting growth culture within the business with targeted rewards and progression

Merger characteristics

Mergers can be between two firms from the same or different industries. If from the same industry, a merger will be informed by size and, therefore, scale, both operational and geographical, if international. They can result in takeovers where one dominant partner assimilates the other. This is often determined by the subsequent legal, management and power structures. It is these very same structures that can lead to failure and, in the end, demerger.

Large mergers may arise from executive ego (though this is a very difficult hypothesis to support through research), bandwagon effects (everyone else is doing it), pressure from shareholders (to increase shareholder value) or necessity. Of necessity, a number of bank mergers during the financial crisis were initiated to save one bank collapsing, and, by definition, the collapse of the financial system in totality. For example, in the UK, Lloyds Bank merged with Bank of Scotland (Treanor 2017). In Germany, Commerz Bank merged with Dresdner Bank (Commerzbank 2009).

Away from banking, notable industry mergers include:
- *Automobile manufacture* – Fiat/Chrysler and PSA: "Both share the conviction that there is compelling logic for a bold and decisive move that would create an industry leader with the scale, capabilities and resources to capture successfully the opportunities and manage effectively the challenges of the new era in mobility" (Kollewe and Jolly 2019).

- *Media* – Viacom and CBS: to create "a premium content powerhouse with global scale, including leadership positions in markets across the U.S., Europe, Latin America and Asia" (ViacomCBS 2019).
- *Mining* – BHP and Billiton: "BHP Billiton Managing Director and Chief Executive Officer Paul Anderson said the combined Group will have the financial strength, international scope and enhanced skills to deliver major growth opportunities and value to shareholders, customers, employees and local communities" (BHP 2001).

Acquisitions characteristics

Acquisitions can be consensual or hostile. They too can be the result of external pressures from governments such as the financial crisis of 2008. Many more financial institutions were simply taken over than actually merged. Indeed, in some cases states "bought" and retained debt, while other institutions acquired active accounts and branches. For example, in the UK Banco Santander bought the assets of a range of recently demutualized banks, including Bradford & Bingley, Alliance & Leicester and Abbey National. In the United States, JPMorgan Chase acquired Bear Stearns and Washington Mutual; Bank of America bought Merrill Lynch.

Hostile takeovers arise from a number of sources. The executives of acquiring firms may be looking for scale, resources (for example, intellectual property) and capabilities, skills, market access or new markets. For listed firms, they become hostile when the putative acquirer's offer is rejected on the grounds that the assets are under-valued and/or the senior management of the target firm seek to retain independence and reject the argument presented that purchase would realize value for the shareholders. This was the position with two pharmaceutical industry players, Pfizer (US) and AstraZeneca (UK/Sweden). Pfizer sought to purchase AstraZeneca, itself the product of a merger, for £69 billion but was rebuffed by the executive management. Not all shareholders were happy with this rejection. Eventually Pfizer withdrew. The chairman of AstraZeneca at the time, Leif Johansson, emphasized the importance of the independence of the company and said, "We have attractive growth prospects and a rapidly progressing pipeline. In the coming months we anticipate positive news flow across our core therapeutic areas, which underpins our confidence in the long-term prospects of the business" (BBC 2014). The issue of the "rapidly progressing pipeline" is both attractive to acquirers and assuming that the acquirer's pipeline is not so progressing, while also being attractive in the longer-term to existing investors. But not all.

Hostile takeovers can also involve apparent asset stripping. There are some firms that specialize in deconstructing acquired firms, reselling assets and realizing value greater than the purchase price. This was the case with Melrose's takeover of GKN (Finch 2018). Melrose was much smaller than GKN, but GKN was deemed to be under-performing. Melrose offered shareholders 40 per cent more than the list price for their shares. Shareholders voted marginally to accept the offer. GKN's unsuccessful defence plan involved selling the powder metallurgy business and merging the automobile drivetrain business with a US rival, Dana. Arguably that constituted an asset-stripping strategy similar to that contemplated by the acquirer.

A contemporary example of such a deal is that of the £6.8bn takeover of UK supermarket group Asda. The buyer is private equity group TDR Capital, that also owns EG petrol forecourts. The financial structure created £3.5bn of new debt as a mix of bonds and loans. The sale of Asda's distribution centres is estimated to generate £950m. These are to be leased back immediately to Asda. The Asda petrol forecourts then become part of the EG Group amounting to £750m (Butler 2021). The previous owner, Walmart, retains an investment of £500m in the firm and a seat on the board. Regulations against corporate raiding, as it is also known, are few, though it is lightly regulated by the EU (European Union 2011) – chapter V, section 2, articles 26–30.

Joint venture characteristics

Joint ventures are partnerships based on joint ownership of a newly created entity that provides goods and services to particular markets and/or in the development of a new product or service. Their purpose will be legally determined, and the nature of the assets held by the entity are recorded, valued and apportioned. There will also be agreement on the management and governance of the entity, agreements on selling stakes and dividends or winding up. Despite such agreements, joint venture partners can find themselves subject to the opportunism of a partner, for example, exploitation of intellectual property or even theft.

The example of Sony Ericsson is revealing. The entity was incorporated in 2001 to exploit the capabilities of Sony, then a small player in the mobile handset market, and Ericsson, at that time the third largest manufacturer behind Nokia and Motorola. Ericsson's handsets were seen as unstylish vis-à-vis those of competitors, but were an integral part of the Ericsson business that also included mobile network technologies. The new entity included most of Ericsson Mobile Communications company and was complemented by Sony's handset division.

Ericsson's objectives were to:
- find a partner that could provide know-how and experience of consumer products to supplement Ericsson's technological expertise
- give priority to the high end of the market, more expensive, and more profitable models rather than the mass market
- focus on product development and outsource actual production to subcontractors (Karlsson and Lugn n.d.)

Sony met the criteria but, despite the apparent longevity of the joint venture, the management noted that "getting Sony Ericsson to function as a tightly knit company was complicated and took time. When two such different cultures meet, the loyalty of the staff is put to the test in many ways, for instance in attitudes to working hours and the length of holidays" (Karlsson and Lugn n.d.).

In 2011, Sony bought Ericsson's share for €1.05 billion. On completion, Sony moved the operation to Japan.

The case reveals a number of factors: the importance of shared strategic vision, the strengths and weaknesses of each partner and cultural compatibility. Ericsson had engineering expertise without the retail flair, a strong point of Sony. Despite that engineering expertise, it was still operating at the low-mass-market end of the market. There was also much to be gained by focusing on the research and development capability, rather than manufacturing.

A more recent example of a joint venture can be found in the 5G spectrum auction in the USA in 2020/2021. 5G in the USA is the mid-range/speed spectrum clustered from 3.7 GHz to 3.98 GHz. The three big incumbent players, Verizon, AT&T and T-Mobile, bid against new entrants, in particular a joint venture between two cable companies, Comcast and Charter. The 50–50 equity-based JV was founded in 2018 to launch cost-effective mobile services for cable customers using Verizon's network. That JV was then leveraged in the 5G auction to provide 5G services, independent of Verizon and at scale. The JV was a learning platform (Leswing 2021).

Strategic alliance characteristics

A strategic alliance (SA) is a voluntary agreement between firms, explicitly in pursuit of strategic objectives. The firms do not merge or create joint ventures, but they may exchange some equity by way of security. They are time-limited, though they can be extended. The partners complement one another with resources (financial, physical, intellectual property and human) and capabilities (know-how). Strategic alliances can:

1. Meet their objectives and be wound up
2. Meet their objectives and be extended
3. Not meet their objectives and be wound up
4. Not meet their objectives, but meet unanticipated objectives and be extended (Doz 1996)
5. Meet/not meet their objectives and result in the dominant partner purchasing all or part of the smaller partner

They can be project-based or functional for example, shared procurement.

Doz's (1996) qualitative study of project-based international strategic alliances ranging from alliances between a large pharmaceutical business and a small medical device intellectual property owner, an American telecommunications company and a European office equipment manufacturer, and an American engineering conglomerate and a French aircraft engine manufacturer, revealed many facets of strategic alliances over time that were not easy to pick up with survey-based studies. In particular, Doz's (1996) study reveals the importance of:

- clearly articulated initial conditions:
  - where partners are positioned (environment/industry)
  - task (what is to be done)
- learning:
  - behavioural (what managers can do better to handle the new relationship)
  - cognitive (managers' understanding of environment and how the relationship *should* be handled)
- provision and use of an alliance interface: when and how to meet and capture learning
- task definition and the supporting mutual organizational routines that enable execution of tasks
- early achievements, even if only organizational and not task-related
- timing: certain decisions can be premature or overdue
- readjustment in light of experience, learning, change and emergence of new opportunities
- evolution of trust
- commitment (preferably developing over time)

Recently a strategic alliance delivered the first Covid-19 vaccine (Pfizer and BioNTech). Pfizer set up an alliance with BioNTech in 2018 to develop flu vaccines using a genetic approach (messenger ribonucleic acid (RNA)) that prompts in recipients the production of therapeutic proteins to launch an immune response. The alliance had the following propitious aim: "The alliance partners hope to offer a vaccine that can be quickly adjusted to the latest viral mutations, which can also be a major advantage in case of a pandemic threat from avian flu" (Reuters 2018). The alliance, therefore, centred on BioNTech's gene technology and Pfizer's expertise in human trials and commercialization.

The perfect partner

Each of our growth strategies involving a partnership with a new entity requires considerable due diligence in the decision-making process. Big mergers have different risks associated with them relative to strategic alliances, despite their shared property of strategic intent. Table 6.5 is a checklist of factors informing the perfect partner:

Table 6.5: Perfect partner search criteria for mergers, acquisitions, JVs and SAs.

Criterion	Merger	Acquisition	JV	SA
Strategic intent	Yes	No/maybe	Yes	Yes
Consensual	Yes	No/maybe	Yes	Yes
Complementary physical/human resources	Yes/ maybe	No/maybe	Yes	Yes
Track record – performance/industry/market/ technology	Yes	No/maybe	Yes	Yes
Open to new strategic opportunities	Yes/ maybe	No/maybe	Yes	Yes
Similar size	Yes/ maybe	No/maybe	Yes/ maybe	No
Willingness to be acquired/merge	Yes	No/maybe	No/ maybe	No/ maybe
Willingness to share/exchange equity	Yes	No/maybe	Yes	No/ maybe
Willingness to optimize product/process systems	Yes	No/maybe	Yes	Yes
Cultural convergence	Yes	Yes/no	Yes	Yes

Source: Author's table.

The two essential criteria analysts should seek in partners are strategic intent and cultural convergence. Without strategic intent, the rationale for a partnership is at best compromised, at worst, dangerous. Some firms have been known to merge or acquire on the basis of friendship between owners or executives. That is not a good foundation on its own, though it might qualify as cultural convergence, at least at executive level.

However, acquisition does not necessarily need the strategic intent of the acquired firm to be explicit, especially if it is hostile. The acquirer certainly needs to be motivated by strategic intent, even if that is only to add to a diversified conglomerate or to asset strip. In such cases, the strategic intent is growth by acquisition; there may also be no need for cultural convergence.

Cultural convergence does not mean that firms need to be culturally homogeneous, that is, the same. What is does mean is that partners should, through behavioural and cognitive learning, achieve an understanding of one another, ways of doing things and evolving (Doz 1996).

Partners, acquirers and those seeking to be acquired should ensure strategic intent, and a cultural capability that is existing or feasible. The feasibility of this is difficult to ascertain through basic due diligence; it may require courtship and a period of "living together" before formalizing the relationship. Strategic alliances can be a way of courting ahead of more formal arrangements being agreed.

Summary

This chapter has considered firm-level growth and modes for achieving it. Growth can be fostered by diversification of product and/or market. It can be vertical or horizontal. With regard to vertical integration a manufacturer incorporates suppliers (upstream/backward) or retail space/distribution (downstream/forward). Horizontal integration sees firms extending scale (building a chain of firms with similar capabilities) and, feasibly, increasing scope intentionally or unintentionally. If intentionally, it may be that existing core competences can be deployed.

Growth can be achieved organically using internal resources and capabilities, and by acquisition, merger, alliance or joint ventures. Each have different risk profiles and have implications for control and wider governance of resources, particularly intellectual property. However, growth is generally regarded by core stakeholders not only as inherently good, but expected. It is the job of the executive management to grow the activities of the firm and increase shareholder value.

In revisiting Ansoff's product lines and product missions in the context of climate change, the product mission can be reconfigured to ensure the natural environment and labour are not exploited detrimentally.

Implicit in the discussions around diversification and modes of growth delivery is the question of corporate strategy. Diversification and growth go hand in hand with broader questions of governance. As firms become more complex and diversified across products and geography, how do managers optimize their decision-making? It is to this that the book now turns.

Questions

1. What is a product mission? Compose a product mission for one of the following products: an electric scooter, smartphone, a book, a bed, a streetlight. For each product mission, are there any *unintentional* jobs that the product does?
2. Using Ansoff's framework, why is conglomerate diversification qualitatively different from the other strategies of market penetration, market development and product development?
3. Why is organic growth difficult? What might strategic managers do to overcome obstacles to organic growth?
4. Can a joint venture be a strategic alliance? Can a strategic alliance be a joint venture? If yes, why? If no, why not?
5. Doz's (1996) study offers nine criteria for managers looking at entering a strategic alliance and measuring its performance success. What is the role of trust and how does it change over time?
6. Why does similarity in partner size not matter in SAs? Why is it more of a factor for merger and a JV?

Chapter 7
Strategic management of portfolios

Growth can be achieved through diversification strategies in the form of organic development, mergers, acquisitions, joint ventures and strategic alliances. The results, however, generate dilemmas about corporate governance. How are diversified and complex businesses evaluated? The corporate strategic manager has options when it comes to frameworks; indeed, some business strategy terms are widely used in ordinary language such as "cash cow". Care is needed when applying these frameworks. Practitioners really do need to understand the axes and indicators. However, creative strategic managers can adapt these frameworks for the benefit of decision-making in the context of climate change.

This chapter considers:
- corporate portfolio management tools
- reconfiguration for tools of corporate portfolio management and governance for adaptation and mitigation

Portfolio management

Partial or fully diversified corporates need to manage their portfolios. In what should they invest? In what should they divest? What are the limitations or challenges? There are a number of tools available to help decision-making. These include the Growth–Share matrix (Henderson 1982), Industry Attractiveness-Business Strength matrix, and the Heartland matrix. In deploying the tools, it is necessary to draw the distinction between uses (Untiedt et al. 2011):
- as a prescriptive guide – the grid says X so this is the decision
- as diagnostic tool – what is the problem, for example, low market share, too competitive industry, wrong location?
- synergy – what is the added value of the parent vis-à-vis the subsidiary?

It is possible further to classify portfolio management tools into those that simply seek to guide decision-makers on financial performance, and those that seek to capture issues of synergy such as efficiencies derived from the pooling of resources and/or removing duplication, knowledge exchange and, ultimately, sustainability.

Tools establishing performance – prescriptive/diagnostic

The Growth–Share matrix (Stern and Deimler 2012) has two axes: market share and market growth. Table 7.1 summarizes the positions. Subsidiaries that have low growth and low market share are seen to be dogs. They should be divested. Those

https://doi.org/10.1515/9783110718430-007

with high growth and market share are stars. Question marks offer high growth but low market share. Occupying a space of low growth but high market share is the cash cow, which has become a familiar term in corporate business lexicon and beyond. UK students recently described themselves as cash cows in explaining their treatment by universities in the Covid-19 emergency (Wall 2020). The cash cow, however, makes little sense stripped from its context of rising stars, dogs and the question mark/problem child. A cash cow could be a business unit that is being "milked" to provide resources for other units – question marks, and in some cases, stars.

Table 7.1: Growth–Share matrix.

Growth/market share	Symbol	Option
high/high	Star	Still needs investment, but will pay off
high/low	Question mark/ problem child	Develop – how much investment is needed? Uncertain whether they will pay back
low/high	(Cash) cow	Milk for all it is worth; it will become a dog
low/low	Pet/dog	Divest

Source: Author's table, derived from Stern and Deimler (2012).

Dogs are meant to be euthanized, occupying a zone of low growth and market share, and hence being a drain on resources. A key function of cash cows, using this matrix, is to provide resources to develop rising stars and question marks. The old dog works against this objective.

There are at least five substantive weaknesses to the approach:

1. It assumes that resources for new products, strategies and marketing are largely generated internally. This may be true of corporates developing organically, but other sources of finance are available and widely accessed for investment.
2. What is market share? It depends very much on the fragmented nature of an industry. A share of 10 per cent could be viable in some industries, unviable in others. A little more nuance is needed (Hax and Majluf 1995a).
3. Market share and growth (low–low) indicates divest, but there may be other reasons for keeping a dog or pet. The strategic business unit or subsidiary may well be the home of a signature product/range; it may then have a value over-and-above the revenue it generates, even assuming that market share is a good indicator of revenue. It could also be a favourite of the owner or patriarch, or a key component of an ecosystem, without which the other "organisms" wither and die.

4. Which markets are being discussed? How easy is it to quantify their value? Is a single "proxy" measure sufficient? By way of illustration, in one study (Wind et al. 1983) the fifteen subsidiaries of a Fortune 500 corporate were positioned on the grid applying four different definitions of market growth and market share. Only one of the fifteen subsidiaries was consistently positioned, in this case as a star!

5. What if the dog is the product-sector leader in sustainability? In which case it has value because of its wisdom and keen sense of smell. Maybe it can be taught new tricks after all?

Other portfolio management tools plot SBUs on grids with axes of rather more subtlety and with genuine meaning in the middle ground. The Industry Attractiveness-Business Strength matrix devised for General Electric (GE) is a case in point (Hax and Majluf 1995b). GE is famous for strategic planning, so the complexity of this matrix does not come as a surprise. This matrix has nine cells bounded by two axes – industry attractiveness and business strength. Industry attractiveness is the external environment captured by external macro factors such as PESTEL and five-forces: factors such as market size, growth, pricing, profitability and technology. The business strength measures internal controllable factors such as market share, strategic business unit growth rate, price competitiveness and experience curve effects. Adding further layers of complexity, SBUs can be represented by circles of various sizes and demonstrated with coloured sections representing market share (red in Figure 7.1). SBUs do not need to fit perfectly into a single cell. The matrix can additionally be used to map the dynamics of SBU performance from one year to the next; for example, comparing 2020 and 2021 where would the SBU be positioned in the matrix cells? It can also be used to determine whether to invest (top left) or to divest (bottom right). The middle areas require further consideration, especially at the extremes – high SBU strength but low industry attractiveness and vice versa. These are decisions to be made on the basis of careful analysis and whether the parent can add value such that a SBU can become stronger or there is some change on the horizon to suggest that the industry's attractiveness will improve.

Arguably, this grid replicates a number of the weaknesses of the Growth–Share matrix before it around capital, ecosystems and sustainability. While it does not use a single proxy measure like the Growth–Share matrix, industry attractiveness and SBU strength may still be only indicative. Though Hax and Majluf, (1995b) and Wind et al. (1983) developed a robust list of factors for each axis. Whichever matrix is used, the likelihood of the self-fulfilling prophesy emerges. When a subsidiary becomes either a cash cow or a dog, motivations are affected as the fate becomes known, and performance necessarily declines fulfilling the prophesy.

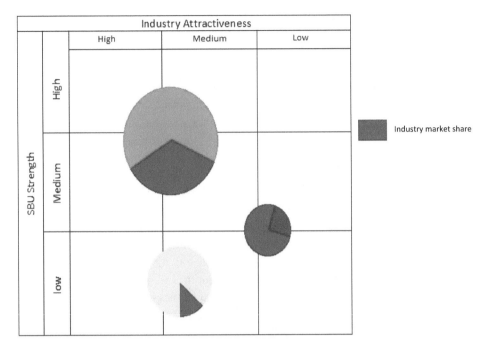

Figure 7.1: Industry Attractiveness-Business Strength matrix.
Source: Author's figure, derived from Hax and Majluf (1995b).

Portfolio tools establishing synergy

Some corporate managers value synergy in their portfolio – the extent to which the parent adds value to the subsidiaries and to isolate any *value destroying* negative synergies. To that end, Campbell et al. (2014) developed the Heartland matrix. This matrix has two axes (Figure 7.2): the vertical captures the risk if subtracting value by the parent not adjusting to the situation of the business; the horizontal captures the potential to add value.

The ideal location is in the top-right where the risk of the parent subtracting value is at its lowest and the potential for the SBU to add value from the parent's resources and skills is the highest. The place not to be, but easiest to evaluate, is the alien territory, where the risk of the parent subtracting value is high and the SBU is unable to add value. There are two areas that require particular attention:

- ballast: low risk of parent subtracting value, but low potential for the SBU to add value. This leads to much central management effort/resource being used with little added value being generated
- value-trap: high risk of parent subtracting value but high potential for the SBU to add value drawing directly from the parent. This may seem implausible. In

this situation, corporate managers need to find a way of reducing the risk maybe by understanding the business/SBU more fully and pushing it into the *edge of heartland* territory.

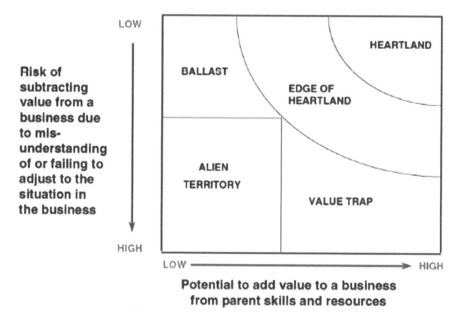

Figure 7.2: Heartland matrix.
Source: Campbell et al. (2014), reproduced with permission.

Portfolio tools including sustainability – prescriptive/diagnostic

There are few tried-and-tested portfolio matrices specifically facilitating sustainability. Sustainability can be classified as an issue of performance, though only if the corporate has sustainability as a defined purpose (Mayer 2018). But even if sustainability is not written into a firm's legal articles of association or licence to operate, a portfolio management method with sustainability at its heart is feasible and increasingly important.

Corporate strategic managers may be minded to create their own or adapt existing approaches. The Growth–Share matrix can be adapted in a number of ways. What follows is some guidance on how this could be approached. Drawing on the innovation literature and principles, a study of research and development portfolios in the automobile industry by Brook and Pagnanelli (2014) provides some guidance for metrics.

Corporates should be mindful of risk. Does the SBU sell products that are breakthrough (Wheelwright and Clark 1992), platform or derivative? The riskiest products here are likely to be *new to the world* and as such must have high standards of sustainability and comply absolutely with butterfly/circular concepts of business. They may be disruptive (Christensen 1997). They may also appear not financially accept-able when measured using conventional indicators such as discounted cash flow.

Platform products are improved incrementally, based on existing infrastructure, designs, etc. For SBUs that work on platforms, their products should incrementally achieve sustainability targets that are set centrally and/or from the industry in which they operate. In Brook and Pagnanelli's study, this was an automobile manufacturer developing hybrids (electric/diesel/petrol). Many automobile brands build their cars and trucks on platforms shared by a family of vehicles across subsidiaries.

Finally, SBUs that create derivative products need to ensure that what is deriva-tive, or possibly copied, already has high-sustainability properties. In the automobile case, this was illustrated by the improvement in the efficiency of diesel and petrol en-gines. In 2021, this is unacceptable as governments are readily putting end-dates on the business of marketing and selling such technology. These products typically offer only short-term advantages from existing knowledge and capabilities.

Risk is not the only factor. The corporate parent should ensure strategic fit. In tra-ditional terms, strategic fit relates to long-term objectives defined by growth, alignment of resources and capabilities, including personnel. The ideal corporate parent in the future scenario will have sustainability as a core purpose. Again, drawing on Brook and Pagnanelli (2014), there are three measures of sustainability:
- ecological, such as GHG emissions, recycling, sourcing
- social, serving not just elite customers, but reaching out to excluded groups
- economic; viewed in terms of conventional competitiveness

In addition to strategic fit, a corporate parent should be evaluating brand value, customer perceptions and approvals, market potential, profitability, emissions and waste, and value to the group in terms of its core soft and hard technologies, capa-bilities and spill overs/alliances.

All of these factors have metrics, and all of them will define the viability, accept-ability and value of a SBU into the future. Low performing SBUs under these metrics should be closed: they will have no corporate value. These businesses should not be sold as going concerns as this would be like reselling a dirty diesel van or truck in-stead of scrapping it. Governments could help firms with an SBU scrappage scheme, similar to those used to remove old vehicles from the roads, and provide support for personnel losing their jobs and livelihoods. The climate emergency is such that SBUs knowingly damaging the environment have no place in a modern global economy.

Variations on portfolio matrices

Figure 7.3 offers a sustainability and stakeholder utility matrix (revised Growth–Share matrix) defines sustainability in term of three measures: ecological, social and economic. Stakeholder utility is a measure of value created for stakeholders from new market opportunities and the advantage derived from that value.

Using the symbols of the Growth–Share matrix, instead of a cow, there is a friendly dog whose stakeholder utility remains high and is agile enough to adapt. Humans keep fewer of them but look after them very well; some eat plants rather than meat, and they keep people fit and happy.

Instead of the dog there is a rat. Rats are destructive, readily carry disease, and reproduce fast. They have to go.

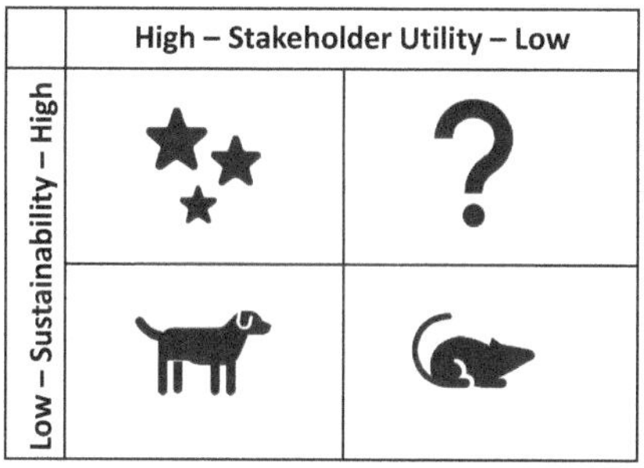

Figure 7.3: Sustainability and stakeholder utility matrix.
Source: Author's figure.

Likewise, the Industry Attractiveness-Business Strength matrix can be modified. Portfolio managers can adapt the criteria for attractiveness from pure profitability to ones incorporating sustainability. Here, the strength of the SBU equates with its internal resources and capabilities aligned with the industry in question. Consider a conglomerate with a cement manufacturer subsidiary. The cement industry contributes significantly to carbon emissions. Where the SBU has strength, the focus can be on research into the development of lower-carbon cement products. The industry is likely to remain attractive, but only if its carbon emissions can be reduced. A SBU that does not have resources and capabilities enabling research and development will need investment in that capability, or to leave the industry. It is an industry whose carbon emissions will be regulated in the future.

With regard to synergy, the Heartland matrix (Campbell et al. 2014) can be deployed. Where value is derived from sustainability, the:
- parent's value-adding/creation insights are focused on sustainability (edge of heartland)
- critical success factors (CSFs) for SBUs incorporate measures of sustainability (edge of heartland)
- parent fully complements an SBU's sustainability value-creation strategy (heartland)

- SBU's CSFs are not sustainability driven, indicating a failure that cannot be/is not being reconciled by the parent (ballast to alien)
- parent's value creation insights are misaligned with sustainability value creation, but the SBUs are aligned. In this case parent interventions can prove to be value destroying (i.e. a value trap)

Summary

This chapter has considered approaches to strategic portfolio management. Tools can be prescriptive or diagnostic, guiding strategic managers in decision-making, and be synergistic in highlighting value added by parents and subsidiaries alike. The tools have to be used with caution because the metrics are imperfect. In translating complex phenomena into easy-to-use tools, nuance is lost. There is no substitute for embedding decision-makers in key functions at the corporate centre and SBUs. The Heartland matrix captures this for situations where the parent does not understand the SBU, its business or industry.

Notwithstanding the caution needed with respect to application, a little creativity can lead to advances in understanding factors affecting sustainability across a portfolio. Dogs can indeed be more valuable than bald metrics would indicate.

Assuming that sustainability is advanced by geographical diversification, there are other considerations to internationalization. It is to this that the book now turns, starting with a very short history of colonialism.

Questions

1. What are the Growth–Share matrix's key weaknesses? Are these weaknesses successfully addressed by the Industry Attractiveness-Business Strength matrix?
2. Why would corporate managers strategically retain a dog, but not a rat?
3. Under what circumstances do parents destroy value in SBUs? Provide some examples.
4. As a corporate manager, what might you do to move an SBU from value-trap to edge of heartland?
5. How might product platforms contribute to, and diffuse, corporate sustainability (design, manufacture and disposal)?

Chapter 8
Internationalization

The international system and backdrop in which firms operate was introduced in Chapter 1. Responsible and progressive strategists need to know their history and learn from it. This chapter first introduces the international system through an account of its history, before building on the diversification issues to evaluate internationalization as a viable growth strategy for firms and select the tools of execution. The distinctions between international strategy and global strategy are highlighted. The implications for environmental sustainability complete this chapter.

This chapter offers:

- a brief history of international trade – a story of colonialism
- insights on internationalization options for firms
- clarity on the difference between international strategy and global strategy
- implications for climate change arising from internationalization

History and its contemporary value for international and global business strategic analysis

The contemporary economic and business challenges are rooted in history. The modern concept of the limited liability firm dates back to the East India Company – founded in 1600 under royal charter – with monopoly trading rights in the region backed by its own army with which it conquered and controlled territories in South East Asia. While its main commodities were spices (pepper, ginger, nutmeg, cloves and cinnamon), textiles (cotton and silk), indigo dye, saltpetre and tea, later it traded in opium. The company was also leading in the slave trade, transporting African slaves initially from Madagascar to St Helena and then more generally between Asia and the Americas. Its stockholder merchants became very rich, bought large swathes of land in England, claiming common lands farmed by peasants and created a very powerful lobby in the British Parliament to protect and further its trading, property and wealth interests. At the same time other extractive and exploitative colonial enterprises were established, including the Muscovy Company, the Hudson's Bay Company and the Royal Africa Company, also profiting from the capture and transportation of African slaves. Other colonial powers had their own enterprises, notably the Dutch East India Company (Hirst et al. 2009). Subsequent forms of capitalist enterprise were informed by the experience of these early mercantilist companies in terms of mitigation of risk, finance, trust, employee motivation, shareholder satisfaction and societal responsibilities (Roy 2016). These joint stock companies were arguably the original Born Globals (Kudina et al. 2008).

https://doi.org/10.1515/9783110718430-008

The Industrial Revolution has its origins in textiles manufactured in north-west England and southern Scotland. It is here that the terms of production and consumption were established, including technological innovation, labour relations and political control of the factors of production. For example, Malm (2016) demonstrates that the coal-powered steam engine as the force that came to dominate the provision of motive power for machinery and distribution was not a foregone conclusion. Water was by far the most efficient source of energy for milling, but two overriding *strategic* factors substituted coal and steam for water. First, coal was portable and possible to be located in population centres such as Manchester and Glasgow. Second, it ensured that labour power (trade unions) could not control the use and deployment of steam-powered motive force. The steam engine returned the power of capital to the factory owners and sustained it for generations. It also set humanity on a path to climate stress by way of its emissions.

Dicken (2014) notes that there has been for more than 300 years a global division of labour; it is not a recent phenomenon. The pre-war, colonialist global economy functioned as a core–periphery configuration, with manufacturing concentrated in the core, and exports and imports to/from the periphery. These are quite benign terms that hide a sometimes brutal subjugation of the people of conquered nations on the continents of Asia and Africa that guaranteed markets for the manufactures of the newly industrialized economies of Europe. In more modern, decolonized, times, these very same nations have acted as low-cost sources of labour and manufacturing for the former colonizers, particularly after China embraced this role as it rapidly industrialized under Deng Xiaoping in the 1980s. In the post-war period (1945–1989) the world economy, its interests and conflicts were defined in terms of the capitalist West (first world) and the communist East (second world). The rest of the world was seen as merely the third world, generally referred to now as the developing (or newly developed) world or countries.

Slavery was once seen as a legitimate business and was legal. These practices have not been left behind in the preceding centuries. The Black Lives Matter movement of the twenty-first century is part of that legacy and modern-day slavery continues through large-scale people smuggling, often of women into prostitution or servitude. People working for subsistence wages, often below the legal minimum, from taxi drivers to garment workers, are also part of this narrative (Bushby 2019; Perraudin 2019).

The meaning of these concepts varies in different countries. For example, racism in the USA has deep and enduring ideological foundations that incumbent corporates and those seeking entry need to understand. Corporate support for Black Lives Matter can have significant business implications, as in the case of Ben & Jerry's ice cream (Ciszek and Logan 2018), a company with a declared commitment to social justice. In the UK, racism also has its origins in the slave trade and the obscene defence that those enslaved were sub-human. However, the UK has an additional colonial history rooted in exploitation of resources and people (Fryer 2018). In modern times, the British political establishment consistently draws on race to build electoral coalitions of which Brexit is a recent example. Corporations and firms are complicit in this, consistently discriminating against non-white people in recruitment, promotion and pay (Office for National-Statistics 2020).

As Kelton (2020) notes, post-war trade arrangements continue to favour rich and diversified developed economies over less-diversified developing economies. Ricardo's concept of *Comparative Advantage*, for example, has been taken by developed economies as meaning extreme specialization, leaving some countries dependent and vulnerable to developed countries' consumption requirements (see also Mazzucato 2018b). Kenya's production of perishable foodstuffs and Bangladesh's dependency on textile manufacturing are examples of this specialization. Arguably, responsible and sustainable trade would involve developed nations sharing green technologies, know-how and resources.

The so-called post-war consensus brought into existence a number of international organizations established primarily to facilitate world trade and to support global economic stability. Primarily among these organizations are the World Trade Organization (formerly the GATT), the World Bank (see also the International Finance Corporation (IFC) – its commercial lending arm), the International Monetary Fund (IMF), the Organisation for Economic Co-operation and Development, (OECD), and the European Union (European Bank for Reconstruction and Development). Kelton (2020) takes what might be seen as the normative, progressive approach to the role of these international organizations. She argues that countries like the USA *should* be global leaders in reforming trade arrangements, in setting high environmental standards and promoting labour protections. Critically, "[a] revamped WTO could mandate these sorts of provisions in trade agreements as well, rather than entrenching existing privileges for powerful multinational corporations, as it does today" (Kelton 2020, p. 154).

However, non-governmental organizations are also important. The World Economic Forum, for example, convenes annually the global financial and political elite at the exclusive Swiss town of Davos. Additionally, there are many privately funded conservative think tanks and lobbyists with agendas that are neoliberal and free trade. These include, in the USA: the Heritage Foundation, Cato Institute, Heartland Institute and the Ludwig von Mises Institute; in the UK, the Adam Smith Institute, Centre for Policy Studies, Institute of Economic Affairs and the TaxPayers' Alliance. Progressive think tanks, such as the New Economics Foundation and the Work Foundation, are often absent from dominant conservative policy forums. Attempts at creating strict laws curbing carbon emissions have been subject to tangible lobbying efforts (Massiot 2020; Holden et al. 2021). There are also cases in which state investments have been made that actually hasten climate change (Wasley and Heal 2020).

Internationalization, globalism and hyperglobalism

The debates and negotiations related to the UK's departure from the European Union (Brexit) have helped familiarize many people with the concepts of the single market, customs, tariffs and barriers, both trade and non-trade. The post-war consensus in trade terms has been focused on reducing barriers to trade (led by the WTO). The WTO, and its predecessor the GATT, negotiated global agreements on trade in a series of "rounds". These rounds are complex as the WTO members – in all of their diversity and interests – negotiate global tariffs and subsidies. The last completed round was the Uruguay Round in 1986 after 87 months of negotiation between 123 countries. The current Doha round started in 2001 and involves 159 countries. It remains unfinished.

Countries build their trade agreements around these basic WTO rules in bilateral agreements. Increasingly, countries come together and negotiate as a bloc. This is the case of the EU, and it is why the UK negotiated, and continues to negotiate, with the EU rather than individual member states for access to the single market. In trade negotiations, the debates are usually about convergence, bringing together states or blocs around standards for product, process, labour, environmental protection, tariffs, and dispute resolution mechanisms, among others. What is unique in the Brexit negotiations is that the free trade agreement of December 2020 was negotiated around how to diverge standards, tariffs and state aid, rather than how to converge. This was explained very well by the former Spanish Foreign Minister, Arancha González, in an interview on Sky News on 13 December 2020 (Zorzut 2020).

Corporate international and global strategy

It is important for firms to understand the nature of trade as there are resource and capability implications. In corporate strategy terms, an international strategy is one where products are manufactured, sold or services provided either by means of export from the home country, or through subsidiaries in countries other than the home country. These subsidiaries can replicate existing products in new territories with their own supply chains, customers and strategy. For diversified companies, subsidiaries may be unrelated, that is, manufacturing or selling products or services unrelated to those by other subsidiaries. In this case, the parent becomes a holding company of diversified subsidiaries and the corporate entity.

By contrast, a global strategy is one in which the subsidiaries are inter-related and inter-dependent. They may supply one another, provide research and development expertise such as competence sharing. However, a global strategy may not involve ownership. Automobile manufacturers, for example, can lock-in suppliers to their just-in-time manufacturing systems in exchange for exclusivity, quality control and, in some cases, research and development expertise. Global strategies depend on states and governments having global perspectives that enable trade on that basis. Hence trade agreements and customs arrangements are very important for just-in-time production. Global trade agreements in services are fewer and less easy to negotiate. The European Union has one of the few such arrangements across its member states.

Globalization in the business world often takes the form of outsourcing, that is, sourcing components or services once internally provided from external companies. Outsourcing (see Porter's value chain) has enabled major cost-cutting where outsourcing involves buying from low-cost countries or exploiting *comparative advantage* (Mazzucato 2018b). The market in products and services becomes globalized. The WTO works to enable frictionless global trade through its rounds of negotiations.

Internationalism and globalism are informed by political and economic movements. Globalism equates with neoliberal economists who believe that markets can distribute resources efficiently and optimally. The role of the state should become increasingly limited. Indeed, one of the few functions of the state should be negotiating the reduction in global trading barriers. The end goal for this perspective is hyperglobalism where:

- there is a high degree of functional integration of economic activity. Consider the (hyper)global nature of automobile manufacture, with extended supply chains and just-in-time delivery facilitated by frictionless cross-border transfers or similarly consumer electronics
- a high degree of geographical spread of these activities; for example, over four or five continents (Dicken 2014)

This end state is hyperglobalization; any trend towards this has been put in check in recent years with the re-emergence of nationalism and populism, and the crucial role of the state in managing a global pandemic and responses to climate change.

Hyperglobalists believe that unrestricted trade benefits all, albeit within the rules agreed through the WTO. Indeed, some economists such as Rodrik (2015), with considerable justification, argue that millions of people have been lifted out of poverty by the globalization of the world economy; but there is much debate as to whether there are limits to globalization both in terms of poverty alleviation and environmental sustainability. Globalization is not, however, a new phenomenon; only its mechanism is new. Colonial powers in the nineteenth century employed globalist principles locking-in countries to the supply and purchase of products and services. In modern times, globalization is driven by economics and trade, with the richest countries exercising their power through mechanisms such as foreign direct investment (Eurostat 2021). The Eurostat data show the extent of investments held offshore in low-tax jurisdictions such as the British Virgin Islands, the Cayman Islands and Jersey. Whichever view is taken, Jessop (2002) quoted in Dicken (2014: p. 6) captured its essence in this definition: "globalization is a . . . supercomplex series of multicentric, multi-scalar, multitemporal, multiform and multicausal processes".

At no point in human history has the world been hyperglobalized. The case for partial globalization or internationalism is made on the basis of trade, investment and migration data in the period 1870–1913. Comparison is not straightforward, as very different financial systems operated in the earlier period vis-à-vis modern times, including the Gold Standard and short-/long-term capital variations. However, their analysis supports the claim that "we have at the beginning of the twenty-first century an extraordinarily developed, open and integrated international economy. Thus the present position is by no means unprecedented" (Hirst, Thompson, et al. 2009, p. 40).

Rodrik's Trilemma

With these concepts in mind, Dani Rodrik (2012) poses his Trilemma (Figure 8.1).

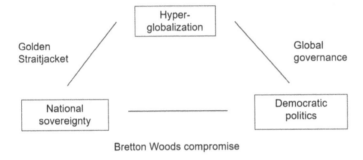

Figure 8.1: Trilemma.
Source: Rodrik (2016), reproduced with permission.

The riddle of the Trilemma requires some knowledge about the global twentieth-century history when many of the concepts in the Trilemma were invented or constructed. The Trilemma puts at the three points of a triangle, national sovereignty (self-determination), democratic politics (government by election and engagement in decision-making including opposition) and hyperglobalization (high levels of economic integration and geographical spread). These are explained in Table 8.1. The points are mediated by the following factors:

- Bretton Woods compromise: the creation of the World Bank, the IMF and the GATT; capital controls, liberalization and rule-based trade in the context of domestic politics and economic policy to maintain employment and social insurance systems
- Goldenstraitjacket: trade liberalization, free capital markets, free trade, free enterprise, small government (Rodrik 2012, p. 189)

- global governance: global government, alignment of legal and political jurisdictions, global institutions of standards and regulation, reduction in transaction costs associated with national borders (Rodrik 2012, p. 202)

The challenge now is to choose two of the three because all three dimensions are not options at the same time. Why is this?

Table 8.1: Combinations in the Trilemma.

Dimension	Rationale/challenge
Hyperglobalization – democratic politics	This combination requires some form of global governance/ government. A one-world approach to international order
Hyperglobalization – national sovereignty	This combination gives the opportunity for executives (governments) to globalize their country's economy not subject to democratic control; such control might militate against the export of jobs, environmental degradation, displacement, etc. Can lead to reduced poverty as happened in China; European countries' colonial enterprises are also examples
National sovereignty – democratic politics	This combination restricts (hyper)globalization. The UK opted through Brexit for sovereignty and democratic politics over a regional (EU) "partial globalization" dimension while pursuing "global Britain". Globalization had resulted in manufacturing jobs being "exported" to developing nations for comparative advantage. In democratic systems this is a difficult trade-off. By contrast, EU member states pool sovereignty in a regional economic bloc of twenty-seven countries of circa 500 million consumers. The EU project of "a United States of Europe" remains an option though not without the democratization of the institutions and further alignment of political, legal and financial institutions (in turn eroding individual national sovereignty). This is increasingly challenged by citizens of member states.

Source: Author's table, derived from Rodrik (2007, 2012, 2016).

We may ask, can the Trilemma be used to rationalize climate change? Climate change, ironically, looks to a hyperglobalization to solve the fundamental issues of carbon emissions and biodiversity loss. There are clearly challenges for democratic politics. There exist both forces of conservativism that recognize the need for change, but only if lifestyles and the economy are unchallenged, and radicalism whereby climate change is an opportunity to reset the economy to one that is fair and just. Sovereignty is challenged as states will be bound to international agreements and law, albeit entered into as a sovereign state. Pick two, any two!

International systems and business/corporate strategy

Why does this matter for business and corporate strategy? Firms that internationalize are subject to the terms of trade between countries and trading blocs. It can determine *inward and outward foreign direct investment* decisions, or indeed whether to internationalize at all. For example, the inward investment that the UK received from the automobile industry throughout the latter part of the twentieth century, most notably Nissan in 1986, were made on the assumption that the UK would remain a member of the EU and that the UK would be a good location for its European operations because of its educated population, flexible workforce and potential market (not to mention regional aid payments). In the age of Brexit, such investment decisions might have been different. This is, of course, a counter-factual, but the automobile manufacturers factored into their investment decision the political and economic reality and expectation that the UK was a member of the EU and hence inside its single market and customs union. To have been outside, the UK government may have needed to offer firms considerable compensation for the costs associated with borders and tariffs; otherwise it would be logical for the multi-million pound/euro investment to be made in other EU-member states in order to retain the benefits of global supply chains and just-in-time delivery to an assembly plant in a globalized sector/industry. In other words, components arrive when they are needed and not held in stock. Border checks and payments work against this way of manufacturing and are costly. The margins on each vehicle become squeezed. They are non-tariff barriers.

Firms enter foreign markets in a variety of ways, captured in Table 8.2.

Table 8.2: Modes of internationalization.

Method	Risk	Comment
International division	Low	Firm controls all aspects of the product, though may employ agents for sales support
Franchising	Low	Product is controlled by the franchise owner through conditions of franchise agreement. Franchisee may have local knowledge that give a degree of freedom (menus, language)
Licensing	Medium	A product or technology is licensed to partners located in a new territory. The ability to control the product, its manufacture and sale is diminished
Joint venture	Medium	A joint venture shares the investment risk. If the partner has experience in the chosen territory, this can mitigate risk
Wholly owned subsidiary	High	Foreign subsidiaries – starting from scratch – are capital intensive and are high risk because of the uncertainty of the new territory and market

Source: Author's table.

International divisions are simple, as they work largely as a department or function (a capability) within the firm. Orders can be taken directly and dispatched. There comes a point, however, when an export business becomes difficult to maintain because of volumes and increasing costs. In such cases it might be appropriate to set up a subsidiary, either wholly or joint-owned. Joint ventures tend to be formally constituted with equity shares held by partners. Tesco, the UK supermarket multinational, has employed both forms with varying degrees of success. The Fresh & Easy brand in the USA was a wholly owned start-up but became an expensive failure, despite considerable research into the format and significant infrastructural investment (Bateson 2012); other overseas ventures have involved the outright purchase of existing retailers such as in Poland, the Czech Republic and South Korea, and joint ventures such as China and Thailand. These are dynamic arrangements, however. As businesses develop, so do ownership structures. In Thailand, for example, the joint venture became wholly owned and then sold in December 2020.

Technology can also be licensed. A licence grants a licensee rights over a technology, trade mark or patent in return for a fee. The licence owner is bound by the terms of the agreement that may or may not allow for inputs from the licensor. There is an intellectual property risk associated with licensing and may require significant compliance and use monitoring. Arm Holdings, the chip maker, operates a licensing approach.

Franchising is a familiar format, particularly for global fast-food companies such as McDonald's, but also Swarovski (retail), TONI&GUY (hair care), Regus (property) and to a lesser extent, IKEA. Franchising has a number of advantages. The form of product can be controlled as well as the way that it is sold (shop format, for example). Franchisees can share the financial risk, lead on all matters of HRM and adapt the corporate strategy to local conditions and manage local stakeholders, in some cases, the state itself.

Supply chains

In the era of globalization firms extended their supply chains, particularly global firms vis-à-vis international firms. Sectors such as automobile, consumer electronics and semi-conductors, particularly so. Vehicles have about 30,000 parts, constituting some of the most extended and complex global supply chains. Vehicles are assembled in factories in which these parts arrive *just-in-time*. Modern enterprise resource planning (ERP) systems can manage these networks, in many cases as just-in-time supply. Just-in-time production dates from the 1980s and the Toyota manufacturing system in the auto industry (Womack et al. 1990). The system is built on the idea that firms can order components or commodities and have them delivered at the point of use rather than stored as expensive inventories in warehouses. The ability to do this owes much to the shipping container and the supporting infrastructure that engendered efficiencies so much so that transportation costs changed from being major to marginal. The history of "The Box" is told by Levinson (2016). At its most advanced, Levinson describes the process at Rotterdam's Maasvlakte 2 terminal, which opened in 2014:

> [A]n automated system notified the drivers when to bring an outbound box to the terminal. At an appointed time, a driver would be admitted through an automated gate after sensors had verified his credentials and scanned the truck and the container, and another automated system would instruct him where to back up to the security fence that surrounded the storage yard. There a computer-controlled vehicle would lift the container off its chassis, bring it over the fence, carry it to its assigned location, and stack it at the proper level. (p. 373)

The driver was the only human actor in this process. It is anticipated that the driver will not be needed in future years.

Disruption to these schedules can add significant cost to operations whose margins are narrow. These supply chains have, on the one hand, enabled complex products such as cars and computers to be affordable to mass consumers, while, on the other, contributed significantly to the breakdown of natural systems as they are resource intensive in not just energy, but also minerals and metals mined in sensitive environmental and political areas of the world. Examples include cobalt and lithium used in batteries for electronics and cars that are increasingly strategic in their importance for states, much as oil has been in the past (Frankel 2016).

Moreover, semi-conductor manufacture is concentrated in specialized regions. One region of China is responsible for assembling 70 per cent of the world's smartphones; a similar concentration is true of laptop computers. With as little as two weeks' worth of inventory, disruption to supply chains can quickly affect availability and impact on production (*The Economist 2020d)*. For example, in the wake of the Japanese tsunami in 2011, automobile production in the UK was cut back due to a shortage of parts (Kollewe 2011), and, more recently, Covid-19 not only affected the supply of components but also affected demand which, in the case of garment manufacturing in Bangladesh, Cambodia, Myanmar and, Vietnam, significantly impacted on the largely female sewers themselves (Kelly 2020). Covid-19 also affected the global supply and distribution of accredited personal protective equipment (PPE). So dependent is public and private procurement on the smooth functioning of supply chains, when disruption occurs it can cost lives and impact domestic, regional and global economies. One answer to this is to shorten supply chains and designate certain products as strategic. Dependence on global supply chains can be reduced by allowing domestic or regional production and *storage*. Some commentators, however, respond with reframing the problem as merely being about distribution and advise only to shift from ships to planes (DeHoratius 2020) with the attendant impact on carbon emissions. An unintended consequence of Brexit is exporting calves for veal using air freight rather than trucks due to delays at borders (McSweeney 2021).

Motivations for internationalization

Firms internationalize for many reasons. Chief among these are growth and competition. Many firms, particularly those publicly quoted, need to grow to satisfy shareholders. Shareholders in these firms expect consistent and growing profits. These profits have to be generated either through diversification into new products and services, or by entering new markets with an existing product. Tesco entered overseas markets for this reason. The domestic market was reaching its limits and there were no realistic new formats or related diversification to provide the growth. Regulators were also watching the big UK supermarkets and made it clear that they would act if these companies achieved too high a market share. The competition regulator had already intervened in Morrisons takeover of Safeway in the UK and later over the Sainsbury's takeover of rival Asda.

Prudent and successful executives and boards can sometimes miscalculate. Many British companies have tried to enter the USA for reasons of common language and perceived culture. Terry Leahy, former Tesco plc CEO, recognized the danger in this expectation on the launch of the company's Fresh & Easy US subsidiary. In constructing a totally new format for the brand (new territory, new product), Leahy (2012) discusses the need for courage and the importance of difference, rather than similarity, when entering international markets. In order to design a brand around difference, Tesco undertook considerable market research that included setting up a secret store in a warehouse, and living with potential customers to experience their lives. Leahy records the positive feedback received and the need for further refinement and modelling "to test the idea to destruction" (Leahy 2012, p. 92). The company also built considerable supply infrastructure. In 2013, Leahy's successor, Philip Clarke, exited the US market in failure (Butler 2013).

UK transport operators such as Stagecoach (Harper 2000) and FirstGroup (Topham 2019a) have struggled in the USA with scheduled coach operations, the latter succeeding only in its school bus business where demand is known, reliable and is a significant contributor to overall profits. Another notable miscalculation was Royal Bank of Scotland's (RBS's) rapid growth through acquisition in the UK. Just before the financial crisis of 2008, RBS, under its ambitious CEO, Fred Goodwin, put together a consortium to acquire ABN AMRO, a Dutch bank. After a bidding war with Barclays, the consortium's offer of €71bn (€10bn more than Barclays) was accepted. Notwithstanding the premium price, RBS's due diligence did not fully capture ABN AMRO's exposure to the sub-prime mortgage liabilities (Bowers and Treanor 2011), leading to the collapse of the group.

Firms also expand and internationalize because that is what the competition is doing, much like any fashion or trend. For example, during the privatization of the UK railway industry in 1994, the body in charge of selling rail franchises used the active participation of a single private transport operator in the UK, Stagecoach, through the sale of South West Trains providing services out of London's Waterloo station, to sell its other twenty-four franchises (Grantham 1998, 2001). International companies such as Connex, Abellio and Deutsche Bahn entered the bidding process. Deutsche Bahn partnered with an incumbent and, separately, through buying a general transport operator, Arriva, that had train operating franchises in its portfolio. More recently, this phenomenon can be seen in the popularity of cryptocurrencies, in particular Bitcoin. Its popularity can partly be explained by a media interest, the entry of traditional financial services firms and the currency's likeness to gold as a reliable store of value.

Finally, firms internationalize because of trade barriers. Much foreign direct investment into Europe is motivated by access to the EU single market. In the automobile industry Honda, Nissan and Toyota, for example, established manufacturing subsidiaries within the single market. Fast-moving white good brands owned by non-European companies are also manufactured in the territory of the single market, for example, LG in Poland.

More recently, many UK firms have internationalized by relocating manufacturing or distribution functions to countries within the single market and the customs union. Post-Brexit, firms evaluated the costs associated with exporting in light of significant non-tariff barriers being erected. A UK company based in the South Coast English town of Littlehampton, Mediwin, relocated a production line to Amsterdam, the Netherlands, in order to ensure delivery of its products in a reliable and timely fashion. As a supplier of critical drugs with a large customer base in France, any delay risked losing business, and potentially lives (O'Carroll 2021). The counter to such a decision in situations where export is a small part of the overall business is to withdraw completely. There are also cases of products made in the UK but distributed from Europe becoming unavailable for direct delivery to UK customers, for example, Brooks saddles (Reid 2021).

Trade agreements and their impact on mode of entry

Firms located in one country seeking to trade in other countries need to understand what is allowed and what is not. The most recent trade agreement between the UK and the EU provides a good example of how careful and informed decision-makers need to be. While there are no money tariffs on the transfer of goods between the UK and EU member states, there are non-tariff barriers. A non-tariff barrier comprises anything that prevents *frictionless* trade between countries. The UK government has negotiated a free trade agreement with the EU; however, it is free only to the extent that it is money-tariff free. There are costs linked to standards, including safety, quality, permissible materials, testing regimes, veterinary health and rules of origin. Anything that has to be declared ahead of its transfer between the UK and the EU is a non-tariff barrier. Moreover, VAT is collected and is payable by importers. To illustrate the point, on 31 December 2020 the UK government published a series of case studies illustrating non-tariff barriers for a series of sectors (HM Government 2020).

For firms in service industries, there is no provision for trading on any terms. From 1 January 2021, business personnel are permitted to enter the EU for ninety days in any six-month period. They can attend trade shows but not sell directly to customers without a work visa. Sam Lowe, senior research fellow at the Centre for European Reform, uses the case of fashion models and musicians to illustrate the restrictions on human trade. Prior to 1 January 2021, a fashion model could work on the Milan catwalk and a musician could tour Europe freely. Subsequent to 1 January 2021, both need work visas from the country in which they intend to work. Such restrictions are important for firms and personnel to understand (breaching these regulations can result in a fine) before committing to internationalization (Barnard et al. 2020). Lowe has also created a list of state exceptions to the trade agreement (European Commission 2020).

Sole traders and small and medium-sized enterprises (SMEs) are particularly disadvantaged. They tend not to have the resources or capabilities to manage this complexity and cover the costs of bureaucracy. This is why states have been keen in the past to remove barriers to trade, rather than to erect them. In the UK, services and cultural products are hugely valuable to the economy and are a major export. Larger companies and those predominantly in the financial services sector have reassigned and transferred their assets to European bases and subsidiaries. For example, easyJet, the low-cost airline, transferred assets to a new subsidiary, easyJet Europe: easyJet Europe Airline GmbH (Topham and Sweney 2017). This was a strategic management decision.

Proximity and culture

The trade agreement between the UK and the EU illustrates a number of other issues surrounding internationalization and international trade. Firms seeking to internationalize, particularly those doing so incrementally, choose countries that are both geographically and culturally similar. If internationalization is conceptualized as a process of risk management, this is a logical element of a growth strategy. IKEA, the furniture maker and retailer, founded in Sweden in 1943, opened its first retail store in 1958, was likely to be an international, if not global, firm. The Swedish market was small and the scale economies were to be achieved in a much bigger market. Scale economies are a component of cost-leadership. IKEA learned its business in Sweden before establishing stores in other countries. Not surprisingly, the management selected Norway (1963), Denmark (1969) and Switzerland in 1973 before entering the biggest European markets, Germany (1974), France (1981) and the UK (1987).

This internationalization strategy can be explained and predicted from a concise framework known as the Uppsala model (Johanson and Vahlne 1977; Forsgren 2002). The Uppsala model broadly assumes that:

1. Organizations learn from their own operations and apply that learning to new markets
2. Firms manage their risk in new markets by incremental expansion; they learn about operating in a new market and build commitment before entering another one
3. Individuals working in those new markets gain the operating knowledge
4. Investments are made in countries with similar psychic distance (cultural similarity) to the home country

On the face of it, IKEA applied this Uppsala approach. It was twenty years before IKEA opened in Norway and a further six years before a move into Denmark was attempted. These countries have a low psychic distance, though they are not the same. It took thirty-eight years to enter France, which culturally was quite different, but still close in proximity. So far, so good, for Uppsala alignment. Though what explains IKEA's entry into Japan (1974), Canada and Australia in 1976 and the USA in 1985? Entry into Canada was undertaken as a franchise operation, sufficient to establish the brand in the country speedily, draw on local knowledge and develop the necessary continental logistics. In the USA, IKEA was not an immediate success on the East Coast; the standardization of products did not work. Eventually, local adaptations were introduced into the product range to align products with the market and consumers. The company also took over a West Coast competitor, Stor, to build the economies of scale (Schmid 2013).

Forsgren's (2002) research offers a number of additions to our understanding of how firms learn about new markets. While experiential learning is important, firms can learn *without* doing, particularly in modern digital economies. As indeed do students of strategy. Detailed case studies provide insights into new market potential. Moreover, case studies can be from different industries and still offer valuable learning.

Additionally, firms can employ people with internationalization experience, that is, people who bring the capability, having done it before with another firm, or indeed in a partnership with an incumbent. It is also the case that *more-of-the-same* has diminishing returns. In the case of IKEA, the market in the USA and Japan were, ultimately, very different to each other and to the home/regional markets. For firms looking to be truly multinational or global, there may be the imperative to enter significant markets such as the USA before others do and erect barriers to entry such as reputation and scale. These territories may also have access to factors of production such as land, raw materials and know-how. It may also be true that investment in a new territory can provide *real options* in the future. Care is always needed in interpreting business timelines, however. All is not what it might seem. Allegedly, the IKEA strategists selected to open a store in Konstanz, mistaking it for Koblenz (Collins 2011). While this may be apocryphal, most managers experience such lapses, even if the implications are not quite so costly.

Host country characteristics

Decisions to enter a new territory are often determined by an assessment of the host country and its factor conditions, domestic demand conditions, support and related industries and industry structure and rivalry. These are the components of the so-called Diamond Model (Porter 1990; 1998) Table 8.3 captures the four components:

Table 8.3: Diamond Model.

Issue	Description
Factor conditions	Land, labour and raw materials
Domestic demand conditions	Performance or acceptance of products in new territories. For example, Honda's 250cc motorbikes did not cope well with the continental distances in the USA, unlike US domestic machines like Harley Davidson; likewise, Tesco's Fresh & Easy did not appeal to consumers' expectations for personal customer service and ready-made meals and were met with incomprehension in a country where fast food outlets proliferate.
Support and related industries	Suppliers of raw materials, components, finance and expertise – universities both educate future employees and generate patents and further develop products.
Industry structure and rivalry	States determine structures when they regulate, invest, subsidize and protect.

Source: Author's table, derived from Porter (1990; 1998).

A further point of note about structure, from the UK's liberal economic perspective, even firms operating in strategic industries can be sold to overseas buyers. Examples include companies like Arm Holdings (semi-conductors, sold to Softbank in 2016) and DeepMind (artificial intelligence (AI), sold to Google in 2014), Eurostar (transport, sold to a Canadian-British fund consortium in 2015) and GKN (engineering, sold to Melrose in 2018). By contrast, in Germany, firms operating in strategic industries including biotech, energy and digital economy are now protected (Gow 2008; Reuters 2020). The role of the state, in these cases, can be a determinant in decisions to enter a territory.

Born Globals and transnationalism

Some firms operate in sectors for which borders and domestic markets are blurred. The digital economy is an example. Digital products and the equipment used to access them are global. Microchips that drive mobile devices are standardized products. Mobile devices have slight adaptations for sale in particular territories. These may be language capabilities on mobile devices/computers and videogames, for example. The companies behind these products are often what are termed, Born Globals. Take, for example, Arm Holdings, a designer of semiconductors/microchips running many of the world's mobile devices. It licenses its intellectual property in return for a fee. In so doing, it was able to maintain commercial links to numerous firms, many of which were in competition with one another – Apple and Samsung, for example (Davies 2020). It was a spin-off from Cambridge University. It is also potentially a strategic firm as it supplies into the defence industry. It was always a Born Global.

Kudina et al. (2008) define born-global firms as

> business organizations that, from inception, seek to derive significant competitive advantage from the use of resources and the sale of outputs in multiple countries [and] companies who have reached a share of foreign sales of at least 25 per cent within a time frame of two to three years after their establishment. (p. 39)

The home country – the UK or Germany, for example – does not offer a viable market for the product. In the Porter sense of the Diamond, the host country has important factor conditions such as land and labour and university-educated scientists and technologists, and related and support industries, including the university and finance. The host country may also have a robust legal system sufficient to protect intellectual property that is developed domestically.

Kudina et al. (2008) demonstrate a number of other properties of born-global firms. They are often de facto global standards-setters. In other words, their product or key technology becomes the industry standard. Being an international standards-setter is a good competitive strategy for small firms without the resources to secure international patents.

The managers of born-global firms often have an international mindset; they fear neither internationalization nor international markets. Where they compete, moreover, it is usually not on cost. They differentiate their products, which are often few in number; that is, the scope of the business is limited and hence focused. They are *differentiation-focused*. Their technologies are hard to imitate; in other words, they are *inimitable*. Born Globals grow fast, often by international acquisition. Developing proprietorial technology is a slower growth strategy. These are significant strategic management considerations, namely, where, when and in what, to invest. These are also firms with trust-based relationships. As a network of professionals, they are less transactional than their traditional counterparts. This trust potentially facilitates research and product development, with the ability to share knowledge with clients and vice versa.

Finally, Born Globals establish international subsidiaries very quickly in order to support the product and develop and protect the standard they set. Moreover, they are likely to be not only international and global, but also networked. The networked firm or corporation (also known as transnational) is not exclusive to Born Globals. The network is often digital, but not exclusively so. Networked firms are likely to practise open innovation whereby they draw on expertise, technological and market knowledge from sources external to the firm, often mediated through digital networks. What physical proximity used to do to in Silicon Valley in the twentieth century in clustering expertise in tech firms and their support services such as university research and venture capital, digital networks do in the twenty-first century. What makes them different from merely global is their ability to design and/or make regional product variations, not just standard global products. Castells (2000) has written extensively about the networked society. The first plank in building the networked firm was *informationalism*, understood as the use of data to enhance production whether material objects, food or services. The financial services industry is particularly informational in its operations – digital, global, interdependent, and temporally independent, unrestricted by domestic schedules and time zones. The networking allows SMEs to work cooperatively across borders, making them competitive and, potentially, differentiated from larger rivals. Global and networked education companies, for example Kaplan, can offer country-/discipline-specific curricula and assessments. Many consultancies are networked businesses, for example the civil engineering firm, Arup. Global social movements are also enabled by networked approaches as indeed is public policy and healthcare.

Implications for climate change

Firms internationalize to grow. Their domestic market may be either too small or saturated. Firms look to international markets to maintain growth on behalf of shareholders or other core stakeholders. Whichever mode is adopted it is likely to be carbon intensive with extending supply chains and distribution networks.

Firms globalize to capitalize on resources and capabilities that are located in many different locations around the world. The automobile industry is globalized with component parts manufactured in many different international locations and shipped *just-in-time* to assembly plants in different continents supplying different geographical markets. These supply chains are extended. The products themselves are increasingly globalized and standardized.

Globalization has resulted in cost and price reductions. The smartphone is ubiquitous because the costs of production have been reduced and brought quite sophisticated electronics to retail consumers. Notwithstanding the carbon footprint of the products being shipped, the increased output and consumption creates waste. While much electronic waste has value and is recycled (Dicken 2014), albeit re-exported to be recycled, other products of global production are never re-used or recycled. In the UK alone in 2012, in the order of 300,000 tonnes of used clothing went to landfill, which is the equivalent of thirty-three T-shirts per person per year (WRAP 2012). Carbon emissions associated with the fashion industry and its sourcing and manufacturing processes have actually increased since that report.

Summary

Internationalization is a strategic choice for firms having reached the limits to growth in the domestic market, seeking efficiency savings by outsourcing to low-cost countries or trading in products that are global and where the sales potential in the domestic market are small or non-existent. Strategists, however, need to consider risk pragmatically. Colonial histories are important. History tells us what has been done in the past in the name of mercantile profit and is the basis, in some cases, of responsible investment and behaviour in the present.

History also tells analysts something about the international environment and mechanisms. For the time being, the twentieth century's violent history explains the current global consensus supported by familiar international organizations such as the UN, the Bretton Woods organizations and other non-state actors. However, as recent history illustrates, this consensus, while resilient, is not guaranteed. The rise of populism across the world, fuelled by a backlash against globalization, threatens to undermine democratic and alliance norms just at a time when global cooperation is needed to tackle climate change and a pandemic. The USA's constitution has been severely challenged during the Trump presidency, and the UK's departure from the EU has shown that alliances change as a result of different forces ebbing and flowing in their power and influence. Even *attempting* to reconcile Rodrik's Trilemma helps students of business to understand and control for the global forces that countries are subject to as rule takers; with only the exceptional few actors such as executives being influential over them. In the twentieth century those actors were oil company leaders. In the twenty-first century, perhaps the power brokers are those from social networks, AI and big data analytics?

While the internationalization formulae for selecting territories, choosing entry modes and evaluating host-country characteristics are effective, internationalization remains risky and subject to numerous cultural factors relating to firms themselves and the territories that they enter. The ego of CEOs combined with a misunderstanding of history, international trade agreements and domestic politics can be decisive.

Finally, in the context of climate change, history tells us that it is not inevitable. Coal and steam were choices related to the control of labour and the *extraction* of profit. To pursue business-as-usual is a choice. Firms and states can change course, and they can do so without radical change to political and economic systems. It requires a change in priorities for firms, at the very least investing in carbon neutrality, possibly leading to delaying profit and dividends. Governments, by contrast, need to enact intelligent and enabling policy and diffuse them through alliances (the EU, for example). However, internationalization and globalization are drivers of consumption and ultimately climate pressure. Those changed priorities need to be a re-conceptualization of consumption and to align the firm with objectives met by sustainable production and distribution. In other words, the circular or butterfly economy and shorter or climate/social welfare value-adding supply chains.

Questions

1. What is international strategy? What is global strategy? What is the major difference? Consider the difference in the context of the following industries: automobile, oil, fast food, banking, retail.
2. What is comparative advantage? Which countries have comparative advantage in the following industries: textile manufacture, semi-conductors, unseasonal vegetables, oil, rare-earth metal mining?
3. How can the Trilemma be used to help with mitigating climate change?
4. What are the five entry modes, and which is the riskiest (on what do analysts base risk)?
5. What motivates firms to internationalize?
6. What options do firms have to shorten supply chains?
7. What is the Uppsala model of internationalization? Is it an accurate reflection of how firms internationalize?
8. What is the Diamond Model? What does it tell analysts?
9. What is a born global firm – what characteristics do they have?
10. What is informationalism?

Chapter 9
Innovation

Innovation is a key element of business and corporate strategy. Without it, firms stagnate and, eventually, fail. Successful firms, therefore, innovate and invest. For some it is a core function. Innovation has many components. Firms innovate their products (between generations) and their processes (how products are made, sold, distributed). Innovation can be incremental (step by step) or radical (new platform, technology, corporate form). Innovations can be disruptive, in that they challenge existing providers, offering customers cheaper alternatives, though sometimes with reduced functionality. Innovation can be open or closed, involve users or be exclusively users creating their own products. Innovation is also central to firms' responses to climate change, that is, making products that are sustainable, recyclable, etc., using processes that are zero carbon, low impact and fair.

This chapter introduces the following:
- the concept of innovation
    - as product and/or process
    - open to outside inputs and/or closed
    - incremental, step by step or radical new paradigm
    - disruptive or discontinuous – stripped down, fit for purpose
- innovation as a driver for climate solutions

What is innovation?

It is important to note that innovation is *not* invention. At its most basic innovation is the commercialization of a product or process (Tidd and Bessant 2009). Innovating a product results in a positive change to a product, such as enhanced functionality, appearance, speed or accessibility. Annual releases of iPhones by Apple is an example of product innovation in this sense. Innovating a process involves the commercial introduction of a new enhanced production, marketing or logistics process. Both types contribute to improved firm performance either by selling more units or reducing the cost of each unit.

Innovation has a life cycle. Innovations diffuse (Rogers 1995) in stages: introduction, growth, maturity and decline. The diffusion curves for product and process are different. Product innovation occurs earlier than process innovation. Firms prioritize product innovation in the first instance, as they build market share and lock in customers to the product before turning to process innovation to extract more value from the product indirectly. The two curves are illustrated in Figure 9.1.

https://doi.org/10.1515/9783110718430-009

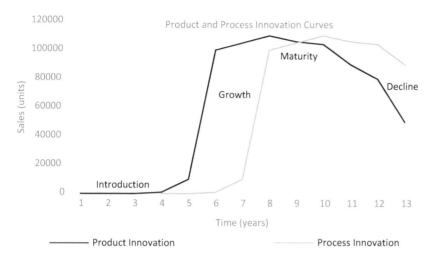

Figure 9.1: Product and process innovation curves.
Source: Author's figure.

Innovation models

How does innovation work? What are the causal links, if any? Rothwell (1994) traced the history of innovation through five phases or models. The first-generation model took as its driving force, basic science. Scientific discovery led to product development and then markets. This linear model (1950s to the mid-1960s) was very much a product of its time. The post-war period, particularly in Europe, was one of rebuilding and renewal driven by discovery and knowledge, some of which derived directly from the wartime experience of production and logistics. Many of the outputs of production were capital items and not consumer products. It made sense for products derived from basic science to lead to design and engineering, manufacturing before marketing and sales. It was *technology-push*.

The second-generation model (mid-1960s to early 1970s) reflected a new consumerism. It was a market-driven model where perceived consumer desires drove product development, manufacturing and sales. This is *market pull*. Both of these models are strictly linear. There are no feedback loops, no parallel activities.

Rothwell's third-generation model synthesized these two approaches whereby both market and basic science impacted on product and market development. It covers the period from the early 1970s to the mid-1980s. Figure 9.2 shows how the linear flow of the first two generations become "coupled", and a two-way interaction refined innovation inputs. The model hints at private corporate maturity generating communication channels and linking functions together, not least with technologists, conceivably external to the firm. Critically, however, this remains a linear model where activities are sequential.

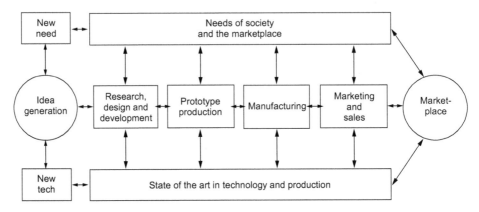

Figure 9.2: The "coupling" model of innovation (third generation).
Source: Rothwell (1994), reproduced with permission.

As technology advances, supply chains become stretched and organizations become global in reach, linearity begins to have less explanatory power. Hence the fourth generation, covering the period of the early 1980s to the early 1990s, has activities such as marketing, engineering and manufacturing working in parallel. Some of the activities are undertaken by subsidiaries; others are outsourced. Manufacturing and design technologies were deployed; it was also a period of just-in-time production, a factor that transformed the automobile industry and many others as well. However, this model, illustrated in Figure 9.3, precedes widespread use of the Internet.

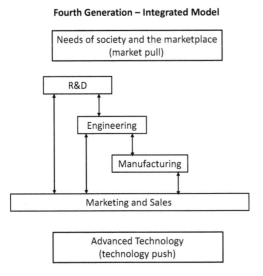

Figure 9.3: Parallel working and technology model (fourth generation).
Source: Author's figure, derived from Rothwell (1994).

A fifth generation of mid-1990s forward sought to capture the dynamics of a digital transformation of science, design, manufacture and sales. Sharing many similar features of the fourth generation's parallel working, it envisaged an impact associated with the integration of sophisticated information technology supporting innovation activities. At the time Rothwell was writing, he did not know how sophisticated these technological networks would or could be. This time was pre-Internet/Google and pre-smartphone. In innovation terms, this fifth generation was radical, where the others had been incremental.

Firms with fifth-generation innovation approaches:

- optimize organizational features such as project management, flat hierarchies, agility, intrapreneurship, and quality systems
- have strong inter-firm vertical linkages with supplier and customers
- leverage external horizontal linkages, competitors, partners and buyers
- may deploy sophisticated enterprise resource planning (ERP) systems to manage them

There are a number of ways in which the fifth-generation model works for firms. They can use their networks to work around the clock. When one group shuts down for the night, others take up tasks associated with product development. For example, digital businesses building platforms or games can spend a day in one territory developing functions and hand these over to other territories for "overnight" testing. Tested modules or features can then be ready for designers in the morning to fix issues and/or further develop the product. The fifth generation is radical in its utilization of information technology and increasingly the incorporation of artificial intelligence, such as machine learning, processing and interpreting big data.

Fifth-generation innovation and vaccines

The rapid development of Covid-19 vaccines demonstrated features of the fifth-generation model (Davis 2020). All societal stakeholders were seeking a plurality of vaccination options to roll out at the earliest safe opportunity. There were millions of doses of the vaccines available immediately after regulators passed them as safe. The pharmaceutical companies did not need to wait for approval to start manufacturing, as that would have delayed the diffusion of their vaccine; this was made possible only by states pre-buying in bulk, essentially taking away the risk. Additionally, at the beginning of the process, the deoxyribonucleic acid (DNA) of the virus was decoded by a Chinese laboratory and the data made available to all firms and research institutes seeking to develop a vaccine. This is the interplay between international public- and private-sector stakeholders working not as closed competitors, but as open collaborators seeking to reduce timeframes for a collective good. The caveat is, however, that the process of Covid-19 vaccine development was not the norm for pharmaceutical development. For reasons of safety, drug development is mostly linear, sequential and derived from basic science (technology push or technology enabled).

There were also new "platform" vaccine technologies available to pharmaceutical firms, themselves a product of a fifth-generation innovation approach. These technologies work by taking the genetic material of a virus and "slotting" it into a pre-coded delivery module. Once inserted into the body, so-called spike proteins are generated, in turn triggering a natural immune response in recipients. These platform technologies have partial regulatory approval, that made the final approval of the vaccine faster. But equally, the regulatory approval was also undertaken in parallel; at each stage, data were shared with regulators rather than provided at the final regulatory stage. When final time for approval came, elements of the standard regulatory procedure had already been completed. States, moreover, provided generous financial resources that were devoted to vaccine development.

There is a caveat, though. Fifth-generation innovation works well for developed economies, not so much for the developing world. Using the example of vaccines again, developing countries are missing out on access to a Covid-19 vaccine because new technologies and processes fall back somewhat when scaling up manufacturing is important. For example, Dr Peter Hotez, founding dean of the National School of Tropical Medicine, Professor of Paediatrics and Molecular Virology and Microbiology at Baylor College of Medicine, argues that Sub-Saharan Africa needs four billion doses of vaccines that can be administered in places where intense refrigeration is not available, and logistics are generally more difficult. His team is working on a vaccine based on an earlier generation of vaccines, so-called recombinant-protein. These use a technology developed for a hepatitis-B vaccine and are scalable, manufacturable and transportable (Hotez 2021).

Fifth generation and aerospace: Hydrogen and biofuels

The challenge for the aviation industry is to reduce the GHG emissions attributable to flying. The two major manufacturers, Airbus and Boeing, have different approaches. Airbus is committing to hydrogen as a fuel (Ambrose 2021), while Boeing will power its aircraft using biofuels (Reuters 2021). Airbus has revealed three prototypes with a view to taking about 200 passengers up to 2000 nautical miles with zero emissions (water vapour is the primary emission from hydrogen fuels). Airbus is looking to have a version of these planes commercially in service by 2035, after selecting the most favourable variation in 2025. Boeing's fuel of choice, biofuel, is not zero carbon. Nor does it stay within planetary boundaries. The advantage over hydrogen is that biofuels can be used by existing planes and hence be implemented more quickly and cheaply. While the carbon released in burning biofuel merely releases the carbon that was captured in the growing of the crop, there is a significant land requirement. Growing crops for biofuels potentially displaces the growth of less lucrative but locally important food crops. It may also lead to further deforestation.

The Boeing plan to have its planes in commercial service by 2030 is ambitious and involves significant parallel working in a fifth-generation model. For example, plane makers have significant dependencies. Jet engines are designed and built by suppliers, not by the plane makers themselves. However, jet engines are integral to plane design; that is, they are not designed independently of aircraft. It is not just manufacturers that need to work on these major innovations. Aviation is subject to strict safety regulations. Regulators are very much part of the ecosystem. Moreover, if aviation fuels change, then the infrastructure that delivers them to airports and to aeroplanes also needs to innovate in tandem. There will also be a role for governments. To achieve the change needed within the timeframe, states may well offer financial incentives, if not provide infrastructure and research capability. If biofuels have to be grown, arable land needs to be made available equitably (Mellor 2020).

Fifth-generation model and vertical agriculture

Finally, the case of an innovative vertical farm start-*up like Plenty* poses additional questions about innovation models. Counter-intuitively, it is a technology firm supported by tech venture capital. Plenty claims to produce edible greens and soft fruits using 95 per cent less land than conventional salad farms, with 99 per cent less water. The controlled conditions enable the produce to be genetically modified organisms (GMOs) and pesticide-free, because there are no pests, and the electricity is 100 per cent renewable. It looks like a perfect solution to society's consumption habits and desires. Technology in the form of data analytics, machine learning and robotics combine to produce some of the simplest foods. The question remains, is this fifth-generation model fit for a sustainable future? Is there a sixth-generation model that is more in line with United Nations' Sustainable Development Goals (SDGs)? Is there a planetary generation?

Sixth-generation planetary model

The first new dimension in the planetary model (Figure 9.4) is the incorporation of planetary boundaries. These are determined by the external factors established by Raworth (2017), namely, climate change, water acidification, chemical pollution, nitrogen and phosphorous loading, freshwater withdrawals, land conversion, biodiversity loss, air pollution and ozone layer depletion. Second, the model incorporates social foundations, namely, water, food, health, education, income and work, peace and justice, political voice, social equity, gender equality, housing, networks and energy. Within these constraints are bundled what is termed a *democracy of ideas*. In all contexts this is a political process. Ideally, in a liberal democracy, these would arise from debate, protest, research, representation and community consensus between stakeholders. However, the political domain is not always liberal. Where this is the case, the boundaries are still respected because of international treaties and goals, for example, the Paris Agreement of 2015, trade agreements and the UN's SDGs.

The planetary boundaries and social foundations are not breached in providing the energy that delivers societal needs because it is renewable. The tree is the perfect metaphor; not only does it generate its energy exclusively from the sun by the chemical process of photosynthesis, but it also traps carbon in doing so. The tree provides shade, holds the soils together, creates moisture, generates clouds and finally rain that then provides clean water. A number of the SDGs are met in the process. The tree supports biodiversity. It is the most effective regenerative technology available to humanity. The sixth-generation planetary innovation model is uniquely carbon negative. The innovation system has established that there is enough renewable energy to support human society (Goodall 2016). Human beings can more than subsist without fossil fuels; but to do so means that the economy becomes non-extractive, by which is meant resources are equitably distributed, recycled and re-used. More cannot be taken than is returned. Profit can remain as an objective of firms because profit is used for investment and is distributed to shareholders and the broader stakeholder community. However, it does mean that profit is not the sole purpose of firms (Mayer 2018).

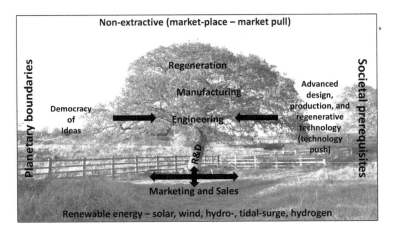

Figure 9.4: Sixth-generation planetary innovation model.
Source: Author's figure, derived from Raworth (2017).

The innovation generations become more complex, incorporate more stakeholders and develop through time (temporally) and geographically (spatially). Policy-makers often do not compose policy on the basis of an understanding of the dynamics of innovation. For example, in the UK, governments tend to apply a first-generation linear model in policy-making and implementation. They focus public investment in STEM subjects (science, technology, engineering and maths) at the expense of the social sciences (including business) and humanities. Writers such as Caracostas (2007) argue that linear models have the distinct advantage of simplicity and are understandable by policy-makers in a way that the forth- and fifth-generation models are not. Balconi et al. (2010) note that one of the limitations of non-linear models, such as the fourth and fifth generations, is that the position becomes simply one of "everything depends on everything else" (p. 11). In such cases, models have to be very specific and detailed in order to be meaningful. In some cases, this can lead to very bad and wasteful policy. For example, Brexit was predicated on a very simple idea, namely, that sovereignty is indivisible. You have it or you do not. The case is that the world is interdependent and pure sovereignty is elusive even for the most secretive and isolated of states such as North Korea. Innovation is a collaborative endeavour where states pool resources and share in the benefits. When humanity is faced with a warming climate, the interdependencies of effects and solutions are evident. Withdrawal from international and collaborative research funding schemes, such as those of the EU, and information/knowledge sharing for security, is rooted in linear thinking and a shyness towards complexity.

Implications for firms and climate

The first-generation model has at its heart public financing and execution of basic or fundamental scientific research. Basic research is not innovation, but it can be the foundation of innovation in product and process. Many of the technologies that can benefit mitigation efforts, such as carbon capture, have come from basic research.

There is no direct link between basic research and firms' ability to innovate, however. Innovation is often a capability. Firms have an innovation capability that might involve extensive networking, partnership in research and/or production, marketing, technology sharing, etc. Firms that do not innovate, decline. Take, for example, firms operating in one of the dirtiest industries on the planet and a major emitter of carbon dioxide, namely, the cement industry. It contributes 8 per cent of all carbon dioxide emissions from eight billion tonnes of material (Lehne and Preston 2018). Every 25kg bag of Portland cement produces 24kg of CO_2 (Berners-Lee 2020)!

Firms emitting such quantities are likely to be regulated into reducing their carbon emissions, or to fail. The firms in the global cement industry need to innovate their way into lower emissions. The source of the emissions is an input of energy in the mining and chemical production processes. Cement plants can improve their energy efficiency, reduce or replace fossil fuels and deploy carbon capture. But there are many processes and materials that are unique to the industry and need industry-wide innovative solutions. For example, clinker is a major ingredient of cement and the harm it causes is potentially analogous to the CFCs used in refrigeration that caused the hole in the ozone layer. Clinker has to be reduced or substituted. Novel cements are needed at scale, globally. There is a complex set of financial stakeholders involved in cement, over and above the international firms that produce it such as Heidelberg and Cemex. These stakeholders include: UN Environment Programme (UNEP), the International Energy Agency (IEA), working with the industry-led Cement Sustainability Initiative (CSI), and the Energy Transitions Commission (ETC) (Lehne and Preston 2018, p. vi). This is both a threat and an opportunity for manufacturers. The innovation capability comes into its own in situations like this where there is both a firm- and industry-wide interest in a tangible outcome and product. It is an industry where patents limit equitable knowledge sharing, leading to duplication of effort and waste and not least of time, which is in very short supply.

So much for manufacturing, is there a solution to climate change and business opportunities in digital technologies and data processes? It is to this that the chapter now turns.

Digitalization and digitization

Digitalization is the exploitation of business or societal opportunities arising from either the conversion of existing data into digital files or the creation of data exclusively in digital form. Digitization is the process of converting data or information into a digital format to be exploited by information and communication technologies (ICTs). Digital transformation is a process by which economies, businesses, society and lifestyles are restructured around the opportunities created by digitization (Rachinger et al. 2019). The digital world incorporates, among other things, cloud technologies, sensors, big data, 3D printing and through these, business models are innovated. The business model defines the value proposition, its delivery to customers and how that value is captured by the firm in terms of maximizing revenue. This is not only an issue of price; it is also one of cost.

Firms and agencies are increasingly accessible online. Services such as issuing passports and drivers' licences, tax declarations, payments and urban planning are largely executed remotely, by virtue of digitalization, digitization and digital transformation. Health service records and diagnoses through AI are digitized and increasingly provided to patients digitally. In the home, smart meters record consumption of electricity, gas and water in real time. The days of the human meter reading are ending. These meters have additional important uses; for example, in electricity supply, peaks can be managed using real-time data such that stand-by carbon capacity, usually provided by gas power stations, does not need to be used to meet demand. It is possible to disconnect certain appliances or factory processes to save enough electricity to cope with everyone arriving home and cooking dinner, though the Covid-19 pandemic may change this demand pattern into the future through home working in the developed world. In this scenario, big and small users agree to go partially off grid at short notice and are compensated as a result (Goodall 2016). This is an example of the Internet of Things (IoT).

Utility companies are hybrids. Their core business is production with tangible inputs and outputs. Inputs of fuel and funnelled through generating plant, with an output of electricity. Their digitalization strategies are around the service aspect of the business generating efficiencies and, potentially, benefiting customers. The same is true of airlines and traditional retail banks. However, there is a whole economy now that is purely digital. So-called big tech companies like Google, Facebook and Twitter were always digital companies. They generate large datasets that are crucial to their business model. Users pay for services in data rather than money. The data are monetized largely by charging advertisers looking to target likely customers. New businesses have piggybacked on these platforms and the professional influencer has emerged.

The digital world is an ecosystem. Firms that are assumed to be independent are indeed not so. For example, Apple is a hybrid big tech firm creating hardware on the one hand and digital services such as cloud servers on the other. When the company announced changes to the privacy options on its iPhone operating system (v14.5) in the wake of growing concerns about transparency and use of data, it immediately sparked a response from firms in the ecosystem. The revised privacy settings and options ask users whether they want to be tracked or not, rather than users having to search the privacy setting on the operating system. Why is this significant? It is significant because other players in the ecosystem are potentially denied monetizable data should the app-tracking facility be disabled by the user. This is deemed to be worth $350bn to so-called data brokers (Naughton 2021a). This is the ordinary business of digital marketing companies.

Digitalization presents many challenges. At one level, it excludes those without access to the digital marketplace. At another level, the more that is digitized, the more is shared among those in the ecosystem. While Apple is offering users a degree of secrecy, competitors such as Google less so. The sharing between commercial apps is one thing; the sharing of data from non-commercial apps such as healthcare (services and records) has major implications for the owners of data. For example, if insurance companies can access health records, they will use them to exclude risky policies, or at least make them unaffordable. However, even in the commercial world, app usage can reveal lifestyle choices that can be inherently risky for insurance companies. A regular visitor to a bar may be seen as a higher risk than a person who is an infrequent visitor. Conversely, regular gym-goers may see their premiums decrease.

In societal terms, digitalization changes employee profiles and necessary qualifications. Employees are retrained, let go or recruited with the skills of digital business. Customers also need a compatible skillset to access and use the products of digitalization. Many customers train themselves in order to access services and platforms. This is a cost saving for suppliers and potentially monetizable further though video tutorials on new media platforms.

There is also another societal benefit to digitalization and digitization, that of investigative journalism. Investigative journalism has been in decline in recent years as media organizations have both digitized and digitalized. Their business models have been challenged and operations have been scaled down. Data, however, are the key resource for investigative journalism where networks of professional and amateur journalists use digital open-source resources such as geo-location, digital maps, mobile phone records and audio to uncover wrong-doing. Indeed, they now provide admissible evidence to the International Criminal Court (ICC), prosecuting crimes such as the loss of flight MH17, summary executions and people smuggling (for example, Bellingcat.com). They are financed by donation and subscription models.

Whether digitalization totally transforms the business model, or just a part, it is disruptive or discontinuous.

Disruptive (discontinuous) innovation

The concept of disruptive innovation is the work of Clayton Christensen. Christensen (1997) identified a dilemma for innovators. Innovation within firms can often focus on the perceived needs of key customers and not, more broadly, on the needs of potential customers. Take, for example, Microsoft Office and the ever-increasing functionality of the programs in the suite. Most customers use only a fraction of the functionality but pay for the whole. Is there a point where customers choose alternatives with reduced functionality and which are cheaper to buy or access? The fact that Microsoft Office remains the most widely used suite of products suggests not. However, Microsoft has managed to lock-in its customers building links and user synergies between the programs and its cloud computing business. Effectively the Office Suite became the de facto industry standard.

This is not the case with other products in other industries. The compact disc (CD) was disrupted by MPEG-1/2 Audio Layer III (MP3) files. Music companies' value proposition to their core music customers was a constant improvement in the quality of the sound. However, many consumers could not tell the difference between CD quality and MP3. What the MP3 users knew, however, was that MP3 files were considerably smaller than "lossless" files and so could be packed on to music players and mobile phones. MP3 files could also be infinitely copied and shared causing leakage to the revenue system and undermining the business model of the music firms. Moreover, the mode of consumption changed. CDs and the vinyl products that preceded them came as carefully composed albums, for which every track earned its place on the track list and also its position. It was inconceivable that consumers might choose only to listen to and purchase a single track. Though that is precisely what happened, and the integrity of the album was lost. The MP3, and the businesses that sold them, disrupted the music-production industry. Streaming has disrupted the industry again with a new distribution system that further relegates the creative in the global value chain vis-à-vis the platform owner.

Retail banking has recently been disrupted. Anne Boden had a long career at Royal Bank of Scotland and later as chief operating officer (COO) at Allied Irish Bank, charged with restructuring, modernizing and introducing new technology. Her exposure to that technology convinced her that she could set up a new retail bank; a disrupter, as she called it, a challenger, in government language. Starling Bank would not be a bank with digitized services, like an app; rather it would be a digital business. It would not replicate existing services (as an app replicates a counter service) and it would be very narrow in its product offering. Essentially, it would offer a current account-plus. Like other disrupters in other industries, the bank would strip down the service to the minimum, and its profit would be derived from its customer service around those few products. The profit comes from excelling in that service, not just matching existing providers. Moreover, Boden (2020) notes:

> It is in fact, very rare that anyone ever has a truly unique idea. The thing that all these businesses have in common [Google, Amazon, Facebook] is they are disruptors. The foundations of their businesses are not unique. They have identified a problem that a large number of people were experiencing with an existing business or service and then found a way to make it more accessible/fast/cheap/efficient. If they pitch it right, in a short space of time, the disruptors become successful enough to replace, or at least displace, the conventional product or service in the sector they've made their own. (p. 23)

In some instances, an industry is disrupted not by products of lower quality but sufficient utility. Instead, they are disrupted by products that do the opposite. Apple's iPhone, for example, disrupted the mobile phone market and business models. Apple introduced a product that could access the mobile Internet using an intuitive operating system; it also disrupted the business model of mobile operators, being offered only to those willing to revenue share. This itself was an innovation in the business model of mobile phone manufacturers and the network operators. Prior to the iPhone, manufacturers did not increase their revenue in line with how much extra bandwidth was accessed by users through their devices. Apple executives knew that the iPhone was particularly valuable to operators with excess bandwidth to sell, but with no devices, mobile phones, at the time, with the capability to enable its use. That was a real challenge for firms already in the industry. Cain (2020) observed Samsung's strategy in relation to such disruption:

> Samsung watched how disruptive products like the iPhone fared on the market and then, when the path to success was clearer, released its own smartphones. Seeking an edge, its mission was to improve the smartphone's hardware features in small steps: a bigger screen, a longer-lasting battery, a water-resistant exterior. *Gaeseon* is what Koreans call this process of "Incremental innovation". To the Japanese it is *Kaizen*. (p. 18)

Samsung was effectively a *fast-second*. The fast-second is a common and successful innovation strategy. The benefits to being first to market – so-called *first-mover* advantage – are the following:
- experience curve
- pre-emption of scarce resources
- buyer switching cost
- reputation
- scale benefits

Samadi (2018) notes that the experience curve assumes "that technology costs decline as experience of a technology is gained through its production and use" (p. 2346). To illustrate the experience curve, imagine assembling flat-pack furniture. The first-time assembly of a bookcase will take a long time as the purchaser reads the instructions, finds the components and assembles amidst the uncertainty of the process. Then imagine assembling the same piece of furniture for a tenth time. Assembly becomes much easier, quicker and less uncertain. There is another factor to consider. Keeping innovative ideas and products secret is very difficult. In pre-Internet times, Mansfield (1985) investigated the rate at which information about development decisions leaked out to competitors or into the wider business community in a number of sectors, including chemicals, pharmaceuticals, petroleum, primary metals, electrical equipment, machinery, transportation equipment, instruments, stone clay and glass, fabricated metal products, food, rubber and paper. One-fifth of firms reported leakage occurring within six months. At best, rivals had critical information about products from twelve to eighteen months. Leakage regarding process innovations was slower due to better internal capabilities to generate them with less communication and interaction. In other words, causal ambiguity makes copying processes difficult.

There are three variants to the experience curve: learning-by-doing (supply side), learning- by-using (demand side), and learning-by-interacting (users engaging with suppliers to improve product or process). The experience curve has been particularly influential in the reduction in the manufacturing costs, and the selling price, of photovoltaics (Goodall 2016). In the case of photovoltaics, for every doubling of global manufacturing capacity, costs decrease by 20 per cent (*The Economist* 2012). This can be illustrated with respect to photovoltaics (Figure 9.5).

Not unrelated to the experience curve, firms can achieve rapid scale economies with first-mover advantage. This also creates a barrier to entry for followers. The first-mover can also gain access to scarce resources and, potentially, make it more difficult for followers to access them, through price and/or availability. This includes skilled labour, contractual obligations as well as a natural resource. Switching costs are also a factor, especially if the first-mover has a complementary ecosystem to support users, as Apple quickly achieved with the iPhone through apps, music, payments, etc. The reputational benefits are also tangible – though only if the launch is successful and the product is reliable and safe. Samsung's launch of Galaxy Note 7 provides an example of what can go wrong if a product is prematurely launched. The mobile phone's battery was liable to spontaneously combust (Cain 2020). The service of Boeing's 737 Max plane is chastening in the realization that haste can be deadly (Jolly 2020).

Notwithstanding the failure of the Galaxy Note 7, Samsung was a fast-second in the smartphone market. The iPhone launched in 2007 to a competitive field of smartphones from Nokia (N95), Motorola (Q), Blackberry (Curve) and Samsung (Blackjack). In June 2008, Samsung released its competitor product, the Instinct (Cecere et al. 2015). The learning from Apple, and the determination to overturn Apple's dominance, was progressively achieved in terms of performance, units sold and

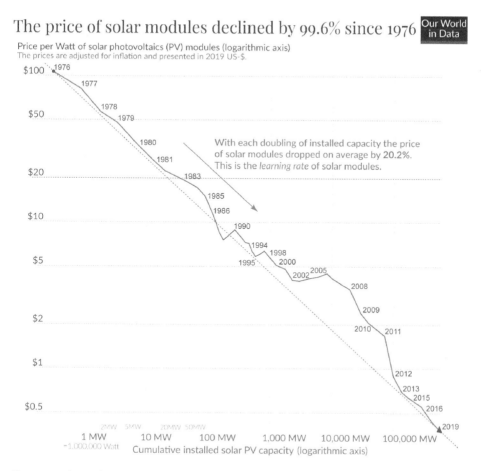

Figure 9.5: Photovoltaics experience curve (Swanson's Law).
Source: By Our World In Data – Max Roser – https://ourworldindata.org/cheap-renewables-growth,
CC BY-SA 4.0, https://commons.wikimedia.org/w/index.php?curid=106245005.

design (Cain 2020). In the second quarter of 2019, Samsung shipped 75.5 million units against Apple's 37 million accounting for global market shares of 27.5 and 13.5 per cent respectively (O'Dea 2020). The experience of the Galaxy Note 7 is illustrative of how important being first to market can be, especially in the field of consumer electronics. It also shows the pitfalls and how competitors can learn from errors made by others in their market.

Open and user innovation

The standard model of product development and innovation is a closed approach where the focal firm has well-resourced research-and-development facilities that funnel viable options through a series of approval points, with a view to only successful products reaching the market. This is still prevalent in pharmaceuticals and consumer electronics. The pioneer of this model was Thomas Edison who established the Menlo Park (1876–1886) and West Orange and Fort Myers (1886–1931) research facilities. AT&T, likewise operated Bell Labs, and more recently, Xerox's Palo Alto Research Center delivered some of the most familiar computing innovations such as laser printers, the ethernet and the graphical user interface (GUI) while AT&T's Bell Labs gave the world transistors, lasers, photovoltaic cells, the Unix operating system and various programming languages. This closed innovation approach requires control and degrees of secrecy.

Increasingly common now is open innovation (Chesbrough 2003) where many sources of innovation are external to the firm, for example, in small start-ups with unique but under-developed technologies or users. Open innovation is an innovation system where there exists an exchange between producers and other stakeholders such as technologists, scientists and patent owners. The exchange may well involve payment. By contrast, user innovation (von Hippel 2005) involves co-operation. For example, a surgeon seeking new tools and medical devices cooperates with producers to enhance the toolset and surgical options. Elite athletes work with clothing and shoe manufacturers to perfect equipment to maximize performance. This leads sometimes to branding opportunities (such as Michael Jordan/Nike). One step further, users often coalesce and congregate around a community such as open-source software development (Christian and Vu 2021). Some large firms have specific innovation managers to facilitate open innovation/intrapreneurship; for example, Siemens (Bessant 2015a).

In terms of the relationship with other innovators, Bogers and West (2012) show that in:
- producer or traditional closed innovation, there is no relationship and spillovers are blocked
- open innovation, the relationship is that of exchange, and spillovers are transactional and paid for
- user innovation, co-creation is co-operative and spillovers are free (open source/creative commons)

Spillovers are knowledge or product opportunities not captured by the core firm(s) in a network. There were many spillovers from Menlo Park and Bell Labs. Such opportunities can be the foundational resource or intellectual property of a new firm. Arm Holdings, for example, was a spillover from Cambridge University. Some spillovers are unplanned where the knowledge simply "escapes" the confines of the laboratory or workshop. User innovation is a planned spillover where sharing and free-revealing is purposeful. While it is possible to monetize the spillover, it is not possible to prevent others from doing the same.

Diffusion

For Rogers (1995), diffusion is a social process: "[D]iffusion is the process by which an innovation is communicated through certain channels over time among the members of a social system. It is a special type of communication, in that the messages are concerned with new ideas" (p. 5). Innovations diffuse and spread in the form of an S-Curve.

Rogers classifies adopters into five ideal types, that is, stylized characterizations of the people within the category. These are captured in Table 9.1.

Table 9.1: Adopter categories.

Adopter/size of group in social system	Headline	Position on S-Curve	Properties
Innovators 2.5%	Venturesome "cool, let's try"	bottom left – time 0; low adoption	Obsession with innovation/newness; "cosmopolites" and networked into cliques; often outsiders with financial resources to offset losses associated with failure; able to cope with uncertainty; daring; not risk averse; technically knowledgeable. Essential for launching a new product/innovation
Early adopters 13.5%	Respect "that looks like a useful innovation"	bottom left – t1; initial adoption	So-called "localites"; opinion leadership (respect of peers over adoption); sought by "change agents" to speed up innovation; reduce uncertainty for those in the early majority
Early majority 34%	Deliberate (over adoption) "the reviews are largely good"	mid-point on upward curve; t2	Adopt just before the majority; willing but not leading; interconnection with the diffusion system's inter-personal networks
Late majority 34%	Sceptical "I suppose I'd better adopt before it is too late"	upper point of growth curve; t3	Adopt because of economic necessity or missing out/pressure from peers; scarce resources so are always cautious about potential losses; adopt when uncertainty is removed

Table 9.1 (continued)

Adopter/size of group in social system	Headline	Position on S-Curve	Properties
Laggards 16%	Traditional "Do I need this (now)?"	plateau/ decline; t4	Most "localite" of all; interact with other laggards; suspicious of innovations; very limited resources

Source: Author's table, derived from Rogers (1995, pp. 262–266).

Different classes of users purchase or use the innovation, starting with innovators and early adopters – often either willing to pay a premium to use the innovation, or by being part of a user community leveraged by producers to test and diffuse the innovation by promotion, word of mouth or review. The steepest part of the curve occurs when the majority join (early and late) before tapering off.

At the point where only the laggards remain, the innovation is heading for decline. The decline, negative growth, can be as steep and rapid as the growth phase when it reaches a tipping point. The response of technology holders to this impending decline is to innovate further and create new S-curves with new innovations. Alternatively, disruptive innovations can also become part of the equation. For example, with smartphones, the main established product innovation is captured by the main curve, while smaller curves represent niche innovations – maybe devices with large digits, voice-activation, or just extravagant decoration.

Institutional isomorphism and dominant design

Many competing products when they reach the mature phase of a product life cycle tend to look similar to one another. This results from institutional isomorphism (Meyer and Rowan 1977; DiMaggio and Powell 1983) whereby the environment that firms inhabit shapes them. Those that survive do so for three reasons:
1. *Coercive* – where they have conformed and complied with standards
2. *Mimetic* – where they have copied successful competitors
3. *Normative* – where they are all influenced by professional expertise; engineers, marketeers, designers, all having similar educational and life experiences and shared norms of decision-making (Mintzberg et al. 2009)

It is not only the businesses that exhibit isomorphism. The products they make tend to resemble those of competitors and vice versa. They are also subject to the impact of the environmental forces coming from customers, technologies and regulatory frameworks. There comes a point in the life cycle of a product where a dominant design emerges (Utterback and Abernathy 1975). In the early part of the life cycle, producers release unique products with considerable variations of size, shape, operating features and price. Despite these differences, a product category is created. Dominant design defines the look, operation and functionality of many products, ranging from televisions and automobiles to cement and glass (Cecere et al. 2015).

The smartphone, as a product category, is a suitable example of the emergence of dominant design. In 2007 Apple launched the iPhone into a market for mobile phones where each producer in the industry supplying a market had variations, particularly evident in operating systems. The journey to a dominant design took a major step forward with the adoption of the Android operating system (OS) in September 2008 by many smartphone manufacturers. This itself was based on an open-source kernel (Linux). Android created a rival ecosystem to Apple's iOS. While the operating systems are different, the user interfaces and device functionality bear similarities such that users are able intuitively to operate either system. Both systems worked within the limitations of the hardware technologies built to international standards necessary for accessing the transmission frequencies owned/licensed by mobile network operators. The factors indicating dominant design are cameras, music players, wifi, touch screens, weight and 3.5mm jack option (so-called vertical factors) and screen size and width (horizontal factors). A study by Cecere et al. (2015) reveals that dominant design had been established in the vertical factors, but not in horizontal factors.

There are sustainability implications arising from institutional isomorphism and dominant design. As noted in the examples of smartphones, even partial fulfilment of dominant design factors indicates a formal and informal standardization of handset and infrastructural hardware and software. This impacts on price, adoption, diffusion and network effects. Key technologies in mitigating climate change and adaptation benefit from this convergence. Wind turbines and photovoltaic cells are examples. The dominant feature of photovoltaic cells is silicon technology for the supply of power modules (Parida et al. 2011). Though the variations within this technological paradigm are many. Any dominant design that does emerge, however, will not necessarily be a superior technology (Furr 2018). Superior technologies may be rather more difficult to manufacture, or to source raw materials. They can also be blocked by dominant industry actors.

Dominant consumer technologies can be determined by consumer preference or decisions by suppliers and business customers as to which they will support. For example, Blu-ray (Sony) and HD DVD (high-definition digital video disc) (Toshiba). Blu-ray won the battle after the Hollywood film studios opted to supply exclusively on the format. Sony (Betamax) had lost out to a previous home-entertainment format, VHS (video home system) (JVC) in the 1970s and learned the importance of broader stakeholder support in winning so-called *standards wars*.

For business organizations, isomorphism may well determine survival in a warming world. Should governments and states engage fully with the Paris Agreement, regulation and conformity may be a pre-requisite of a licence to operate. Firms will have greater responsibilities towards reporting on their activities, trading carbon and mitigating externalities. They may even be required to change their purpose and move away from shareholder approaches to broader stakeholder-based business models.

Business model innovation

A business model at its simplest is a statement about how the firm will make money – how value is created and captured (West and Bogers 2014). It determines the value proposition and is normally expanded to include assets, capabilities, the ownership and development of intellectual property, routes to market and marketing. In modern times, costs associated with GHG emissions and other externalities (for example, pollutants, health and safety) will also be included. Firms offering a sustainable product will also include return, recycling and re-using costs and revenues. There may also be the opportunity to state social value, social welfare and social returns.

Business models can also be innovated as activities change either incrementally or radically. They may be adapted to deal with:

- disruption and disruptive technologies as Fujifilm did on the arrival of digital photography (*The Economist* 2012)
- decisions to enter new markets as Nokia did when it entered the mobile handset and network infrastructure markets in the late 1970s and exited wood and rubber
- moving through the value chain to higher-value activities as IBM did moving from mainframes, PCs to cloud services (Drucker 1994)
- occupying more of the activities in global value chains, for example, selling coffee in coffee shops, roasting and distribution
- becoming a purposeful business and/or provide for customers at the bottom of the pyramid (Mayer 2018)

Innovating the business model to do good, in addition to doing well, is not so easy to express in business model terms. Mayer (2018) cites an example of Mars Wrigley entering a difficult and unfamiliar territory in Nairobi, Kenya. They named the project Maua (flower). Its success is founded in the direct involvement of local micro-entrepreneurs as a route to market. This has provided work opportunities and skills development and the attendant wider social benefits. The challenge was in supply chain and distribution, partially solved by working with local stakeholders, non-governmental organizations (NGOs) (such as Technoserve that specializes in creating economic opportunities for women) and government agencies. In 2015, Mars Wrigley reported a positive bottom-line contribution of $4.5m. This went some way to assuage shareholders, but actually quantifying the social benefits required the company to invest much in exploring suitable metrics to measure non-financial forms of capital – human, social and natural.

Routines

All organizations and individuals rely on routines to function. These can be basic individual acts such as starting the day with coffee and checking email. Routines are also part of the innovation process. There are routines of new product development, open and user innovation. They can be productive, for example, providing stability, predictability and efficiency. They can also be a source of rigidity and inhibit innovation. These are the routines and to change them is to upset the status quo that, currently, delivers stability. Routines contribute to a firm's direction of travel, a so-called path dependence (Becker et al. 2005). The routine that enables interaction between individuals and groups across organizational boundaries can act as a source of external knowledge and innovation; but at the same time, such interaction can be a challenge to existing routines. They evolve over time as the environment impinges on those acting out the routine. When they are codified or explicit, they can be used as tools of management. However, many routines are implicit, not codified and, in some cases, are anti-managerial. They are sufficiently embedded to thwart management, as they control all space and work freedoms and autonomous action. Routines, therefore, are at the interface of innovation and organizational change.

Sources of finance

Securing investment is difficult for new and innovative ventures. Banks evaluate risk narrowly, particularly after the financial crisis of 2008. Anne Boden, founder of Starling Bank, catalogues her attempts at winning investment for her Internet-only bank, even though she was a banker herself, albeit without the coding skills needed to build a banking platform. Innovative thinking and ideas sometimes promote innovative approaches. Boden *eventually* found a clutch of investment funds willing to support the venture.

Smaller entrepreneurial firms may need to step outside normal finance. For example, Claire Vallee, a restaurant owner in Bordeaux, France, has been awarded a Michelin star for her restaurant's food. There is nothing extraordinary about that; though, a Michelin Star is a resource that can bestow competitive advantage. However, this restaurant would serve only vegan food. The banks applied their risk algorithm and rejected loans on two grounds. First, vegan food in France is not so common and is unlikely to compete with French cuisine. Second, the chosen location, Bordeaux, was seen as being "not promising enough" (Agence France-Presse 2021). Vallee turned to crowd-funding (Cumming and Hornuf 2018) to finance her venture, in combination with a loan from a so-called green bank (Le Nef), where investment criteria include business ethics and sustainability.

Agitu Gudeta was a refugee from Ethiopia who set up a successful diary business in the rural region of Alto Adige in northern Italy. In 2010 she bought fifteen indigenous goats (by 2020 the herd was 180 and growing), to provide the raw materials for her business. Her further expansion into hospitality (linked to the dairy) was a community project made feasible by her networking and links to the nearby towns and villages in which she operated, and a desire to limit the debt placed on the existing business. Gudeta, therefore, innovated a product (dairy/cheese), a business model (local sales, organic growth and related diversification) and finance (re-investment of profit, borrowing and local political economic development grants). Her story is told in a television documentary (Deutsche Welle 2019).

Summary

Innovation is an outcome of a radical and applied economics. The study of innovation created models of innovation explained in part by the application of information technology to modes of working and global de-regulation of trade arrangements. Innovation is dynamic, and can be locked into organizations through structures, ownership and protection of intellectual property. It can equally be democratic as in user innovation. Innovation is simultaneously the pursuit of efficiency and profit, and the means to economic and environmental sustainability. At its most expansive, innovation incorporates a wide range of stakeholders – suppliers, customers, finance, and communities of users. Members of these groups can be multiple stakeholders, especially where finance is derived from crowd-sourcing where one can be both a customer and be a crowd-funder. It is not always so. Innovation in finance and financial instruments led to the financial crash in 2008. On that basis, there is an important role for governments, states and trading blocs in regulating innovation that does not enhance social welfare.

Questions
1. What is the difference between innovation and invention?
2. Apply a linear model to the process of vaccine development and implementation. Apply a fifth-generation model to the process of vaccine development and implementation. What is revealed about the models and the product?
3. What is the difference between digitalization and digitization? Why is digitalization important for businesses in the twenty-first century?
4. What is disruptive innovation? Which of the following products/technologies are disruptive? Uber taxis; iPhones; music streaming; cloud computing; low-cost airlines; fast-food; fast-fashion; wind turbines; AI; mobile banking; video-conferencing?
5. Provide three reasons to (a) adopt a closed innovation model and (b) adopt an open innovation model.
6. Why do many products from different producers look the same?
7. What is crowd-funding and where does it fit with innovation models?

Chapter 10
Financial evaluation of strategy and investment for sustainability

Having undertaken strategic analysis, strategists are left with choices. The choices need to be evaluated, potentially against one another, in order to select the option that is achievable, meets the objectives of the firm and satisfies the needs and wants of its stakeholders, whether they are shareholders, employees, local communities or others. This chapter discusses the quantitative tools of evaluation. It is a discussion because no single measure or ratio provide a definitive answer. Ultimately, decisions are not determined by the evaluation; rather it is a guide. Decision-makers have to apply not only a financial logic, but ideally also ethics. This is particularly important in the age of climate change. Firms may well need to make investments that the existing tools cannot evaluate effectively where sustainability becomes a strategic objective. Adapting a business to an uncertain environmental future requires investment over extended timeframes. Existing tools generally bias quick returns over longer-term investments.

This chapter:
- considers investments and the indicators of their value, short-, medium- and long-term
- posits strategy as a project
- explores the utility of evaluation methods and tools
- compares evaluation methods against long- and short-term investment criteria and alignment with stakeholder expectations
- highlights how these methods can be adapted for use addressing climate-change challenges

Accounting protocols, financial and environmental reporting and business models

Chapter 4 discussed financial and management accounting. Financial accounting has a purpose of informing external stakeholders about the health of a firm. Management accounting, by contrast, facilitates management decision-making and strategic options. The outcome of financial accounting is a balance sheet reflecting the performance of the firm. Performance reveals to stakeholders whether the firm is meeting its objectives. However, that may not be enough in the age of climate change. Mayer (2018) asks, what is the purpose of a firm? Is it merely to meet the earnings expectation of shareholders? Taking the example of Google, while it is hugely profitable and meets shareholder expectations, its stated purpose is something else entirely. Google's mission statement is "to organize the world's information and make it universally accessible and useful" (Google n.d). Indeed, to write this book, the author has extensively drawn on Google Books as a database and downloaded references direct to bibliographic software. Google has created an extraordinary – albeit private – database of published books available previously only to the most privileged

https://doi.org/10.1515/9783110718430-010

of scholars working at elite universities. The question is, how does this serve the interests of shareholders? Google Books does have a revenue model. After searching, it is possible to buy e-versions of books. Though that is hardly in the league of what is achieved in revenue terms by Google Search and YouTube. The answer is that Google products are part of an ecosystem. Google Search leads to Google Books, YouTube, maps, local businesses, etc. Many of these business unit initiatives had opportunity costs and, indeed, represent real options for Google. Without them, other innovations would not have been possible or be simply missed.

Increasingly, financial accounting has the function of presenting sustainability reports that are either integrated into annual reports or published separately (though their function has evolved over time). Sustainability reporting embraces the presentation of data demonstrating a firm's ability and commitments to meet environmental targets for carbon emissions and other pollutants. With carbon emissions potentially attracting penalties for non-compliance, financial accountants quantify the costs associated with the firm's less desirable activities, namely, its *externalities* such as carbon, that have traditionally been kept off the balance sheet. Carbon is, however, tradeable. Where firms produce too much, it may be necessary to buy carbon credits; where they create less carbon than budgeted for, firms can trade the excess and generate revenue.

Accountancy standards and protocols are changing. The environmental damage that firms do is increasingly being costed. It is worth, however, just highlighting what is wrong with many existing protocols. Take, for example, exploiting oil concessions (licences to prospect for and exploit oil reserves) in an environmentally sensitive region, such as the Arctic. Putting aside the fact that in order to meet the targets set under the legally binding Paris Agreement of 2015, all non-exploited reserves of fossil fuel need to remain in the ground, exploitation involves a number of destructive activities that impact on the natural environment. Habitats will be destroyed or disrupted by road and other infrastructure construction and use, water courses changed and/or polluted and indigenous people displaced. These destructive activities remain largely un-costed and disregarded. They are externalized and the costs borne by the local community, government, future generations or the natural environment.

A retrospective price could be paid by corporations for violations, particularly if the firm knowingly and wilfully transgresses; so-called Big Oil is currently being litigated on this basis (McGreal 2021). In evaluating strategic options, for as long as these external impacts have zero cost, such a strategy generates increased shareholder value satisfying the Friedman doctrine. In this case, the executive management's responsibility is to shareholders, and profit more specifically (Friedman and Friedman 1962). If the costs are factored in, environmentally and socially damaging strategic options may be less attractive. Firms may need to offset the damage caused, adapt their plant, provide for the local community in terms of jobs, infrastructure and the development of social capital. It also may be that firms will need to ensure a future for as-yet unborn generations. The costs can mount up. Alternative options may become more attractive and sustainable (in both business and environmental senses).

It is largely through management accounting that strategic options can be evaluated and decisions made ahead of releasing the necessary resources to execute strategy. There are two components to evaluate strategic options. It is assumed that:

1. Strategists know what the purpose of the firm is and have undertaken a strategic analysis in line with macro- and micro-level analyses (Part 1 of this book) as well as some form of stakeholder analysis. In short, firms know in which sector they are operating, or seek to operate in, have audited their resources and capabilities and considered stakeholders and their needs and potential responses. Firms are also confident that a strategic choice is made on the basis of feasibility where the resources and capabilities are available or can be procured.
2. Costs and benefits of strategic options have been evaluated and presented in the form of traditional and non-traditional financial ratios and other indicators of value and worth.

Common evaluation measures are: Accounting Rate of Return (ARR), Return on Capital Employed (RoCE), Payback Period (PP), Internal Rate of Return (IRR) and Discounted Cash Flow (DCF). These measures and ratios are explained and applied extensively in Atrill and McLaney (2019). In Table 10.1, these tools are compared with a view to deciding which tools and measures are fit for purpose.

The comparison reveals the following:

- Simplicity is seen as a virtue. Decision-makers often have *limited capacity* to reflect on complexity and the arithmetic that factors in risk, time and environmental sustainability.
- Risks of all kinds are not captured by these measures, environmental and social risks, particularly so.
- Speed is seductive to decision-makers. A short payback period is inherently good.
- High returns on tangible and discrete assets are good. High net present value (NPV) is better than lower.
- Short-term shareholder wealth is prioritized over longer-term investments such as firm infrastructure, skills and stakeholders more generally.
- Environmental sustainability is not well served by these measures.

In cases where strategy is viewed as a top-down, with decisions made by company executives informed by strategic analysis, it may be helpful to view strategy as a project.

Table 10.1: Comparison of evaluative tools.

Tool	Understandability (to decision-makers)	Factors in the impact of time on value	Factors in risk	Utility to compare different strategic options	Accommodates shareholder wealth	Factors in environmental sustainability
Accounting Rate of Return (ARR)	High: expressed as an annual percentage	Yes	Yes: financial liabilities	high	Yes	No
Return on Capital Employed (ROCE)	High: profitability ratio	Yes (defined timeframe)	Yes: financial liabilities	Low (firm-level analysis)	Yes	No
Payback Period (PP)	High: months/years	Yes	Yes: financial liabilities	High	Yes	No
Internal Rate of Return (IRR)	High: break-even point	Yes	Yes: financial liabilities	High	Yes	No
Economic Value Added (EVA)	Medium: absolute and/or monetary indicator	Yes	Yes: financial liabilities	Low	Yes: value-oriented	No
Sustainable Value Added	Low to medium: absolute monetary indicator plus non-financials	Yes	Yes: financial, environmental and social risks	Low	Yes: value-oriented; including environmental and social efficiency and effectivity (avoiding damage/harm)	Yes

Discounted Cash Flow (DCF)	Medium (complex calculation)	Yes	Yes: financial risk captured in discount rate	High	Yes	Yes: when assessing environmental investments
Net Present Sustainable Value	Medium: complex encompassing three different capitals	Yes	Yes: financial, social and environmental	High	Yes: assuming wealth is also derived from investments in environmental and social capitals	Yes: social and natural capitals

Source: Author's table.

Strategy as a project

All strategy can be viewed as a project, though not all projects are strategic. A project has a justification, resource implications, objectives, is time-limited, has appropriate measures and a risk profile. Consider a decision to build a new factory. As a project, the decision to go ahead ordinarily is subject to an investment appraisal considering costs, benefits, returns and risk. Seeing strategy as a project provides some rigour at both appraisal and implementation stages of strategy development and execution. There are many project management methodologies available and strategists often have additional project management qualifications (Cobb 2011; Nicholas and Steyn 2017). Mitigation and adaptation measures inside firms lend themselves well to being viewed as projects.

Projects have many explicit costs that are relatively easy to represent in a project proposal. There are also implicit costs that can be missed at the proposal stage but can have serious implications at implementation if not fully accounted for. Consider the building of a new sustainable factory again. Costs include land purchase, design/architectural services, building materials and construction, fitting out with furniture, plant, hardware and support infrastructure such as supply of utilities, software such as an enterprise resource planning (ERP) system that could be off-the-shelf, proprietary, hosted on own servers or in the cloud, removals from former facility, decommissioning of old facility, training/change management, new staff and recruitment, insurance, etc.

The practice of sustainability investment decision-making

Ecover products were categorized as differentiation-focus in the context of Porter's generic strategies. The products are premium, high cost and niche. The materials are manufactured and packed in a state-of-the-art factory in Malle, Belgium. Built in 1992, the factory incorporates sustainable low-impact materials. Its design optimizes ventilation, cooling and heating. For those times in the year when the temperature dips below what is comfortable, employees layer their clothing.

When firms consider whether it is worth building a factory to high standards of sustainability that exceed industry norms, there are a number of appraisal questions. Decision-makers will consider what sustainability actually means in relation to buildings. Meins et al. (2010) declare that "a property is sustainable if it provides long-term environmental, social and economic benefits or at the least avoids harm in these areas" (p. 285). The sustainability of the building will need to demonstrate that there is a future benefit that compensates stakeholders for the reduced current *consumption* that would have been possible without the investment or with an alternative investment. The forfeited consumption could just be a dividend for investors, or bonuses for senior managers (Nordhaus 2013). Social benefits are potentially harder to quantify for a private building. Ecover, for example, claims an obsessive carbon measuring regime. The green roof provides habitat for insects and a food source for others, including ospreys. What is the added value of the roof ecosystem worth? How is that value calculated? Clearly, there is a marketing value. The firm matched its environmental claims with a tangible investment in environmental and business sustainability. It creates employment that is valued by society and its workers. Its employees work in a safe environment and do work that is meaningful for a purposeful firm (Mayer 2018). They are less likely to be absent due to illness or lack of motivation. The firm itself is more efficient. The company develops and manufactures products that are valued by customers and do not cause harm when used, thus avoiding generating unpaid-for externalities. It has B-Corp accreditation. Back in 1992, so many of the variables factored into the investment decision were less-well understood than they are today. The private-sector investment risk, therefore, may well have been high. The finance market at the time may not have supported investments for sustainability.

Discounted cash flow (DCF)

DCF is a common method for assessing the value of an investment at today's prices. It is defined by White and Jenyson, quoted in Meins et al. (2010, p. 283) as a:

> method of dynamic investment valuation that discounts future cash flows (revenues and expenditures) to a single reference date to obtain the present values which are added afterwards. The sum of the present values results in the net present value.

Put simply, practitioners need to estimate the cash flows in the future and put a value on them at today's prices. This is a process that throws up a few challenges. The primary challenge is to determine the discount rate, which is an interest rate that is used to discount future cash flows into today's money value and is a measure of the cost of capital. Like many interest rates, the greater the risk, the higher the rate. Increasingly, the discount rate is higher for firms that have poor ESG ratings (Schoenmaker and Schramade 2018). The rate, therefore, requires a detailed assessment of the risk factors for the project or strategy.

What might constitute risk? Firms are likely to consider factors such as changes in the market for goods or services, regulation, slippage (not delivered on time), cost escalation or errors. In a time of climate change, depending on the project, it might be that environmental conditions may not support the activity in the future. Farmers and infrastructure developers (for example, intensive livestock facilities, roads, electricity grids, communications) must consider such a situation.

Firms that are rigorous with their preparation can mitigate these risks by testing assumptions; for example, by generating hypotheses. News media often report the outcome of hypothesis testing. For example, researchers in the field of health and lifestyle test hypotheses such as the link between diet and climate change, obesity and susceptibility to Covid-19, income and educational attainment. It requires considerable expertise to undertake hypothesis testing even in cases where data exist. Where data are limited, such as linking a business practice and sustainability, they might be unreliable and subject to dispute. There are two options here. The first is to build scenarios (Table 10.2). The second is to ensure that the project is itself properly constructed with ownership and benefits assigned to particular individuals and groups. That way, responsibility is assigned to named individuals who take ownership and ensure compliance/effectiveness. This can be ensured if strategy is managed as project and not merely as an extra task for managers.

DCF is, however, a method that ordinarily biases projects that deliver their value in the shortest period of time on the assumption that investors can then reinvest their money in other projects. Essentially, the method values return *over* sustainability. For example, two projects with the same investment capital, one with high sustainability properties, the other without but delivers faster, would be selected. The project with the high sustainability properties might take much longer than the traditional investment option to deliver its value. Moreover, cash flows are often based on historic market data. In the era of sustainability, SDGs and pandemics, market data lag behind what is actually valuable in the future and the further into the future the project goes, using existing methods, the lower is the present value likely to be.

Nobel laureate William Nordhaus (2013) recognizes both the importance of discounting for investment decisions and the difficulties associated with it. Traditionally, practitioners have had to deal with rates of inflation and the erosion of the value of payments in today's prices. Nordhaus notes that humans consume to satisfy both needs (food, shelter/housing, etc.) and wants (entertainment, consumer electronics, cars, etc.). When climate change is factored into calculations, the difficulty arises in reconciling the forfeit of consumption today for consumption tomorrow. Put another way, invest now and consume the benefits at some point in the future. For example, if we consume fewer flights today, we can enjoy holidays in national parks in the future. For most people, that is not really an attractive option. Some people may not like or care for the countryside; others will see the natural resources underneath the national park as being far more valuable than the trees, wildlife and ecosystem the parks support and protect.

Prescriptive/normative vis-à-vis descriptive approaches

Assuming that the natural world is valued into the future, economists use discounting to put an investment value on it. There are two ways of thinking about this:
- a normative, prescriptive approach
- a descriptive, opportunity–cost approach

The normative view is found in the work of British economist Nicholas Stern (2006), and separately American political scientist John Roemer (Llavador 2015), who propose that the discount rate is kept low (at about 1 per cent). This is problematic. For the discounting to have the right effect, there will be a difference between discounting of goods and services and that of human welfare through housing, education, and environmental technologies such as carbon capture and storage. Discounting consumption of goods in the future may be somewhat perverse in a warmer world. Moreover, it is assumed that future generations will be richer than earlier generations; a low discount rate rewards the rich. Though an assumption that future generations will be richer is debatable in an age of climate change and global pandemics.

The descriptive approach, by contrast, draws on the concept of opportunity costs; namely, money could be invested in some other technology, product or service that presents a benefit that is equal to or greater than alternatives to the investor. Therefore, rather than setting a low ethical discount rate under the normative/prescriptive approach, the selected rate reflects a realistic market rate of return in the private sector. Nordhaus (2013, p. 190) offers a theoretical case of a $10m investment today that delivers $100m of reduced CO_2 damage in fifty years' time. Using the basic formula, $(1+r)^{-50}$ where r is the discount rate of 4 per cent, he calculates a positive benefit of US$14.1m, making the investment economically justifiable (US$4.1m higher than the US$10m initial investment – the saved damage has a higher present value than the original investment). However, if the discount rate rises to >7 per cent (the rate at the time of his writing and recommended by the US Federal Government to its agencies), there would be a net present value of -US$6.6m (minus). The selected discount rate, therefore, is fundamental to the outcome. The discount rate of 7 per cent is a real market rate; but governments do not have to borrow at market rates. A 4 per cent discount rate, in this case, can be justified. The UK Treasury's Green Book (Treasury 2018), sets the discount rate at 3.5 per cent.

The situation in developing countries can be stark where the opportunity costs of investing in conservation and supporting biodiversity, rather than agriculture, are quite high. Norton-Griffiths and Southey (1995) illustrate how the Kenyan government subsidized conservation to the tune of US$203m. This is equivalent to the difference between the estimated return of agricultural produce vis-à-vis tourism and forestry. For developing nations that is a high opportunity cost.

DCF explicitly factors in risk to an investment proposal. This is captured in the discount rate: the higher the rate, the higher is the risk anticipated to be. Risks, moreover, are uncertain and dynamic. For example, one of the risk factors for Meins et al., (2010) was energy prices. They created a scenario where fossil fuels would become scarce and/or priced significantly higher. However, at the time they were writing, renewables, particularly photovoltaics, were more expensive and much less efficient than they are today (Goodall 2016). The modelling of the future makes assumptions about economic growth, consumption and energy use. Should these change, due to external economic factors, then so will present values for investments related to climate-change mitigation. In

Nordhaus's case, the benefits might be reduced over the accounting period. Decision-makers may be sensitive to reductions and not support a project or policy initiative.

DCF is regarded, along with other Capital Budgeting Techniques (CBTs) such as Internal Rate of Return (IRR), Modified Internal Rate of Return (MIRR), Profitability Index (PI) and Real Options (RO) as being Sophisticated CBT. By contrast, techniques such as Payback Method (PB), Accounting Rate of Return (ARR), Return on Assets (RoA), Return on Equity (RoE), Return on Investment (RoI) and Discounted Payback (DPB) are classified as Non-Sophisticated CBT (Sarwary 2019).

Investing in photovoltaics

Installing photovoltaics is a climate mitigation measure; though reduced costs and efficiency are also important factors for firms in evaluating investments. Firms adapting to climate change may well choose to invest in photovoltaics to secure supply of electrical energy. Beloev et al. (2017) provide an example of an investment appraisal as a simulation to install photovoltaics on petrol stations in Bulgaria. The stated motivation for the investment was to reduce CO_2 emissions.

Table 10.2 summarizes the appraisal based on two scenarios each with a different mix of benefits and cost. The investment appraisal tools used are RoI (return on investment) and NPV (net present value). NPV tells decision-makers the current value of the investment by discounting the value of future cash flows (DCF). It is assumed that the company has the resources to make the investment; though the return is contrasted with a decision to keep the money in the bank offering a 1 per cent interest rate. This acts as a useful measure of the opportunity forfeited by making the investment.

What do the simulations tell those who make investment decisions? Simulations are subject to fluctuations. In this case, the changes in the selling prices of renewable and conventional energy affect the return on investment. In scenario 1, this is quite pronounced; however, both NPVs are above the estimated investment and hence attractive. The NPVs for scenario 2 are much less, though for a much lower investment, still positive and attractive. The return can take up to twenty years to be realized. The differences between NPVs in each scenario represent a *sensitivity analysis* (what ifs?) for fluctuating prices. If the selling price goes up, this is the effect on NPV.

The investment appraisal does not account for battery storage; this is particularly important for scenario 1 where excess electricity generated could be stored and used through the winter; indeed, the scenarios as presented only work if all of the generated electricity is actually used.

What sets this example apart is that it additionally quantifies the outputs of the photovoltaics and contrasts the winter and summer months. This is important because the rationale for the investment was to save CO_2 emissions, and not specifically to make money. For a petrol station, that is an interesting rationale. There may be a number of reasons for this omission:

Table 10.2: Investment appraisal for photovoltaics on petrol stations in Bulgaria.

Scenario 1:	Scenario 2:
Investment: 50 kW PV park Annual nominal rate of return: 1% (from bank if investment not made) Annual inflation: 2% Buying price of PV energy: 0.2 €kWh^{-1}	Investment: 10 kW PV park Annual nominal rate of return: 1% (from bank if investment not made) Annual inflation: 2% Buying price of PV energy: €0kWh^{-1}
Investment outcome	Investment outcome
The investment price estimated as €81,000 RoI has been evaluated to be 150% NPV (1) at the end of the period is: €214,000 with *influence* of purchase price (PP) of renewable energy (RE) at €0.3kWh^{-1} €144,000 with influence of PP of RE at €0.2kWh^{-1} €74,000 with influence of PP of RE at €0.1kWh^{-1} Investment will return in five to ten years (optimistic–pessimistic projections) NPV (2) at the end of the period is: €193,000 *influence* of the daytime selling price (DSP) of conventional energy (CE) at €0.21kWh^{-1} €144,000 with influence of DSP of CE at €0.14kWh^{-1} €95,000 with influence of DSP 0.07 €kWh^{-1} The investment will return in six to nine years (optimistic–pessimistic projections)	The investment price estimated as €16,000 RoI has been evaluated to be 103% NPV at the end of the period is: €40,000 with *influence* of the selling price (SP) of conventional energy (CE) at €0.21kWh^{-1} €20,000 with influence of SP of CE at €0.14kWh^{-1} €720 with influence of SP of CE at 0.07 €kWh^{-1} The investment will return in six to twenty years (optimistic–pessimistic projections)
Carbon-dioxide savings	Carbon-dioxide savings
December (representing winter months) 15–21% June–July (summer months) 32–50% Average annual saving: 27 tons/year	December (representing winter months) 3–4.5% June–July (summer months) 17–29% Average annual saving: 11.1 tons/year

Source: Author's table, derived from Beloev et al. (2017).

– Investors cannot know what the carbon saved in ten years will be worth, especially if the motivation for the investment was not overtly financial; that is, merely to save carbon. The carbon price may be subject to political influence, regulation and climate change effects.

– Governments' policies are insufficiently robust with respect to providing firms with a means to cost CO_2 emissions to enable the savings from appropriate investment to be quantified and discounted. Carbon markets exist and prices can be estimated on the basis of increasing scarcity of carbon credits the closer economies get to 2030 and 2050, which are going to be the critical years for carbon accounting. Trading schemes are not perfect. Some schemes omit some industries such as aviation.

Analysts could go further and actually put a price on the carbon saved and even on the environmental damage avoided, similar to investment decisions made in the construction of large-scale power generation such as wind turbines (Table 10.3). Goodall (2016) reminds investors that mitigation makes good business sense. The price of photovoltaics and the costs associated with installation and maintenance are simultaneously decreasing while improving in efficiency.

Table 10.3: Additional earnings from saved carbon emissions.

Scenario	Saved carbon (t)	Carbon price (€)	Duration (yrs)	Value (€)
1 (now)	27	60	20	$(27x60)20 = 32,400$
1 (future)	27	180	20	$(27x180)20 = 97,200$
2 (now)	11.1	60	20	$(11.1x60)20 = 13,320$
2 (future)	11.1	180	20	$(11.1x180)20 = 39,960$

Source: Author's table.

Net present sustainable value (NPSV)

There have been attempts to reconfigure DCF to accommodate sustainability. Liesen et al. (2013, p. 179) have developed the strategic investment measure of Net Present Sustainable Value (NSPV) that:

> determines the anticipated future returns that an investment creates with the use of financial, environmental, and social resources compared to the company's minimum rates of return. These future values then have to be discounted to their present values.

Put differently, in NPSV calculations at least three different capitals are used: financial, environmental and social. The NPSV score is an indicator of improved performance of *all* capitals, not just the financial, from an investment.

Liesen et al.'s approach takes into consideration opportunity costs in a similar way to Nordhaus (2013). It is explicitly strategic in its application in that "it makes sense to commit financial, environmental, and social resources to a specific investment" (Liesen et al. 2013, p. 177). It also makes it imperative that a sustainability commitment is recognized as a *strategic objective* for the firm. The method has seven steps (see Figure 10.1) and leads to a relatively simple addition of all NPV contributions of the resources deployed. This sum is then divided by the number of resources that were part of the evaluation.

A firm could commit to incremental reductions in CO_2 emissions being a strategic objective. In such a case, a firm sets a target for so-called CO_2 "efficiency", defined as a rate-of-return on the capital employed to achieve it; this could be expressed as

Step	Description	Calculation
1	Determine the target efficiency of resource i for each period t through the defined minimum rate of return F of resource i and the targeted yearly improvement rate c_i.	F_i = ratio between targeted return and targeted use of resource i as defined by sustainability strategy. c_i = targeted yearly improvement of F_i. Target efficiency of resource i in period t $= F_i(1 + c_i)^t$
2	Determine anticipated efficiency of resource i in period t.	R_t = anticipated return of the investment in period t. U_{it} = anticipated amount of resource i used by the investment in period t. Anticipated efficiency of resource i in period t $= R_t/U_{it}$
3	Determine the value spread (VS) for resource i by subtracting the target efficiency of resource i from the anticipated efficiency of resource i for each period t.	$VS_{it} = R_t/U_{it} - F_i(1 + c_i)^t$
4	Determine the value contribution (VC) of the use of resource i by multiplying the anticipated resource use with the value spread for each period t.	$VC_{it} = VS_{it} * U_{it}$
5	Determine the net present value contribution (NPVC) of resource i through discounting the value contribution of each period t using the financial discount rate r and summing up.	r = financial discount rate for similar projects. $NPVC_i = \sum(VC_{it}/(1 + r)^t)$
6	Repeat steps 1 to 5 for every resource i considered.	
7	Determine the NPSV by summing up all the net present value contributions of all the resources and dividing by the number n of resources considered.	$NPSV = \sum NPVC_i/n$

Figure 10.1: Summary of steps for carrying out an NPSV analysis.
Source: Liesen et al. (2013), reproduced with permission.

€EBIT per tonne of CO_2 emitted, for example. This is a static view measuring only the return associated with CO_2 efficiency. It becomes an opportunity cost that can be compared against other strategic investment options.

However, Liesen et al. push their framework further. It is possible to move from a static to dynamic approach by linking strategic factors together. They take a hypothetical case of a firm over the five years of an investment committing both to an annual growth rate of 3 per cent, and an annual cut in CO_2 emissions of 5 per cent. To achieve this, a CO_2 *efficiency* 8.42 per cent is needed to achieve the financial *and* environmental targets. These targets may seem to pull in opposite directions but, in the context of NPSV they are complementary, as the firm's strategy will have objectives for all of its capitals: *financial, social and environmental*. All targets are challenging; that is the point in setting them. The strategic balancing of capitals inside and between firms is aligned to stakeholder approaches to management and are not antithetical to profitability.

The investment measure is not without limitations. Liesen et al. (2013) list them as follows:

– Some of the social resources associated with sustainability are not easy to measure. Factors relating to employee motivation or the inherent value of a resource such as a forest, for example, are qualitative in nature and will need to be appropriately sourced and quantified. This is an expensive and labour-intensive task and is open to challenge.

- The measure of NPSV indicates the efficient use of a resource or resources in a firm seeking to implement a strategy that has sustainability as a core objective. The scores do not indicate that the use of resources in a firm are sustainable or whether the strategy or strategies of the firm are likely to lead to a sustainable use of resources. In this way it is not dissimilar to traditional NPV approaches, which simply state that the investment (financial capital) represents an efficient deployment. It says nothing about the profitability of the firm, though that would be expected to be an outcome.

So far, the discussion has highlighted the importance of getting a meaningful discount rate and the difficulties of measurement and consensus. The chapter now considers social return on investment as a technique and value for firms with environmental and stakeholder purpose.

Social return on investment (SROI)

The New Economics Foundation (NEF) is a think tank in the UK and has developed Social Return on Investment (SROI) as a way of calculating the added social value of investments or business strategies. SROI is:

> a framework for measuring and accounting for much broader concept of value [than under normal investment measures]; it seeks to reduce inequality and environmental degradation and improve wellbeing by incorporating social, environmental and economic costs and benefits. (Cabinet Office 2009, p. 8)

The approach uses monetary values to *represent* social, environmental and economic benefits. As a common unit, money is easy to understand, but SROI is more than monetary. It is expressed as a ratio, where, for example, 3:1 indicates that an investment of €1 delivers €3 of social value. As a technique it can be applied to a whole organization, or just a part of it such as a function, department or activity.

On any investment, a conventional investment appraisal might indicate that a payback period is five years, or the RoI is 5 per cent, or it has a positive NPV. SROI adopts these measures, but raises the potential that such measures do not fully capture the true value of the investment. For example, if a firm installs photovoltaic cells on the roof of a factory, its own investment appraisal, using existing tools, will consider the value to the firm in terms of reduced costs, increased capacity and revenue generated in selling the excess back to the grid (similar to the case in Table 10.2). SROI asks analysts to quantify the *additional* social value *derived* from an investment. Investment in simple photovoltaics has linked economic, environmental and social benefits:

- Economic – trade in photovoltaic cells, installation, maintenance, energy and materials research

- Social – keeping temperature rises down costs society less in the longer term, due to
  a) reduction in unpredictable and damaging weather events impacting insurance premiums
  b) reduced human stress and illness for those affected and for the next generation
  c) eliminating unnecessary compensation, enabling society to focus on creating value rather than destroying it
  d) lower/manageable sea-level rises avoiding the need for mass relocation and migration, conflict and possibly even disease
- Environmental – creates additional electricity-generating capacity from renewables, which
  a) has a mitigating effect on rising temperatures because less CO_2 is emitted
  b) enables the state to meet international carbon emission budgets and commitments

These are all quantifiable. While the investment and contribution of one firm is modest, overall, the social value that is generated can be significant, and should be factored into an investment appraisal.

At a more personal level, consider a case of an individual deciding to get fitter. Some empirical measure of fitness is the objective. The approach or strategy taken involves a daily exercise regime made up of cycling, running and swimming. In order to do these things, there are economic, social and environmental costs and benefits:
- Economic – investments are necessary in a suitable bicycle, year-round clothing, shoes and possibly some form of computer to monitor fitness levels and calculate kilometres covered, and in time allocated to the activity.
- Social – activity may displace other activities involving family, friends, hobbies or work. Benefits are potentially significant in terms of well-being and reduced likelihood of illness or injury (Lee et al. 1997), and companionship if the activities become social.
- Economic/social – society itself benefits; fitter people potentially make fewer demands on health services, are more productive, creative and have fewer absences (due to ill-health and motivation). It can prompt governments to invest in infrastructure such as cycle paths, pools and running tracks. More cycle paths that are safe, illuminated and well maintained can lead to more people cycling. More people become fit, and cycle-related services are needed and provided such as cycle hire, repair and servicing. There is a social return on the individual's personal investment in fitness. Fewer traffic accidents.
- Environmental – more cycling, fewer journeys made that generate carbon. Improved diet and a move away from unsustainable levels of meat consumption.

The ability of firms to think of investments in this way is, of course, affected by the purpose of the firm (Mayer 2018) and its relationships with its stakeholders. If the only stakeholder category that matters is owners/shareholders, then SROI is unlikely to be adopted. Firms that have a purpose beyond pure profit will go some way to reporting on a social value for their activities. It might be that having evaluated strategy, products and services using SROI, the firm may choose to diversify away from activities that generate little or no SROI. SROI can become a measure *for* strategic intent.

Calculating SROI is not a trivial activity, especially if firms have not done so before. There is a commitment in time because some of the indicators of social value are intangible and qualitative, have no monetary value, relate to the future and are possibly subject to changes in government policy. The potential for improved cycling paths is a case in point. SROI in firms can be evaluative (what has already been done) or as a forecast (what a future value might be).

The NEF/UK Cabinet Office have created a step-by-step guide to calculating SROI, which is summarized in Table 10.4.

Table 10.4: Stages in calculating SROI.

Stage	What it is	What it entails
1	Establishing scope and identifying key stakeholders	Clear boundaries are set for what the SROI analysis will cover, in particular, who will be involved in the process and how. Once the scope has been established the stakeholders can be mapped and identified. However, stakeholders can be core or periphery and may have higher or lower power and interest at different points during a project or business cycle. If the scope is too broad, even having achieved stage 3, it may be necessary to return to stage 1 and redefine the scope if it was too broad (or indeed too narrow). – It may also be that practitioners discover that stakeholder groups are not necessarily homogeneous. The classification "young people" disguises the differences between young people who have different backgrounds, interests, experiences and needs.
2	Mapping outcomes	Stakeholders should largely benefit, but there are some that might lose out or suffer unintended consequences. These should be anticipated. – An example used by the Cabinet Office (2009) involves taking disadvantaged children to Greece for a holiday and educational experience. This has a positive social return. However, the unintended consequence is a contribution to carbon emissions and the perpetuation of demand for air travel.

Table 10.4 (continued)

Stage	What it is	What it entails
		The SROI methodology requires practitioners to draw up an impact map, or an illustration of change, demonstrating the relationship between inputs, outputs and outcomes. Outcomes may lag considerably the outputs. The completion of a new piece of railway infrastructure might be an output: − the outcome enhances individual mobility and other development opportunities that are realized well into the future and may be subject to their own investment appraisal − when the building is completed, labourers are no longer employed in that capacity
3	Evidencing outcomes and giving them a value	Some outcomes are tangible and can be measured directly. Increased mobility can be measured by passenger usage. Some outcomes may rely on proxy indicators. If the outcome being investigated and promoted is self-confidence, that is, the infrastructure facilitates mobility by people with disabilities, it may: − be necessary to ask what self-confidence "looks like" or means to the user as it may be very different to able-bodied people − not only be about having the confidence to use the train − help in broadening social networks, employment or volunteering opportunities more generally Practitioners are advised to measure what matters rather than what is simply measurable. Care is needed not to double-count inputs.
4	Establishing impact	Practitioners need to avoid being blinded by potential. In any project, the outcomes might be achieved without the project or intervention. This is known as *deadweight*. Increased mobility can have different causes, not just the building of new infrastructure. Another factor is *displacement*: an intervention moves an activity to somewhere else. − Criminalizing rough sleeping in town centres does not end rough sleeping, it only causes *displacement* to other locations. − What is needed is some measure of *attribution* – how much of the change can be attributed to the intervention or investment? − Over time, enthusiasm for investments wanes: something may have a novelty value for stakeholders that declines over time – perhaps the price of train travel goes up and chokes-off some demand, therefore reducing the value of the outcome. This is known as *drop-off*.

Table 10.4 (continued)

Stage	What it is	What it entails
5	Calculating the SROI	The calculation by this stage is relatively straightforward. The value of the outcome (impact) is calculated by multiplying the total number of outcomes by the financial proxy; for example: – Twenty people benefiting to the tune of €100 is €2000. This is subject to reduction when *displacement, attribution* and *drop-off* are factored in. Assuming an annual *drop-off* of 10 per cent, *displacement* of zero and *attribution* of 40 per cent, the calculation becomes (2000 x 0.6) x 0.9 = €1080 (year 2); €583 (year 3); €315 (year 4); €170 (year 5). $$PV = \frac{value\ of\ impact\ in\ yr\ 1}{(1+r)}$$ $$+ \frac{value\ of\ impact\ in\ yr\ 2}{(1+r)^2}$$ $$+ \frac{value\ of\ impact\ in\ yr\ 3}{(1+r)^3}$$ $$+ \frac{value\ of\ impact\ in\ yr\ 4}{(1+r)^4}$$ $$+ \frac{value\ of\ impact\ in\ yr\ 5}{(1+r)^5}$$ – NPV is calculated by subtracting the value of investments from the PV. With a *hypothetical* investment value of €700, for example, NPV becomes €3883-€700 = €3183. – Practitioners can then calculate two SROI ratios to complete the picture: $$- \quad SROI\ ratio = \frac{Present\ Value}{Value\ of\ inputs}\ or$$ $$- \quad Net\ SROI\ ratio = \frac{Net\ Present\ Value}{Value\ of\ inputs}$$ By way of example, if total value of inputs is €1000, then the SROI ratio is 3183/1000 = 3.2 which translates as for every €1 invested, a social value of €3.20 is created.

Table 10.4 (continued)

Stage	What it is	What it entails
6	Reporting, using and embedding	Having invested so much in the process of calculation including identifying stakeholders, calculating the associated costs and established attribution, it is important to report the findings to the right people in a clear and unequivocal manner. The final report should provide: – information relating to the firm/organization, including a discussion of its work, key stakeholders and activities – a description of the scope of the analysis, details of stakeholder involvement, methods of data collection, and any assumptions and limitations underlying the analysis – the impact map, with relevant indicators and any proxies – case studies, or quotes from participants that illustrate particular findings – details of the calculations, and a discussion of any estimates and assumptions – sensitivity analysis and a description of the effect of varying your assumptions on social returns – an audit trail for decision-making, including which stakeholders, outcomes or indicators were included and which were not, and a rationale for each of these decisions – an executive summary aimed at a broad audience, including participants (Cabinet Office 2009. Pp. 74–75)

Source: Author's table, derived from New Economics Foundation (2008) and Cabinet Office (2009).

Table 10.4 summarizes the method for calculating SROI, which has embedded within it a number of traditional financial measures and ratios, as well as those that capture less tangible social benefits. Discounted cash flow is one of the techniques. Table 10.5 shares data from the SROI example and demonstrates the application of the discount.

Table 10.5: DCF calculation example.

Present Value (PV)	$=\dfrac{\text{value of impact in yr 1}}{(1+r)}$	$+$	$\dfrac{\text{value of impact in yr 2}}{(1+r)^2}$	$+$	$\dfrac{\text{value of impact in yr 3}}{(1+r)^3}$	$+$	$\dfrac{\text{value of impact in yr 4}}{(1+r)^4}$	$+$	$\dfrac{\text{value of impact in yr 5}}{(1+r)^5}$
Benefit	€2000	+	€1080	+	€583	+	€314	+	€170
Discounted values – 3.5% discount rate (€s)	$PV=\dfrac{2000}{1+0.035}$ $=1932$		$PV=\dfrac{1080}{(1+0.035)^2}$ $=1008$		$PV=\dfrac{583}{(1+0.035)^3}$ $=526$		$PV=\dfrac{314}{(1+0.035)^4}$ $=274$		$PV=\dfrac{170}{(1+0.035)^5}$ $=143$
PV	$1932+1008+526+274+143$ $=€3883$								

Source: Author's table, derived from New Economics Foundation (2008) and Cabinet Office (2009).

Payback period

Another related and attractive measure of investment is payback period. Its very name guarantees the attention of decision-makers. It, too, biases short-term decisions. A short payback period represents low risk. But longer payback periods often deliver more social value and environmental sustainability. Payback period calculations do not discount cashflows with the implication that money in the future is worth the same as currently.

Table 10.6 illustrates this with the example of an investment in photovoltaic panels. Assume an investment of €100,000 and that investment generates €25,000 worth of revenue from electricity generated. The payback calculation then takes the following form:

Table 10.6: Payback period for photovoltaic cells.

Time	Net cash flows (€000s)	Cumulative cash flows (€000s)	
Cost of panels	(100)	(100)	
1 year's time	25	(75)	−100+25
2 years' time	25	(50)	−75+25
3 years' time	25	(25)	−50+25
4 years' time	25	0	−25+25
5 years' time	25	25	0+25
6 years' time	25	50	25+25

Source: Author's table.

In this case, the panels are paid for after four years. For photovoltaic panels there are no guarantees that the generated revenue will be constant as the sunshine is unpredictable. Investors might hope that maintenance costs be minimal and depreciation limited (solar panels do become less efficient over time, but not after four years). Investors might ask, is 4 years a reasonable payback period? Are there alternatives such as wind if it is assumed that one of the objectives of the investment was to mitigate climate change? This is indeed an important point; if alternative carbon-intensive energy projects are presented that seem better, that is, have a shorter payback period, under normal circumstances, they will be selected. Carbon is such a compelling source of energy because of its energy intensive nature. It is why society is so dependent upon it.

Sensitivity analysis

When analysts assess strategic options, they are acutely aware that the assumptions that are made over time may be affected by external factors. A useful check on impacts over the lifetime of a project or strategic change is sensitivity analysis. All investment calculations are based on assumptions on the anticipated performance of the economy, expected sales and costs including factors of production. Sensitivity analysis asks, "what if?" What are the thresholds for a viable project subject to declining indicators? If the project depends on internally generated funds, what if unit prices decline by 20 per cent over the lifetime of a project, would that be enough to sustain the project? Indeed, what is the probability of a 20 per cent decline in prices? What might be the cause? Might there be new entrants, a fall in demand or some other shock? In the application of SROI, sensitivity analysis could also be applied to estimates of:

– deadweight, attribution and drop-off
– financial proxies
– the quantity of the outcome, and
– the value of inputs, where non-financial inputs have been valued

(Cabinet Office 2009, p. 69)

Figure 10.2 checks the sensitivity of an investment in photovoltaics. In this case reductions in cash flows from earnings from photovoltaics demonstrate that while the investment can tolerate positive cash flows of €23,000 per annum, annual reductions of 5 per cent or even 2 per cent would tip the investment into the red. It becomes highly sensitive to sunshine!

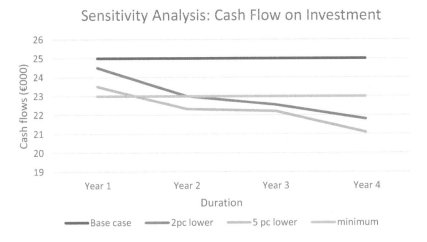

Figure 10.2: Sensitivity analysis.
Source: Author's figure.

Sensitivity analysis can be adapted to incorporate the risks associated with climate change. For example, an investment in a new factory might incorporate a cost associated with the risk of climate-related flooding. Depending on the outcome, the factory might be redesigned, put on stilts, for example, or relocated. By contrast, other risk factors such as extended supply chains might be subject to strategic review and a project to shorten them could be an outcome. Shorter supply chains may well add costs, but against the risk of non-supply arising from severe weather, water or heat stress, the project could have a positive outcome in the longer term.

Real options

This text highlights the fact that strategy and strategic analysis and choice are non-linear. Decisions are based on learning from previous decision experience, what is happening in the macro environment and the dynamic nature of capabilities within the organization itself. DCF is the tool of choice to estimate the value of strategy and the investments associated with it. A limitation of this approach is its linearity. The selection generates a predetermined plan from which there is no apparent deviation. It evaluates a project but does not account for future opportunities that it enables. It also means that projects or assets cannot be abandoned/shut down, restarted, expanded, switched, that is, used for an alternative purpose or alternated with other technologies (Dyson and Oliveira 2007).

One way to build in more flexibility is to adopt a real options approach (Luehrman 1998a). For Luehrman (1998b) strategy involves making a sequence of major decisions. Some decisions are made immediately; others are deferred into the near or distant future. Immediate decisions are made because there is a time imperative; it will not be possible to make the investment at a later date. The resource might not be there, the regulatory environment may have changed, personnel will not be available, etc. Deferred decisions may rely on a better knowledge of the environment or the expectation that it might improve between now and the anticipated investment. Strategists can think in terms of exercising options in the future rather than single, self-contained decisions and investments. CEOs might want to view an investment made now as one that can provide strategic options in the future. Invest in this machine now and have options to expand into X/Y products or services in the future. Decision-making becomes a matrix of invest/don't invest decisions, a chain of real options made possible by computing and improved understanding of options pricing (Luehrman 1998b, p. 90).

Luehrman uses a combination of measures to help in those decisions. The first is the *value-to-cost* approach. This is the calculated NPV and *the time value of being able to defer the investment*. This is calculated as the *underlying value of the assets* to be purchased or built, divided by the present value of the expenditure required to build or buy them (Luerhrman 1998b, p. 91). This is known as the *value-to-cost ratio*. The value and costs are measures of the assets, not the options. Where the *value-to-cost* is from 0 to 1, the project will be worth less than its cost. If it is above 1, the project is worth more than the present value of what it costs.

The second measure is the *volatility* metric. This metric captures how much things can change before the investment has to be made. This depends on uncertainty, risk, future value of assets and the length of the deferral. The riskiness and uncertainty are captured by the variance per period of asset returns; the future value and the length of deferral relate to the option's time to expiration. Where this ratio is 0, time has either run out, or there is no uncertainty. Positive volatility ratios indicate that time has not yet run out and it remains an option.

Luehrman (1998b) uses the analogy of the tomato garden. Not all tomatoes ripen at the same time; some are options for a later date. Investors take ripe ones because leaving them would result in them going rotten and wasting. But there are some tomatoes that are not perfectly ripe but still remain immediate options, and some that can be deferred. The task of the strategist working with a financial team is to decide which options to take, and which not to take using the tools of investment appraisal, NPV among them. Table 10.7 summarises the options.

Table 10.7: Real options using value-to-cost and volatility measures.

Region	Value to cost	Volatility	Outcome	Comment
1	Greater than 1	0	Invest now	Perfectly ripe tomatoes
2	Greater than 1	Low to medium	Maybe now	Some edible and some inedible tomatoes decide on basis of NPV calculation: NPV <0, do not invest immediately; NPV >0, these are real options: edible tomatoes but not perfectly ripe
3	Greater than 1	Medium to high	Probably later	Less promising, but with relatively high volatility there is some potential; time has not run out on them. Cultivate. Some will be picked
4	Less than 1	High(er)	Maybe later	NPV <0; less promising green tomatoes (good for chutney?)
5	Less than 1	Low	Probably never	NPV <0; late blossoms unlikely to ripen
6	Less than 1	0	Invest never	NPV <0; Rotten tomatoes

Source: Author's table, derived from Luehrman (1998b).

There is another dimension to real options. Imagine a firm making an investment in a laser-guided cutting tool in a metal fabrication factory. Not only does this tool enable the firm to cut metal faster and with more accuracy while improving the quality of the existing products. It also creates options for the firm to take on additional work from fabrication firms that do not have the tool and also to diversify into new products in new territories.

There are three traditional investment paths relating to options (Figure 10.3 – options 1–3) and one very specific climate change option to adapt and/or mitigate (option 4).

Invest now (1) provides enhanced performance and new opportunities where the value-to-cost ratio is greater than 1 and volatility is 0. Investing later (2) provides for advantages being realized or "harvested" later after earlier investments have matured and the value-to-cost has potentially increased and/or the volatility metric is higher.

Don't invest (3) when the value-to-cost is below 1 and volatility is 0. Consider investing in situations where the value-to-cost ratio is greater than 1; not to do so risks forfeiting future opportunities. Though there may be other factors preventing investment.

The natural environment real option (4) is somewhat different. Environmental impact remains unknown, or at least uncertain. This would be in line with option 3. However, it is conceivable that the value-to-cost is below 1, even though it would be a strategic investment, prepare the firm for future regulatory compliance, and open the firm up to future leadership in products and services that have adapted to a warmer world and new consumer priorities. On that basis, decision-makers may need to suspend a literal translation of value-to-cost ratio and/or substitute NPSV for NPV. Ultimately, those small unripe tomatoes may still have seeds in them.

Furthermore, much here depends on a firm's overall scanning of the environment and receptiveness to climate change as both a threat and opportunity. Firms that do not invest in order to adapt to future change in, for example, rising temperatures and flooding, gamble on the extent of any impact and the risk. Even in the context of mitigation, firms that do not wean themselves off carbon-rich fuels may find themselves regulated into compliance at higher cost to what would be incurred had they invested immediately. The question of compliance travels throughout the supply chain. If Firm A is a supplier to Firm B and Firm B is a leader in environmental standards and investments, the opportunities to supply are reduced, should Firm B demand compliance from its suppliers. It might also be the case that investment capital is restricted unless the firm has an environmental sustainability plan or record.

Summary

This chapter has explored investment in strategic options. Firms use a range of measures and ratios to evaluate one investment option over another. These range in complexity and what they actually tell decision-makers. Those measures such as NPV and DCF are favoured because they factor in the value of future investments over time and provide a figure of current value on which to make an assessment. Most of these measures, however, do not factor in the value of investments in

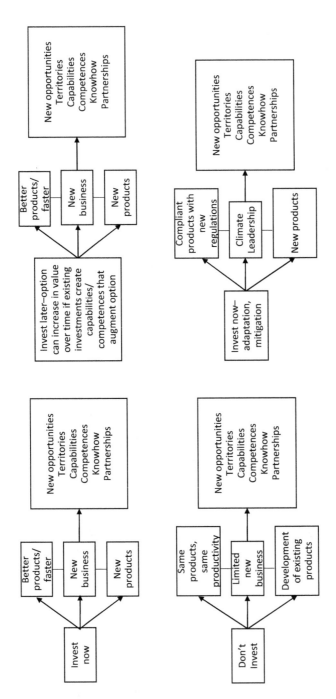

Figure 10.3: Real options configurations.
Source: Author's figure.

climate change mitigation and adaptation. If they do, the value is likely to be less than other options because the investment costs are higher than investment options that do not mitigate or adapt and/or they take longer to be fully realized. There are some measures such as Net Present Sustainable Value that do account for invest-ment in environmental sustainability, but calculations are complex based on unfa-miliar, qualitative or uncertain data. It is also that many small- and medium-sized firms out of necessity focus on business sustainability rather than environmental sustainability. However, with new control regulations likely as the key carbon dates (2030 and 2050) get closer, such investments may be a requirement for a *licence to operate*, or at least to operate without incurring penalty taxation.

Questions

1. What are opportunity costs, and why are they so important in investment decisions, particu-larly those relating to mitigation and adaptation?
2. When making a DCF calculation, what is a discount rate? What discount rate do you think is reasonable for an investment in photovoltaic panels on the roof of a factory?
3. How do firms cost CO_2 emissions? Why is it important to do this now?
4. List some social benefits associated with investment in (a) railways, (b) universities and (c) an out-of-town supermarket.
5. What are real options? Does/should every strategic investment have real options?

Part 3: **Implementation**

Chapter 11
Structures

Organizational structures are often overlooked or ignored. They are, however, fundamental to the implementation of successful strategy. Paraphrasing Chandler (1962), structure follows strategy. A new strategy at business or corporate level will challenge existing structural forms. Templates exist that can be augmented, adapted and customized. Senior managers will think carefully about the structural form that best supports strategy whether it be profit maximization, sustainability, SDGs or some kind of hybrid form. Like much in strategy, it is not prescriptive, though there is a prescription. It is also a creative art. Indeed, organograms are works of art in themselves. Structural forms are not static; as firms evolve, so do the structural forms. As the human and natural environments change, so do organizational structural forms. This chapter discusses:
- factors affecting organizational forms: ownership, innovation and purpose
- prescriptive organizational forms: functional, divisional, matrix, transnational and project
- climate change effects on structures

Ownership and structure

Strategy is not exclusively determined by profit maximization at the business and corporate levels. While the Anglo-American models of ownership and reporting bias profit, in other jurisdictions alternative motivations exist that impact on the way a business is run and therefore structured. A significant motivation is values derived from founders and/or families. Indeed, this was the case in Victorian Britain. Some of the biggest brands of the twentieth and twenty-first centuries, Barclays, Cadbury and Reckitt, have their origins in values-based growth. Cadbury, for example, built Bournville in Birmingham for his employees and their families (Mayer 2018).

The UK is one of the few jurisdictions where – in voting rights – shares have equal weighting. There is no dual system for shares; capital is raised by firms through share offerings, but all shareholdings are diminished as a result. The purpose of a firm, therefore, can change radically in such circumstances. It also leaves firms open to predatory takeover, as happened to Cadbury in 2010, when it was acquired by US food conglomerate, Kraft.

In the United States, a system of dual-class share structures exists whereby founders' shares can be weighted as much as ten times those of ordinary investor shares. Essentially this means that investors buy-in not only to the profits derived from activities, but also the vision and values of the founders. Many of Silicon Valley's most innovative and influential firms have these voting arrangements, including Alphabet (Google), Snapchat and Facebook. More traditional manufacturing firms also adopted these ownership structures such as the Ford Motor Company.

https://doi.org/10.1515/9783110718430-011

With such structures in place, firms benefit from investment but the voting-value of the shareholding of the founders is not, as a consequence, diluted. The founders can pursue the purpose of the firm, often the pursuit of *idiosyncratic value* (Mayer 2018, p. 101) without undue interference. Idiosyncratic value in this sense is the value that the business leader believes that they can generate arising from their vision, which is not appreciated by shareholders. Idiosyncratic value is pursued in trust; it may or may not be protected and reinforced by block shareholdings. Ultimately, if regular shareholders do not like a purpose such as the pursuit of idiosyncratic value, they should simply divest or not invest in the first place. Idiosyncratic value, in modern times, may well be the application of green technology and sustainability initiatives, but only on the understanding that they will *benefit* shareholders in the longer term. Idiosyncratic value is not, and does not have to be, that derived from environmental sustainability.

Innovation and structure

Innovation has structural implications. Product innovation usually involves some degree of research and development, particularly the latter. This requires labs and workshops, engagement with universities and other research institutes. Increasingly, customers are part of the development process as lead users in open innovation mechanisms, for example. Process innovation also has structural implications. An innovation of process can challenge existing structures and those supported by them. Moreover, business-model innovation also affects organizational structures. Bottom of the pyramid (Prahalad and Fruehauf 2005) initiatives such as Mars Wrigley's *Maua* in Kenya (Mayer 2018) is as much a project as it is a diversification strategy. It involves a deep understanding of the cultural and infrastructural context for reaching bottom of the pyramid customers and the development of new and enduring distribution systems (hybrid value chains) that are fit-for-purpose and culturally aligned.

Purpose and structure

Business or corporate strategy should, under normal circumstances, be aligned with the purpose of a firm. When discussing stakeholders, it became evident that the broader the stakeholder engagement and incorporation, of the planet, for example, the greater the need for new structures within the firm to manage those relationships. For many firms the purpose of the firm is very much aligned with the Friedman doctrine (Friedman and Friedman 1962); the optimization of shareholder value on the grounds that to do so also maximizes social welfare. The contemporary situation of climate crisis, the economic hardship created by a global pandemic and financial impropriety in 2008 suggests that social welfare is not optimized when shareholders' interests are the sole concern of a business. Businesses do not operate in a vacuum. They rely on infrastructure provided by the state such as roads, public transport, information technology, education, a justice system, a portfolio of laws and regulations protecting intellectual and physical property and, indeed, the ability to register a company as a legal entity in the first place.

Firms generate externalities, that is, that which is external to the firm, but a product of the firm's activities, such as waste, pollution, noise and congestion. Under the Friedman doctrine, these externalities do not show up on firms' balance sheets, though increasingly they are being included in sustainability reports as a requirement in many jurisdictions. The reasons for this include global accountancy conventions and standards. It is also the case that some jurisdictions restrict, in law, firms' ability to operate in the interests of a wide catchment of stakeholders. The UK is a particular example of this. It is, however, even in the UK, increasingly the case that the state sometimes inadvertently restricts the options open to firms to undertake their business-as-usual. An example of this was the intervention by the courts after a legal challenge by Plan B, a so-called activist environmental group (Rosenberg 2016). The intervention was to prevent Heathrow Airport from building a third runway on the grounds that it would inhibit the UK from meeting its legally binding carbon emissions target agreed in the Paris Agreement of 2015, itself an international treaty *(The Economist* 2020b).

The structure of a firm aligns with strategy, which supports the firm's purpose. Without a purpose, it is impossible to determine how the firm can and should be structured and its performance measured and audited (Mayer 2018). This also determines the nature of success. Under this approach, success is not measured by profit; rather it is measured by its delivery of purpose. In Google's case, arguably it has met and continues to develop and evolve its purpose that by design, and with some luck, coincides with increasing shareholder value. However, that does not have to be the case.

Some firms create structures around social and human capital. In the UK, for example, in 2019, Julian Richer, the founder of Richer Sounds hi-fi retailer, transferred 60 per cent of his shares to an employee-owned trust. Similarly, in the UK, the John Lewis Partnership (JLP) department store and grocery group exists for the benefit of its employees, also known as partners. As Mayer (2018) notes, however, a quirk of UK common law is such that the *non*-transferability of material assets to heirs is frowned upon, if not actively discouraged. This means that cooperative arrangements for asset sharing is not actively supported by company law. Elsewhere, Mayer notes, there exist so-called industrial foundations whose originators deliberately chose not to transfer assets to heirs. They created ownership structures that excluded asset transfers to heirs simply because of birth. Examples include Germany's Bertelsmann (media company) and Bosch (engineering conglomerate), Denmark's Carlsberg (brewer), and Tata (industrial conglomerate) of India. Profits are re-invested and/or donated. In terms of structure, these industrial foundations hold the branded firms below them accountable to the purpose, principles and values of the foundation. Should they digress, the members of the foundation are empowered to act.

Models of firm and corporate structure

Firms do not just adopt a single structure and build activities around it. Business and corporate strategies change over time and are linked to changes in size, scale and scope, personnel and purpose. There exist templates for business managers to superimpose their firms on, and then adapt to particular circumstances. This may lead to hybrid structures. The templates are: functional, multi-divisional, matrix, transnational and project-based.

Functional structures

Business managers are acutely aware of the functions inside firms. A classic manufacturing firm, for example, may have the form illustrated in Figure 11.1.

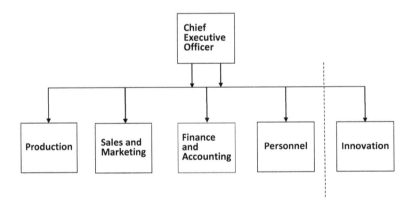

Figure 11.1: Functional structure.
Source: Author's figure.

In this model, the functions are discrete and un/dis-connected. There is much specialist expertise in each function. Functions include, among others, marketing, operations, finance and research and development. The innovation function may well be incorporated into production and/or sales and marketing. In modern digital firms, what Mayer (2018) calls mindful corporations, the innovation function may well be its own function. Moreover, firms confronted with change imperatives – climate change, technological change, etc. – are likely to innovate their way out of such challenges. It is important to configure a functional business structure correctly to secure innovation as a key capability, if not a core competence.

The model has further limitations. The arrows flow in a single direction, from the top down. This leaves the functions disconnected and liable to becoming fiefdoms rather than components of a dynamic whole. A hybrid approach may well connect the functions; an innovation function could well be the unifying component. Mature firms may move personnel between the functions, at least for a short while to develop a holistic understanding of the firm and what it does. Many bureaucracies do this, for example, the UK civil service. It may indeed be good practice for the CEO to spend some time in each function.

The framework, however, overloads CEOs with operational matters at the expense of strategic leadership. Left to their own devices, the functions are unlikely to share knowledge, cooperate and share risks and benefits. Functions do tend to throw problems "over the wall" to avoid responsibility or committing resources to a solution that would benefit other functions.

Multi-divisional structures

While the functional structure has an attractive simplicity for small discrete firms, rather bigger and international firms might consider organizing around subsidiaries or divisions (Figure 11.2).

In this configuration, a head office concedes authority for strategy to each division mediated by central services. Central services may provide accountancy services, human resource management or even research and development, depending on the industry or purpose of the firm. Each division is semi-autonomous and might be totally different businesses. The absence of links between them suggests limited coordination and synergies. They may operate in different territories and/or different markets. In which case, the head office functions as a holding company. The divisions are likely to be governed by central targets that may be financial or market-based (market share might be a short-term objective over profit, for example). Equally, divisions may also have explicit sustainability targets. This structural form is particularly useful in that each subsidiary is a separate legal entity that can be shut down or sold with no impact on the rest of the group. The divisions can also be a good place to develop management expertise with particularly high-performing colleagues rising to more strategic positions within subsidiaries or graduating to the head office.

On the limitations side, again, this structural form offers little in terms of organizational learning. While they may be operating in different territories or markets, this does not preclude learning, especially if they share platforms or other digital functions. Each division is going to be a specialism, and there is likely to be significant duplication of activity in the functions with each division replicating the activities of another unless the central services can accommodate them.

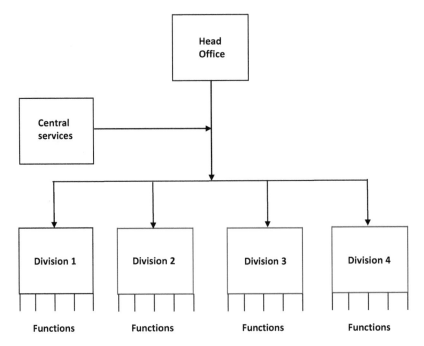

Figure 11.2: Multi-divisional structure.
Source: Author's figure.

The divisions themselves can generate their own subsidiaries and divisions. Division 4 could be a regional division – for example, South America, where a particular product market might require its own entity to deal with regulatory or marketing requirements that are different from the division as a whole. Division 2 could be a manufacturer that establishes a subsidiary to provide parts/components, or a software developer that establishes a specialist audio subsidiary that also supplies other firms.

Matrix structures

The advent of the knowledge economy and eventually to mindful organizations (Mayer 2018) in a global context, initiated a new organizational structure, the matrix. This was designed to facilitate learning across functional, divisional and area boundaries. They were applicable to both manufacturing firms and service sector firms – financial services, consultancy, lawyers. These complex structures were challenging, not least because of language and cultural differences (Bartlett and Ghoshal 1987). The structure can be represented diagrammatically as Figure 11.3.

	Europe	Americas	Asia	Australasia
Production				
Marketing				
HRM/Personnel				
Finance				
	Product Group A	Product Group B	Product Group C	Product Group D

Global reach

Functions

Product groups

Figure 11.3: Matrix structure.
Source: Author's figure.

In this case, the head of marketing reports both to the head of European Operations and the head of Product Group C, taking and receiving information, intelligence and learning with them. Precisely who reports to whom requires careful
consideration and is contingent on the function of the firm and the sectors in which
it operates. There is no generic application. A matrix structure, therefore, is defined
in terms of the existence and need for multiple command or reporting mechanisms
(Davis and Lawrence 1977). The multiplicity comes from increasing differentiation
on product groups, geographical reach, marketing strategies for products and regions and the need for collaborative information sharing and problem-solving. Essentially, a global corporate strategy needs complex structures to support it. Firms
cease to be binary – global versus domestic; centralized versus decentralized – and
the matrix structure reflects a more multi-dimensional perspective and aspiration.
The aspiration is often captured in the vision and mission of the firm, itself a challenge for any senior manager to communicate and instil. Equally, as Bartlett and
Ghosal (1987) note, formal structures are usually matched with formal reporting and
command structures. In matrix structural forms, these mechanisms rely much more
on cultural factors – a willingness to share, cooperate, co-opt and develop – than is
the case for functional and multi-divisional structural forms. Well-known firms that
engaged with these structures were Philips, NEC and P&G. This was all pre-Internet.

Attempts at formalizing reporting mechanisms can generate sub-optimal situations. Returning to the hypothetical case (Figure 11.3), if the production manager
(based in the UK) has to report to the head of Product Group B (based in Tokyo) and
the general manager of the Americas operations (based in Santiago), and each recipi-
ent requires a different emphasis to the received report(s), this amounts to a considerable reporting effort that cannot be used elsewhere more productively. There is a
considerable opportunity cost associated with it. The two people to whom the general
manager reports themselves may also have complex reporting responsibilities across
different time zones, all in the name of knowledge sharing. It becomes unwieldy and

impractical to execute in a meaningful way. The structure potentially distracts managers from what one might call their day jobs, namely, general management, cost control, people management and even strategy. It becomes unwieldy and impractical to execute in a meaningful way. Extended time needed to make decisions is another obvious drawback, but this is not unique to matrix structures.

The principle is not in dispute and could work well for smaller organizations where co-located managers can meet and engage in dialogue. However, many multi-national firms moved away from matrix structures in the 1990s because of the perceived waste of resources and an inability to measure the added value of cross-functional/area/division reporting. Some reverted back to hybrid functional/divisional forms; others moved into transnational structural forms on the grounds that the principles were sound but analogue, physical structures limited the ability of actors in firms to realize and meet their objectives. The advent of the Internet, with its digital networking capability, gave rise to new transnational structures, wholly more suited to the international organizational learning principle.

Transnational structures

The distinction between a multinational corporation (MNC) and a transnational corporation (TNC) is often difficult to comprehend. Rugman et al. (2006) argue that transnational or multinational companies are businesses that produce and sell their products in more than one country and create added value. Usually they consist of a parent company located in the country of origin of the company (home country) and at least five branches located in a host country, for example, of foreign affiliates. A multinational company is considered to be a company that conducts research, production, sales and other activities in different countries, not just where it has its head office. At the same time, TNCs actively create relatively stable, internationally operating corporate networks with their suppliers, customers and cooperating partners. They create considerable profit for investment in research and development, and thanks to the creation of corporate networks, they can influence the choice of technology across the supply chain that is global in scale.

Relative to a multinational structure that might be organized around a multidivisional or matrix form, a transnational structure is less tangible, more digital and more dispersed than the formal functional and divisional configurations. Firms that are structurally and operationally transnational are linked together not by formal reporting structures (though they exist), but rather by networks of stakeholders in relationships of interdependence. They often depend on high bandwidth and secure electronic data transfer networks. Their innovation models are open rather than closed, and they have the ability to provide customized products for regional markets sometimes designed and produced on different continents. They can manage discontinuous/disruptive change. They are agile (Francis 2020), responsive and fast.

Subsidiaries or business units may be distributed according to local special-isms, in some cases such as mindful organizations (Mayer 2018) Silicon Valley tech firms partner with universities and other research institutes. They co-locate them-selves to expand expertise and access resources.

Alphabet

Probably the most familiar transnational corporation is Alphabet/Google. A series of articles (*The Economist* 2015a, 2015b, 2016) illustrate the strategic thinking be-hind creating Alphabet as a notional holding company, and the transnational na-ture of the operation. In *Spelling it out* (2015b), the authors noted "[t]he corporate reorganisation it announced . . . is an acknowledgment of what Google has become: a sprawling conglomerate, albeit with one predominant, profit-generating division in the form of its original internet business". The authors saw in the new structural form inspiration from Berkshire Hathaway, the holding company of Warren Buf-fett's investment vehicle. However, they are very different entities. Berkshire Hath-away diversifies largely through acquisition, not intrapreneurship. Moreover, Buffet has largely eschewed riskier hi-tech ventures.

The structure of Alphabet is captured in Table 11.1.

The Economist reported that in the five years previous to the article, Google had spent $46bn on research and development across the business units that are now reconfigured as subsidiaries. In that time, investors had very little idea about the performance of these business units. To put them into subsidiaries lessens the chance that failure or poor performance will impact on the core Google search busi-ness, the primary source of group revenue. It is incumbent upon the subsidiaries' bosses to manage costs, not least because it enhances transparency and hence makes it less easy to cross-subsidize, something that the shareholders welcomed, but not the less remunerative business units. Subsidiaries can be divested, and the new structure may also assist in avoiding anti-trust action by governments worried about Google's dominance in markets. Not surprisingly, when the new structure was announced, shares in Google/Alphabet rose 4 per cent.

Subsidiaries are represented as being separate entities and not explicitly connected to one another. It is represented as multi-divisional rather than transnational. Look more closely at the Google core business, however, and the reach is significant. Google has offices, engineering and research facilities in many countries, far away from its Sili-con Valley base. In Germany, for example, Google has offices in Munich and Frank-furt. From the Munich office engineers work in collaboration with SAP, one of the largest global enterprise resource planning (ERP) software platforms. Munich is also home to university expertise and collaborative enterprise opportunities. These links are tacit, virtual and rarely formally represented.

Table 11.1: Structure of Alphabet.

Parent	Subsidiary	Business	Purpose
Alphabet LLC	Google	Ads	online advertising
		Android	mobile operating system
		Cloud	web service/cloud computing
		Chrome	web browser
		Drive	file hosting service
		Gmail	email services
		Maps	web mapping platform; satellite imagery, aerial photography, Street View
		Nest Labs	home security/Internet of Things (IoT)
		Pixel	hardware brand: Chromebook, smartphones
		YouTube	online video sharing/channels/social media platform
	Calico		ageing tech – health
	Deep mind		artificial intelligence (AI)
	Fitbit		fitness monitoring/wearables
	Google Capital		finance for growth-stage tech companies
	Google Fiber		fibre optics
	GV		venture capital (VC) for tech companies
	Intrinsic		robotics (software)
	Side Walk Labs		urban innovation
	Verily		human Health
	Waymo		autonomous vehicles
	Wing		drones for delivery and freight
	X		moon-shot projects

Source: Author's table.

Structure in 5's

Structure in 5's (Mintzberg 1980) characterizes all firms and organizations as being made up of different configurations of the following five elements: operating core, middle line, strategic apex, support staff and a technostructure. These are not literal definitions, but idealized *caricatures* of reality. They help strategists, however, to play with organizational forms that match the type of firm currently, or in the future.

For example, a manufacturer of standard products (machine bureaucracy in Mintzberg's terms), would have a large operating core (a factory/call centre/warehouse), a smaller middle line of management, and strategic apex occupied by an elite of the management. The line between the strategic apex and operating core is vertical to reflect the framework and balance of power. The machine bureaucracy balances administrative (operational support) and technostructure (planners, standards-setting, accountants, schedulers, systems managers – often with advisory roles and with access to the strategic apex) governing the operation of the organization in an environment of macro-level stability and predictability.

By contrast, a small entrepreneurial firm has a large operating core and a small strategic apex – probably just the owner/visionary, with little or no middle line. Strategy is the preserve of the owner, with the operating core made up of people who are multi-skilled and self-supporting with regard to technostructure and administrative support. As entrepreneurial firms grow and mature, their structure will change, too. Some will take on the traits of machine bureaucracies over time. The more mature the organization, the more likely is the growth of a technostructure, as activities are standardized and codified. The middle line may expand to accommodate increases in scale and scope.

Universities and hospitals are categorized by Mintzberg as professional bureaucracies with a large operating core made up of professionals (academics/doctors). The technostructure is small, reflecting the relative autonomy of professionals in these organizations. There is a large support staff and a small strategic apex. In recent years, however, professional bureaucracies have been subject to marketization by governments leading to management by targets and performance, the introduction of internal markets, de-professionalization and casualization. The technostructure has grown in size and influence with a new cadre of professional managers being recruited as CEOs. They start to look more like machine bureaucracies (with some specialization at the margins).

Many technology, construction, knowledge-intensive and *mindful* firms employ temporary structures in cases where the product is the output of a project. In Mintzberg's terms, adhocracies. A project is by definition time limited. Many firms that are adhocracies create unique products, for example, each building, motion picture or videogame. The expertise to deliver projects, such as a film, is often located in an ecosystem of firms supplying technology, studio space, location, scripts, catering, etc. They are reconfigured around the project and are effectively "bolted on" to the existing film-company permanent structure. They work in teams and the line (authority)/staff is horizontal. When the project is complete these temporary structures are decoupled.

One of the problems with adhocracies is that they can lead to the focal firm losing its capabilities to do the work in-house. In outsourcing, effectively, many of its functions, power over products and strategy more generally, can move towards the contractors, especially in fast-moving and technological spheres. Very careful contracting and/or trust mechanisms are needed to share the learning and benefits. The configurations are captured in Table 11.2.

Table 11.2: Structure in 5's.

Name	Example firm	features
Entrepreneurial	Tech start-up	Structure centralized (around the boss): small apex and operating core; absent middle and operational support/ technostructure; rapid decision-making; sometimes reverted to in times of crisis by larger firms
Machine	Manufacturer – mature industry; insurance; call centres	Structure centralized around technostructure (planners, time-study analysts): small apex, larger core and middle line; operational support and technostructure
Professional	University, hospital, law firms	Structure decentralized: small apex and middle. Work is standardized. Large core, significant operational support, small technostructure
Diversified	Holding company – autonomous subsidiaries/business units	Structure decentralized: small apex, core and middle are the subsidiaries (subject to central performance-control systems) with additional central administrative support and medium-sized technostructure
Adhocracy	Project-based organizations – aerospace, film, videogames development, advertising agencies	Structure decentralized: small apex, core and middle – team-based facilitating "mutual adjustment". Experts drawn from outside on temporary basis, providing an additional operating core for duration of project; specialized

Table 11.2 (continued)

Name	Example firm	features
Missionary	Business and civil society organizations with shared belief – some Asian/family corporations; religious organizations	Structure decentralized (pure form) vested in an idea or leader personifying the idea: small apex, large cores and middles. Little specialization held together by forces of belief and mission. Forces are centripetal
Political	Government agencies/departments, political parties, dormant firms protected from the market	Structure decentralized: small apex, large cores and middles. Forces are centrifugal – likely to fall apart due to internal disputes or contradictions

Source: Author's table, derived from Mintzberg (1980) and Mintzberg et al. (2009).

Structural dynamism

If structure follows strategy, organizational structures change when organization strategy changes on the basis of whether to grow, diversify, internationalize or turn-around. The structure is not, therefore, an afterthought, and while the models are effectively templates for business managers, they require considerable additional thought to optimize the configuration of resources and capabilities, incorporate external actors (for example, regulators, macro- and socio-economic factors, open innovation opportunities) and expectations for market stability.

The most basic form is a functional structure suitable for unitary firms operating in a single market. What options are available should the strategy of the firm now incorporate internationalization? Much depends on entry modes (agents, licensing, franchising, alliances, etc). The simplest option is to create an international function to manage supply to new overseas customers. The international function would need to provide not only product, but also product support. This will present challenges such as language, standards and logistics. The greater the percentage of sales derived from international customers, the greater the need to reconfigure the organizational structure to meet customer needs. For Stopford and Wells (1972), the choice for firms in this situation is to choose either a worldwide product divisional approach, where international product diversity is growing, or an area division structure, where international sales are increasing as a percentage of total sales. Both paths lead towards a matrix structure as an optimal organizational form where these two variables achieve an equilibrium and an equal importance for firm strategy.

Structure and corporate strategy

Corporate strategy involves the strategic leverage of subsidiaries to meet agreed objectives (financial/social, etc.). Large firms are likely to have a central head office whose internal functions are determined by:
- obligatory activities, such as reporting, compliance, planning and increasingly environmental accounting
- discretionary activities, that is, adding value to subsidiaries through the provision of shared knowledge, expertise, capital, marketing and career opportunities for personnel

Collis et al. (2007) surveyed firms to investigate corporate structures and test for correlations between size and performance. Corporates that are more hands-on with their guidance and management or manage shared resources tend to have larger central staff. Geographical scope (spread) of subsidiaries correlates with larger head-office size. Japanese head offices are larger than those in Europe and North America. However, multinational firms with a complex array of functions/divisions tend to decentralize activities including business-unit strategy. With regard to performance, size of the corporate head office is not detrimental to financial performance; indeed, they found that those with larger head offices outperform firms with smaller head offices.

The design of the corporate structure is, however, an art. It may depend on the personality of the CEO and the board more generally as well as levels of trust and depth of knowledge about sectors and geographies in which subsidiaries operate. Ultimately, does the parent – corporate head office – add value, and, if so, how? This also has implications for portfolio management and questions about whether to invest, acquire or divest.

Structural forms for control and asset transfers

The emphasis so far has been on evaluating structural forms that are clear, balance control and autonomy and clarifying reporting responsibilities for firms and their stakeholders. Many firms, however, may be structured to make responsibilities opaque, at least to outside observers: an organizational structure says very little about ownership. For example, at first sight, Samsung looks to be a classic conglomerate. However, Cain (2020, p. 21) notes:

> The Samsung group consists of more than fifty affiliates in chipsets, shipbuilding, a hospital, smartphones, a theme park, and fashion. But the 'Samsung Group' isn't an actual business entity, nor is it a holding company. It describes a bewilderingly complex web of cross-shareholdings . . . that the Lee family uses to keep control of Samsung with a relatively small stake.

Such complexities are neither unique to Samsung nor exclusively about family control. Many enterprises have such arrangements for financial advantage (Goodley 2015; Shaxson 2018); the case of Alibaba in China provides an international example (Clark 2018).

Structures have been shown to be classifiable, configurable, dynamic and used for purposes not always associated with responsible business. The question remains, what are the sustainability implications for structural forms?

Structure, climate change and sustainability

The simplest functional structure discussed in this chapter included an innovation function. The logic here is that businesses that employ sustainable practices do so as a strategic business innovation with considerations about the value proposition of products and services. The values embedded in the concept of sustainability and the SDGs more generally can be owned by a business function and diffused within the organization by that function.

More complex organizations, such as transnational companies, are often aloof from both internal and external sustainability agendas. Folke et al. (2019) identify the threat to sustainability by TNCs in particular:

> In the face of insufficient environmental agreements and regulations, dominance poses a threat to sustainability. For instance, companies able to set barriers to entry in a sector can stifle sustainable practices and technological innovation in general. They can also impose low prices on suppliers, which reduces suppliers' capacity to diversify and can force them into monocultural practices (particularly in the agricultural sector). Finally, TNCs often lobby regulators to weaken environmental and social standards to the benefit of their own businesses.
>
> (p. 4)

TNCs, however, can also be a force for good. There are many examples of practices directed by TNCs, often in partnership with NGOs/campaign groups, that have led on sustainability. This text has presented examples of Mars Wrigley and Unilever. They can impose sustainability standards and objectives across the supply and value chains. They can also be the de facto industry standard for operations.

Folke et al. (2019, pp. 5–7) list six features of systemic change in the public–private policy interface with implications for sustainable business planning and organization. These are captured in Table 11.3.

Table 11.3: Structural implications for sustainability in TNCs.

Feature of systemic change	Explanation	Implications for structure
1 Alignment of vision	CEOs of TNCs have power to create and diffuse a vision that is resonant with operating sectors and to other business leaders and entrepreneurs. They can change the value base for their own operations, their suppliers and their investors from pure profit to responsibility, ethics, meaning and purpose. Organizations such as the Council for Sustainable Development can facilitate the alignment of vision and its realization.	Alignment of vision in-and-of-itself does not affect organizational structure. Missions and visions are all well and good, but if the articles of association for the firm remain wedded to profit maximization, then the vision is incomplete and probably unrealizable. This is very much a corporate governance challenge. Firms "decouple" the vision and activities, for example: "Companies are measuring the amount of water they use and setting targets to reduce water but they are not aligning this water target with the amount of water available in the local watershed" (Article-13 Undated). If true also of energy consumption, waste generation and management, etc., a structural solution to misalignment is desirable.
2 Mainstreaming sustainability	The UN SDGs are a vehicle for mainstreaming. Composed as normative statements, engagement by firms with them has led to applied approaches being developed and increasingly detailed reporting of those efforts. Substantive reporting, therefore, becomes normalized and expected by stakeholders as a guide to firms' overall responsibility.	Sustainability reports are not trivial undertakings. They can be self-standing or incorporated into the annual report of the firm or corporation. Their increasing importance has implications for structure. If such reporting is as important as the annual accounts, a structural mechanism is needed for validation and releasing the resources necessary to do the reporting. Firms need to extend their engagement with planetary boundaries, not just absolute measures.

Table 11.3 (continued)

Feature of systemic change	Explanation	Implications for structure
3 The licence to operate	Determines the responsibilities of firms trading in a particular jurisdiction. Violation of the licence can result in firms being unable to trade. An example of this was Transport for London removing the licence to operate of Uber in having found drivers uploading inauthentic identities, driving without appropriate insurance leading to safety concerns for customers (Topham 2019b). The UK government also led on the Modern Slavery Act requiring companies to disclose measures adopted to address slavery and human trafficking. Governments can link firms' licence to operate with sustainability practices, indicators and improvement.	This feature is inter-linked with mainstreaming. Evidence of compliance with law (in the future) and voluntary commitments (currently) is contained in sustainability reports.
4 Financing transformations	The financial services sector – in particular pension funds and insurance companies – is slowly moving away from investing in carbon-intensive firms and industry sectors. Governments are initiating regulations "making environment, society, and governance considerations mandatory parts of fiduciary duty, [which] represent another indication that change is accelerating" Folke et al. (2019: p. 7).	The implications for both providers of finance and recipients is significant. Providers need to reconfigure investment criteria and governance structures to avoid knowingly investing in carbon-intensive activities. There are examples of investments that contradict vision and sustainability aspirations. For example, British banks investing in beef production linked to deforestation in Brazil (Howard et al. 2020); arising from the Covid-19 virus, fossil fuel firms were supported with public money (Harvey 2020).

Table 11.3 (continued)

Feature of systemic change	Explanation	Implications for structure
5 Radical transparency	Consumers are familiar with tracking packages ordered online. Many firms remotely monitor their supply chains making them much more transparent. Transparency acts as a driver for sustainable supply-chain management. Those that do not make their supply chains transparent are likely to be asked searching questions about their sustainability policies. Such transparency could become a condition of a global licence to operate.	Firms will be expected to monitor and account for emissions and social effects of their own activities and those of their suppliers (scope 3). This requires enhanced capabilities and structural safeguards.
6 Evidence-based knowledge for action	TNCs in particular have tapped into product expertise found in universities and research institutes around the world. Universities are now the prime knowledge-holders around sustainability and are in a position to co-create and develop the knowledge base to transform the nature and life cycles of their products and services. The co-creation element is important to foster partnership and to optimize change processes.	This factor lends itself to the adoption of transnational structures for large and smaller firms alike. Networking based on trust and cooperative relationships with stakeholders are sources of data, and, hence, evidence. Banks, for example, link to evidence-based knowledge about deforestation and the types of activities and firms contributing to it – unless, of course, banks are investing in these damaging activities knowingly. Here governments can legislate to make such investments harder or removing the licence to operate.

Source: Author's table, derived from Folke et al. (2019).

Summary

All firms have structural forms that should be aligned with strategy. When business or corporate strategy changes, there is an expectation that the structure of the organization changes, too. For example, an internationalization strategy will need infrastructure to support it either in the form of a function acting as an international division/ department or a regional subsidiary managing products in new markets. Over time, international firms combine divisional and area approaches into modern matrix organizations, or build transnational network structures. That is what business-as-usual looks like. The future is different. Climate change, global pandemics and other SDG responsibilities and challenges have structural implications. During the Covid-19 crisis in 2019/2020, firms inadvertently became networked organizations with de facto transnational operations, even if these were not captured by revised organizational structures. Firms found themselves dependent on government guidance, often ad hoc. Depending on the country, firms have relied on government support to maintain their workforce after revenue declined. Many new competences and capabilities have been developed and practised. Some of these will endure.

The same is true of climate change. Firms looking to prosper in an era of climate change will mitigate and adapt and be transparent in their operations, sourcing and impacts. Sustainability performance will be reported openly as sustainability reports act as mandated documentation under the licence to operate. Deciding where to locate this capability (a necessary function/capability to operate) will have structural implications. More generally reporting mechanisms in firms will need to be led by sustainability and not profit. A sustainability function might be what Stuart Clegg (1989, p. 204) calls an "obligatory passage point", that is, a place where all decisions must pass for scrutiny and support.

Structures are a dry subject in business and corporate strategy. They support the realization of strategy by optimizing resource allocation and knowledge acquisition and diffusion. They are a source of identity for employees and badly constructed, they are also a source of inertia. Change is tough. Change takes leadership. It is to that the focus now turns.

Questions

1. What is a dual-class system of shares?
2. What is idiosyncratic value? How might it serve sustainability? How might it work against sustainability?
3. What is bottom of the pyramid, and why do firms operate there?
4. What are the limitations of (a) functional, (b) multi-divisional and (c) matrix structures?
5. What is the difference between a multi-national and a transnational firm?
6. What are the five elements of Mintzberg's configuration? What is an *adhocracy*?
7. What should determine the head office/parent role with subsidiaries?
8. Why are TNCs particularly privileged with regard to pursuing sustainability as a competitive advantage?

Chapter 12
Change management and leadership

Policy-making in politics and strategy in business are straightforward when compared to implementation. Bad policy or strategy often arises from a failure to understand the implications relating
to feasibility. This is not only a question of whether the necessary resources and capabilities are
available or can be procured, but also whether the culture and leadership are there to implement
them successfully. Most strategy involves some form of change, and hence management. It may be
necessary because a firm is failing and needs so-called turnaround. It may be a growth strategy
involving new alliances, new technologies and new locations. This chapter discusses the nature of
leadership, styles of leadership and managing for stakeholders. Implementation, however, is a
strategy development process in itself. Either because it is a bottom-up approach where many
small changes cluster together and generate patterns that become emergent (Mintzberg and
Waters 1985), or because strategy changes as it is implemented. The practitioners such as middle
managers, for example, build on strategy consciously or unconsciously as it proceeds. The more
"top-down" the strategy's origins, the greater potential for change as it diffuses down and across.
The real test of change management for the twenty-first century is whether the transformations it
enables lead to a sustainable society, namely, one that is carbon negative.

This chapter covers:
– change management and styles of change management
– managerialism as the dominant model of management and change
– leadership styles
– international change management
– matching change and leadership styles
– implications for sustainability and climate change

Change management and styles of change management

The discipline of organization development (OD) illustrated well the dilemma associated with implementation. Policy and strategies are agreed by senior managers
and then thrown over the wall for implementation. The link between policy-makers
and implementers, who are primarily middle managers and operational staff, is
weak. This leaves strategy open to misinterpretation at implementation and probably failure (Burnes 2015).

Kurt Lewin

The discipline of OD owes much to the pioneering work of Kurt Lewin. Lewin's original focus was on societal change rather than organizational change, writing and
researching in the aftermath of World War II. His discipline was psychology, and

https://doi.org/10.1515/9783110718430-012

his body of work is complementary and mutually dependent. No one part makes sense without the others, namely:

- field theory – individuals' behaviours are understood in relationship with their surroundings and conditions at a particular point in time
- group dynamics – in groups, members all share the same outcome of a decision and are inter-dependent when undertaking a shared task
- action research – embedded, co-researching

Three-step model

The discipline of organizational change management in firms has largely drawn on Lewin's three-step model that conceptualized change as a process of:

1. Unfreezing – present level of customs and habits
2. Moving – when the change actually occurs
3. Refreezing – new habit or norm is adopted and institutionalized

(Burnes and Bargal 2017)

This is planned change and, in line with his overall objectives of positive societal change, his approach was democratic in the sense that the plan is derived from participation of stakeholders and an understanding of root causes. Hence change managers are advised against taking the three-step model in isolation because it relies on a mutual understanding and application of field theory, group dynamics and action research. In this context, Lewin's approach is not managerialist.

Change as managerialism

Change management as a process is often presented in a linear and prescriptive fashion: do step 1, then step 2 and finally step 3. Prescriptive approaches dominate business management and particularly strategic analysis and choice. For example, Porter's (1980) models for strategic analysis are prescriptive, using generic tools such as five-forces. As discussed for innovation models, steps can overlap and feed back to one another. Judson (1991) created a five-step model in his evaluation of strategy implementation failure: (1) define the firms' operating systems that are relevant to the delivery of strategy, for example, cost accounting and production systems; (2) identify the special demands on operating systems relative to the strategy, such as greater pricing flexibility or customer satisfaction; (3) test these with managers at all levels of the firm, looking for obstacles, dysfunctions and special levers for change; (4) redefine the operating systems and accountabilities, designing out the obstacles and aligning absolutely with the strategy; and (5) measure, track and monitor strategy implementation and the effectiveness of the new operating systems.

The most widely recognized of step-models is Kotter (1996), with eight steps captured in Table 12.1.

Table 12.1: Kotter's eight-step model.

Step	Description	Actions
1	Creating a sense of urgency	scanning the market, identifying/discussing crises, opportunities
2	Building a guiding coalition	forming a group/team with sufficient power – resources, authority – to lead change
3	Forming a strategic vision and initiatives	visions need to be formulated and translated into strategy, or strategies
4	Communicating the change of vision	utilizing all modes to communicate the change of vision driven by a "guiding coalition model" informing the expected behaviour of employees
5	Empowering broad-based action	removing obstacles such as non-functional systems and structures while promoting risk-taking, creative ideas – activities and actions
6	Generating short-term wins	anticipate (by design) visible improvements in performance. Recognize and reward those who make the wins
7	Consolidating gains and formulating more change	change is an ongoing process around the vision – hiring and reward linked to embedding and further delivery of vision and change
8	Institutionalizing change within the organizational culture	leadership development and succession. Broader challenges to existing structures and systems (and normalization). Explicit links between customer-focused behaviour and performance

Source: Author's table, derived from Kotter (1996).

This managerialist approach, while notionally transformational, primarily targets subordinates to remove resistance rather than transform the organization or society in which they work or belong (Burnes et al. 2018).

Moreover, simplicity often wins out over complexity. Step models are simple to articulate, but not necessarily simple to implement because of the inherent complexity of stakeholder interests and formal and informal systems inside organizations. In simplifying, they can miscalculate the extent of change and the impact it has on stakeholders. They are largely managerialist, that is, designed to be applied by managers with instrumental aims relating to financial performance such as increasing shareholder value.

Behaviour is not as linear as step models prescribe. Those subject to change can themselves be classified as instrumental or transformational (Herscovitch and Meyer 2002; Bakari et al. 2017), where:
- instrumental is exhibiting focal behaviour in being either strictly compliant or simply seeking to maintain their employment status
- transformational is exhibiting discretionary behaviours that involve both cooperation (participation) and championing

Change, however, is not something that can be achieved on the basis of a single decision. Organizations need to have readiness for change.

Readiness for change

Readiness for change aligns with Lewin's concept of unfreezing (Armenakis et al. 1993), whereby leaders can ready their employees for change, which in turn increases commitment (and willingness to stay employed and/or reduce absenteeism), adoption and institutionalization (embedding change). Its primary function, however, is to reduce resistance. It is often the job of so-called *change agents* to achieve readiness among the collective and with the individuals. Not all individual interests are met collectively. Individuals may well have different cognitive structures, which means that individuals may read the case for change or the mechanisms differently. They may disrupt the collective readiness for change. It may also be that within the collective are opinion leaders who can be recruited to authenticate the case for, and approach to, change. Employees are not homogeneous, that is, they may not all share the same desires, needs or values. Moreover, organizations that are diverse and embrace conflict as a constructive and critical process may be more open to change. The link between diversity and performance in firms is increasingly being researched and supported by the global consultancy firms such as McKinsey (Hunt et al. 2014).

Readiness as a process has three elements:
- transparency about need for, and form of, change using examples such as new regulations, competition and quality standards where possible
- clear communication of the business model and "deliberate" strategy to meet new desired objectives supported by data
- explicit articulation of what it involves including expectations, workloads and sacrifice in supporting or not supporting change

Readiness is enhanced through participation, which can be active engagement and/or representational. Active participation has the advantage of giving the opportunity for self-discovery of information. Of particular value is participation in genuine and meaningful strategic planning events. This has a positive effect on readiness.

There is also a link to organizational identification. The higher the identification, the higher the expectation that employees will have a positive readiness. This assumes that the change is perceived to have a positive effect on the organization and hence the need for clear communication and a strategy that is aligned with the values of the organizational identification for those affected by the change (Drzensky et al. 2012). What readies stakeholders the most, however, is procedural justice and trust in leaders (Oreg et al. 2011).

Urgency in change may be communicated symbolically by senior managers taking the time to address employees directly. This is important if the nature of the change is fundamental rather than merely incremental. Incremental change in the form of small steps within the existing organizational mindset or paradigm is much less threatening than more fundamental change that requires not only "unfreezing" but also "unlearning" (Tsang and Zahra 2008). Unlearning is the intentional and purposeful removal of routines and knowledge from an organization either simply to discontinue them or in preparation for their replacement with new ones. Drawing on organizational structures, consider the change from multi-divisional form to strategic business unit configuration, as Google did in 2015. The founders created a new parent, Alphabet, and the divisions became stand-alone strategic business units with centrally determined financial targets. This required a major change of behaviour and routines that were not always welcome.

Organizational commitment

An individual's organizational commitment has three components (Porter et al. 1974):
- a strong belief in and acceptance of the organization's goals and values
- a willingness to exert considerable effort on behalf of the organization
- a definite desire to maintain organizational membership

All of these can be affected by demographic issues such as age, length of service, location, education (highly educated individuals have more opportunities), family status (children in school, for example) and leadership style. Organizational commitment, however, can be a *stronger* force on employee behaviour than salary and job satisfaction, hence its importance to leadership and change programmes.

External forces for change

In the models so far, the macro-environment is largely absent. However, the forces of change are often external. Digital information and communication technologies (ICTs), for example, are significant forces for change within organizations. They require new skills to operate them and new working practices and routines. They are often seen as solutions to problems that do not exist or are imposed from external forces such as regulators. They have transformed business models and are disruptive. In manufacturing industries, ICTs have enabled the globalization of supply chains. In some cases, globalization has led to a loss of manufacturing and development capabilities in firms. As such, the change they bring is not always welcomed and embraced. Procedural justice and trust are often absent from such change.

A study by Kwahk and Lee (2008) on the implementation of enterprise resource planning (ERP) systems was motivated by the very low success rate of such projects (up to 90 per cent failure rates in some sectors). The study tested the following factors affecting implementation (Table 12.2).

Table 12.2: Core factors in success of ERP system implementation.

Core factor	Interpretation
Readiness for change	Need for the change
	Belief in positive impact of the change
Organizational commitment	Strength in identification with the organization
	Perceived personal competence

Source: Author's table, derived from Kwahk and Lee (2008).

Readiness for change requires the support of top management through their personal explanation for the change and the benefits to the organization. This may enhance the belief by employees in the system, generating positive effects for the firm and themselves, but, in addition, individuals weigh up the consequences for themselves of not participating and/or trying out the system. The ease of use or, at least, the belief that ERP operations can easily be learned, is important. This also involves some degree of unlearning. Moreover, the sense of "missing out" cannot be discounted as a motivational force in readiness for change.

With regard to organizational commitment, it is important to consider whether the implementation alters the core values and goals of the organization. Fundamental change of this kind is more difficult to achieve than is incremental change. While ERP systems represent a major change in work routines and knowledge and are usually enterprise- and supply chain-wide, affecting everyone, deployment does not need to undermine organizational values and goals. Indeed, they might enhance them. For example, if the aim is good customer service and the system makes it easier for suppliers to coordinate, query and receive timely payment, then this value is enhanced.

It is also the case that leadership in change involves recognizing what is good in an organization, what works and what is not broken. Change can be a blend of new and old. However, this blend can seem more difficult to achieve in reality than a complete "root and branch" reorganization.

Orlikowski (1996) offers three observations common to managerialist frameworks:
1. Centrally formulated policy generates change that is planned and as such fits neatly into the organizational form and culture.
2. There exists a technological imperative. Technology is an independent, external, unavoidable force. In implementing a technological change, organizations can achieve order, predictability in behaviour (routines) and performance, efficient structural forms, appropriate information flows, etc.
3. Change is not gradual and incremental; it occurs as punctuated equilibrium. It comes in episodes that are generated by internal and external forces, such as new technology, process redesign and industry regulation.

Situated or practice-based change assumptions offer a fourth framework. Central to this approach is the claim that change does occur in organizations that is invisible to those with one or more of the above lenses. It may be initiated by, for example, a technological force such as new software, but the change itself is achieved by a process of negotiation between actors such as employees in the organization and over time. This involves adjustment and improvisation. These tend not to be part of an explicit plan. They occur to deal with issues like unintended consequences, which is a common factor in change management programmes. Where software is a driver of change, the act of customization is an example of situated change. Imagine receiving a new smartphone. Customization immediately happens when apps are added, ringtones selected and photographs added to home pages. It is the users who provide the solutions to implementation issues that cannot be predicted by those who create the software code for the program. Situated implementation is key to successful change programmes.

Styles of leadership

Styles of leadership both affect employees' commitment to the organization and the effectiveness of change programmes. Bass and Riggio (2006) present a *Full Range of Leadership Model*, comprising:
- laissez-faire
- transactional
- transformational

Laissez-faire leadership is non-leadership where subordinates are left to their own devices arising largely from a leader's indecision.

Transactional leadership hinges on rewards received when leader-derived goals or performance are achieved. Rewards can be praise, payment/bonus or avoidance of punishment. This is referred to as *Contingent Reward* (CR). Transactional leaders also employ *Management by Exception* (MBE) whereby deviation is monitored and corrective action taken. Transactional leaders do not concern themselves with the welfare of subordinates, including their professional development. Transactional leaders are very good at communicating goals, expectations and strategic objectives. Such a leadership approach does not lead to organizational commitment.

Transformational leaders appeal to higher values and ideals and promote subordinates' notions of fundamental change within organizations and society more widely (Bass and Riggio 2006). This goes beyond serving the needs of the subordinate as in the case of transactional leadership. They additionally provide meaning, understanding, support, mentoring and coaching. Transformational leaders may exhibit charisma in presenting and enabling subordinates' transformational behaviours. Transformational and charismatic are categorically not the same. They are confident and have high self-esteem. Transformational leadership in this sense can be:

- Managerialist – focused on instrumental acts to improve performance; neutralizing resistance rather than constructively using it.
- Authentic – focused on purpose and society. Leadership is moral and informed by followers.

For Luthans and Avolio (2003) quoted in Gardner et al. (2011):

> [t]he authentic leader is confident, hopeful, optimistic, resilient, transparent, moral/ethical future-oriented, and gives priority to developing associates into leaders themselves. The authentic leader does not try to coerce or even rationally persuade associates, but rather the leader's authentic values, beliefs, and behaviors serve to model the development of associates. (p. 1122)

The authentic leader is contrasted with the charismatic leader often referred to in business frameworks. In political terms, the charismatic leader is confident and sometimes coercive. Charismatic leadership is often associated with crisis, turbulence or distress, and charismatic leaders offer a simple message of salvation to followers (Tucker 1968). In business terms the sense of turbulence can be real or imagined. Turbulence can magnify the threats and opportunities, hence the charismatic leader can emerge on the basis of a new idea, product, service or process (Yukl 1999).

Leaders seeking innovative thinking and creativity from subordinates may be charismatic and employ a transformational leadership style. They have a genuine interest in subordinates, their welfare and personal development; however, charismatic leaders are not always transformational. They also adopt transactional leadership styles. Reward remains an incentive for high performance by subordinates. Timeframes may be important in such situations. It may also be the case that some employees respond to transactional styles and not to transformational ones. Many organizations have short-, medium- and long-term objectives that are suited to a mixture of leadership styles. Though in few instances is laissez-faire effective.

Change management presents structural and cultural challenges in a domestic setting, but for firms operating internationally, the challenges are multiplied. How might firms embed change across trading territories?

International change management

The routes for decision-making regarding internationalization – from the export division to transnationalization – generate their own challenges. Culture and cultural difference are factors in the decision-making. Entering territories and markets that are unfamiliar is inherently risky, though firms employ mitigating strategies, such as entering markets by taking over a company operating in the unfamiliar country and retaining the management, using agents or simply being "born global".

The extent to which corporates should or could engage in change management programmes with subsidiaries or business units at a distance, especially if that distance is continental, is debatable. Imposing a global standard in the absence of a deep understanding of cultural and operational norms is risky. Even familiar global franchises provide discretion for regional or country managers to innovate and customize. Cultural differences can lead to conflict in the workplace. For example, in the third quarter of the twentieth century, Japanese firms were internationalizing and entering Europe. Now-familiar work methodologies such as just-in-time production, lean, total quality management (TQM) and even single dining rooms for workers and managers migrated with these acquisitions or start-ups. They were often resisted or misinterpreted by employees.

Tayeb (1994) describes some of these cultural differences and explains why they proved difficult to reconcile. For example, Japanese workers were committed to their firms in a way that British workers were not. Japanese firms offered more than just transactional employment. Work processes and self-development were grounded in collective, rather than individual actions. In the workplace, the collective is not only peers and colleagues, but the firm itself. The firm looked after its employees. Managers discuss not just work issues but also personal issues both in the workplace and socially. They are sometimes configured as missionary organizations (Mintzberg et al. 2009). British workers were reported to find this intrusive and a challenge to their privacy.

Moreover, Japanese workers expected to have job flexibility and rotation. Employees are trained both to perform their allotted job and to participate in the activities of *quality circles*. Sources of finance were also significant. UK and Western firms looked to the City of London for investment funds. In Japan, investment funds were often internally generated or borrowed from closely allied banks or the government. The primary motivation for inward Japanese investment (foreign direct investment) in Europe was access to the European market (Hood et al. 1994).

While the differences between British and Japanese firms and their underpinning cultures may seem extreme and untypical, cultural differences between countries and firms that are geographically close can be equally challenging. German firms, for example, generally have management and supervisory dual boards (Wooldridge 2011). Many firms are family owned *Mittelstand*, which is a form that is not common in the UK. The assumption always has to be that perspectives, routines, expectations and rewards, for example, are not the same in different jurisdictions. Understanding these differences and integrating them into strategic analysis and decision-making is a basic skill of the strategist.

There have been attempts to create frameworks and tools to help managers with these cross-cultural questions and dilemmas. One of the most valuable in recent years has been that of Hofstede (2001). Hofstede created a framework by which it was possible to understand cross-cultural factors that might affect decisions. What was unique about his work in this field was that a simple model was grounded in data and sophisticated data analysis. It was also radical in its time. By entering main-stream management thinking there was an acceptance of cultural difference and the need to manage appropriately as a result (Jackson 2020).

The model is made up of six dimensions (originally four):
- power distance (PD)
- uncertainty avoidance (Uav)/acceptance (Uac)
- individualism versus collectivism
- masculine (M) versus feminine (F)
- long-term (LT) versus short-term (ST) orientation
- indulgence (I) versus restraint (R)

Each dimension has highs and lows, with most societies being somewhere in-be-tween the extremes. The values are relative, not absolute. For example, people are happy or less happy, rather than not happy and unhappy. The model's attributes are captured in Table 12.3.

Table 12.3: Hofstede's cultural dimensions.

Basic problem – shared by all countries	Dimensions of national culture (labels)	Societies where dimension is high/large	Societies where dimension is low/small
How much inequality is acceptable?	Power distance Extent that less powerful people expect and accept unequal distribution of power	Inequality normalized Superiors are superior beings Power first, good and evil afterwards Children learn respect Centralization Subordinates told what to do	Inequality should be reduced Hierarchy but flexible Power used legitimate and everyone is under the same rules of law Children learn independence Decentralization Expectation of consultation

Table 12.3 (continued)

Basic problem – shared by all countries	Dimensions of national culture (labels)	Societies where dimension is high/large	Societies where dimension is low/small
How afraid are we of unknown people, ideas and objects?	Uncertainty avoidance (not risk avoidance)	Uncertainty as a threat Stress and anxiety related to unknown Emotion and aggression revealed Difference is dangerous Rules even if never used Formalization Innovation is slow Limited job mobility/churn Xenophobic and intolerant	Uncertainty is normal Less stress and anxiety related to unknown Emotion and aggression controlled Difference is curious Rules to be avoided and/or broken Deregulation Innovation is faster Job mobility normal and easier Tolerance towards difference
How dependent are we on family/one another (narrow, broad, extended)?	Individualism versus collectivism Loose versus strong ties with groups, tribes, community	"I" Universalism – classified as individuals not group members Competition between individuals Task focus Disharmony can be creative	"We" Exclusion of outsiders Competition between groups Relationship focus (on task) Harmony
How should a man feel? How should a woman feel?	Masculinity versus femininity Emotional gender roles are distinct. Data are different from the genders (only dimension where this is true)	Toughness, assertiveness, material success Work prevails over family Facts Disdain (for the weak) (Sexual) performance Fight (boys do, girls do not)	Focus on the quality of life Balance family and work Facts and feelings Sympathy/empathetic (Sexual) relations Not fight (boys or girls)

Table 12.3 (continued)

Basic problem – shared by all countries	Dimensions of national culture (labels)	Societies where dimension is high/large	Societies where dimension is low/small
Do we focus on the future, the present or the past?	Long-term orientation vs short-term orientation Fostering societal virtues for future rewards vs fostering societal virtues related to the past and present	Perseverance Thrift Adapting to changing circumstances (individuals & society) Norms depend on the situation Humility Learn from other countries Traditions change Contradictory views can be combined Middle way chosen	National pride Preservation of face No adaptation because situations are constant Fixed norms apply Positive affirmation of self Proud of own country (as is) Traditions are constant Contradictory views remain so Extremes chosen (religious/ideological)
May we have fun, or is life a serious matter?	Indulgence versus restraint Feelings of subjective happiness or unhappiness	Freedom is valued; freedom grants gratification of desires Leisure ethic (for example, participation in sports) Positive attitudes Extroverted personalities Feel healthy Friends are important Freedom of speech Control of own life	Freedom is not normalized; gratification is regulated by norms Work ethic Pessimistic/cynical attitudes Introverted personalities Feel less healthy – though objectively equally healthy Friends are less important Societal order is important (free speech works against this) Control over own life

Source: Author's table, derived from Hofstede (2014a, 2014b, 2015b, 2015c, 2015d, 2015e, 2015f).

It is important to note that these dimensions do not change over time. They are relative and passed through generations by nurture, education, ritual and law. Therefore, the purpose under normal business conditions is to use the dimensions to optimize operations in particular societies with combinations of dimensions. Table 12.4 captures some of Hofstede's own insights into what the business implications might be.

Hofstede's dimensions may facilitate managers' strategic choice options when operating, or intending to operate, internationally. His work has been criticized because of the method of data collection and analysis, scope and its conservatism (Jackson 2020). The work was extended by the Global Leadership and Organizational Behavior Effectiveness (GLOBE) team with additional dimensions and measures (House, Hanges et al. 2004).

Table 12.4: Business implications for cultural dimensions.

Dimension	Implication
Power distance (PD) *Source*: derived from Hofstede (2014a)	Society: size of the middle class (low PD correlates with larger middle class)
	Firms: executives in high PD countries are older and long-lasting. In low PD countries they are younger and have shorter tenure
	Innovation: in high PD countries, innovation is only possible if supported by the hierarchy. Low PD societies are more spontaneous in creating and employing innovation
	Politics: when power distance is high, power is often exercised through oligarchy – societal power is concentrated. Sources of power need to be understood and aligned; low PD correlates with change as evolution – power changes are legitimate, incremental and not due to revolution
Uncertainty avoidance (Uav)/acceptance (Uac) *Source*: derived from Hofstede (2014b)	Society: Uav countries have more doctors relative to nurses because fewer responsible jobs are delegated
	Behaviour: in Uac societies, people take more risks than those in Uav countries as long as they are known risks, such as driving fast on motorways; consumers in Uav countries value cleanliness and purity in products – cleaning products are important to consumers in Uav societies; consumers in Uac countries are attracted to convenience, ready meals are popular in Uac countries Firms: businesses in Uac countries are flatter and less bureaucratic. In Uav countries firms are machine-like
	Politics: Uac are perceived as less corrupt than Uav countries; Uav goes up in the event of crises or war
Individualism versus collectivism *Source*: derived from Hofstede (2015c)	Society: wealth is correlated with individualism. Though wealth is not *caused by* individualism, wealth *causes* individualism
	Behaviour: social media used for active search in individualist societies; collectivist societies search for education or communicating with "in-group"
	Politics: individualist societies specify rules, regulations, contracts; collectivist societies have less specified rules, though norms of behaviour may substitute; collectivist societies have less freedom of the press; individual human rights are less respected in collectivist societies

Table 12.4 (continued)

Dimension	Implication
Masculine (M) versus feminine (F): *Source*: derived from Hofstede (2015d)	Society: no relationship between wealth and whether countries/societies are masculine or feminine; rates of illiteracy and poverty are higher in M societies than F societies
	Behaviour: in M societies women shop for food; in F societies men and women shop for food/household Labour negotiations in M societies focus on salary; in F societies, leisure is at least equal to salary where more and longer vacations are substitutes Social media is used for fact gathering in M societies and developing relationships in F societies Politics: M societies have lower aid budgets than F societies
Long-term (LT) vs short-term (ST) orientation *Source*: derived from Hofstede (2015e)	Society: LT-oriented countries have school pupils who score higher in mathematics (but underrate their performance) than in ST-oriented countries
	Economy: in poor LT-oriented countries, economic growth is faster than similar countries with ST orientation; LT-oriented countries have higher levels of savings for investment than ST-oriented countries
	Firms: businesses in LT-oriented countries seek market share and long-term profits; in ST-oriented countries results are reported quarterly and the bottom-line is most important LT-oriented investors look for family-owned businesses and real estate. ST-oriented country investors trade in shares and mutual funds
Indulgence (I) versus restraint (R) *Source*: derived from Hofstede (2015f)	Society: freedom of speech is important in I societies; R societies look for order over freedom; I societies have higher crime rates than R societies; assuming high levels of education, I societies have higher birth rates than R societies; obesity is associated with I societies; I societies have higher approval of music and film from other countries than R societies

Source: Author's table.

Hofstede's dimensions are eminently understandable and applicable, and are a good example of how to embrace in methods of research and deployment. They do *not* reflect reality. Their utility, moreover, is restricted as it is often merely descriptive. For example, if we ask the question about the appropriateness or transferability of the work practices of a US firm for its subsidiary in the Netherlands, what would the answer be? Hofstede's work tells us that the power difference between the two countries is such that industrial democratic values are higher in the Netherlands than the USA. What this application tells us is that there is a difference not what a manager can do about it (Jackson 2020). This is a limitation of the quantitative method used.

Moreover, despite the resilience of Hofstede's dimensions, Jackson (2020) argues that a new generation of cultural theorists and practitioners need to overcome these limitations. For example, if a country and/or a company notionally signs up to the UN Sustainability Development Goals (SDGs), what structures are needed to deliver them? Is industrial democracy the best way to do it, despite the cultural realities of such things as power-distance? This is perhaps particularly true of lower-income economies that are susceptible to the effects of climate change such as flooding, desertification and migration. The challenge of climate change may be an opportunity to close the power–distance gap in a way that managerialist approaches cannot. However, this is true of not only the power–distance gap, but also the other dimensions, such as masculine–feminine and long-term dimensions–short-term dimensions. The role of stakeholders becomes one of fostering change to sustainability, leveraged by Hofstede's dimensions. Such change has happened before in the transition to managerialism started in the 1980s following the Friedman doctrine.

This leads to the question of aligning leadership and change. For many firms the magnitude of change necessary to embed the mitigation of climate change and adaptation to a decarbonized future is radical. What styles of leadership are needed?

Matching change and leadership

The manager seeking to implement strategy faces many challenges. Change is inherently risky. Resistance can be both internal, from employees, for example, or external. Where the impact has societal or political implications beyond the boundaries of the firm. A manager who has understood styles of change management and styles of leadership may seek to match these to optimize outcomes. The challenges come in the fact that the more transformational the change, the less prescriptive can be the recommendation. For example, a transactional manager seeking incremental change can assess the rewards available, including punishment, and predict the degree of compliance with meeting the goal, order or instruction. A transformational manager seeking fundamental change cannot make a similar calculation; moreover, the timeframes are likely to be different. A transactional leader may be looking short-term while the transformational leader is likely to be looking more long-term. Transformational leadership involves considerable investment in communication, support, mentoring, personal development, etc.

Figure 12.1 illustrates Dunphy and Stace's (1993) formalized approach to change in matching styles and extent of change:

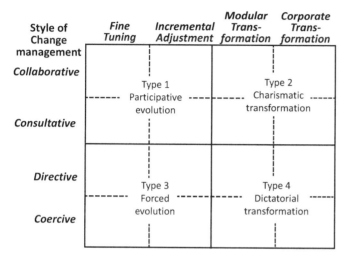

Figure 12.1: Matching types and styles of change: Dunphy/Stace change matrix.
Source: Dunphy and Stace (1993), reproduced with permission.

Where urgency is low, the style of change management can be collaborative or consultative where the purpose is to fine tune or make small and logical adjustments (evolution). Where the urgency is greater, directive and coercive styles of management are employed – though charismatic leadership is not always employed if urgency is a factor. Transformation, however, involves fundamental change, often to the values, products, processes and routines of the organization itself.

Consider climate change in the context of this model. Is the urgency high or low? If it is high, does that mean the style of management has to be directive or coercive? Does the leadership have to be charismatic or merely directive? Maybe authenticity is a better quality for managers?

Change: Implications for sustainability and climate change

Many enduring firms have periodically undergone radical change to their structures, products, processes and purpose. Firms can change incrementally, using collaborative and consultative methods, but there can come a point when change is urgent and transformational, as is the case where climate change is a force in strategic choice and implementation.

Climate change challenges firms' routines and ways of doing things at all levels, in particular, in the way electricity is consumed. Consider a very simple intervention. In many offices, computers and other equipment remain switched on during out-of-office hours. In such cases, computers use more electricity when not being used than when they are (Berners-Lee 2020). Moreover, this consumption is not a trivial amount, especially for desktops. All employees should, therefore, be aware of how to calculate their CO_2e (equivalent carbon dioxide emissions). The calculation is simple and revealing (Editorial 2016).

$$CO_2e = \frac{Hours \times Watts}{1000} conversion\ rate$$

The denominator of 1000 converts to kilowatt hours.

Assume that the average office has 100 desktop computers running 24 hours per day, 365 days per year, to enable overnight maintenance and software updates/downloads or just because users do not switch them off. Each computer runs for 8760 hours. A typical integrated desktop computer (including the monitor) uses 91 Watts of power – this will vary depending on what is being done with the computer. High-end gaming uses much more electricity than word processing and email. The conversion rate calculates the electricity used to a carbon emission in kilogrammes. The UK government publishes this conversion rate annually, which itself changes over time as electricity generating plants progressively move from fossil fuel to renewables. For 2020, the conversion rate was 0.23314. The CO_2e for these machines is calculated viz:

$$CO_2e = \frac{8760 \times 91}{1000} 0.23314$$

$$CO_2e = 185.85kg$$

We might ask what this means. For 100 computers, that is 18,585kg. The question is, is that a lot of CO_2? To answer the question, one might visualize what it would take to offset that amount of CO_2, that is, have it absorbed by trees or carbon capture technology. On trees, the UK Forestry Commission estimates that the average forest can absorb 5400kg of carbon dioxide per hectare per year. That is 3.44 hectares of potentially new forest required annually to absorb the output of 100 computers. The average professional football pitch is 0.714 hectares, making 4.8 football pitch-sized forests needed to absorb the carbon.

In carbon capture terms, one of the pioneers of retail carbon capture, Climeworks, is charging about $1100 per tonne for sequestration. In this case, therefore, the 100 computers emitting 18.5 tonnes cost about $20,350 to sequestrate their carbon emissions. However, a round trip flight from London to New York (economy) generates 1.8 tonnes CO_2. The price to sequestrate, therefore, becomes $1980 (€1680) on top of the ticket price.

The simple business challenge is first to limit business flying as much as possible. Second, at the local level, to determine whose responsibility it is to turn off computers, monitors and printers when they are not in use. Culturally, it should not matter. Reducing electricity consumption needs to be an aim linked to strategic climate mitigation measures or, at the very least, cost reduction. It is not just about electricity consumption; each computer has a carbon footprint from its manufacture that needs to be considered in procurement decisions. These decisions are usually made on the basis of price, not carbon footprints. This is a challenge to procurement departments and, indeed, the considerations of "best value" that are supposed to determine procurement decisions in some sectors and certainly in public administration. Best value needs to change not only to lowest carbon footprint, but also to machine obsolescence. Computers are notoriously short-lived. Buyers are conflicted in that the efficiency of machines increases with every generation of computer chip, but are the efficiencies sufficient to justify purchase rather than repair? Buyers also need to ask what happens to machines that are decommissioned. How much of an old machine will be recycled? Hence, they need to ask manufacturers and suppliers about the life cycle of machines before purchase.

For a university running far more than 100 desktop computers, this single issue generates a number of dependencies. Table 12.5 details potential implications associated with computer electricity consumption.

Table 12.5: Challenges and opportunities associated with IT electricity consumption.

Issue	Responsibility	Options/challenges
Machines always on	Management – corporate	Policy – computers/monitors/ printers turned off during non-business hours
	IT	Optimize software update scheduling; set all computers/ monitors/printers to shut down during non-business hours
	Estates department	Shut down residual IT equipment during non-business hours
Power efficiency of machines/ replacement schedule	Management – corporate	Policy – procurement of energy-efficient office equipment and optimize replacement cycle
	IT/procurement	Source energy-efficient equipment; establish optimal replacement cycle

Table 12.5 (continued)

Issue	Responsibility	Options/challenges
Trade-off between power efficiency gains from replacement vis-à-vis carbon generated in manufacture of new machines and disposal	Management – corporate	Policy – optimize procurement for carbon efficiency
	IT/procurement	Make calculation and recommendation (other factors may be important, such as declining machine capabilities/software availability)
Sustainability training	Management – school/ corporate	Train all personnel in calculating their work-related CO_2e emissions; train all IT and procurement staff in calculating trade-off values
	Human resources	Provision of training
Carbon offsetting	Management – corporate	Policy on renewable energy sourcing and generation (for example, photovoltaics/wind)
	Estates department	Fitting and maintaining generation capacity

Source: Author's table.

It is possible to imagine the application of Kurt Lewin's model of unfreeze–move–refreeze involving all stakeholders for just this one issue. Instead of taking electricity supply for granted, its value and impact on climate is appreciated by all users (unfreezing). Stakeholders act responsibly by shutting down computers and other associated equipment as a matter of course. The university embeds training and trade-off accounting and life cycle procurement (move). New systems are formalized and normalized (refreeze). The change brought about is positive. It is a group responsibility, understood in the context of the institution and its place in society and participants' interdependencies. The data are shared, evaluated and acted upon (equating with group dynamics/field and action research).

Change of this kind can be managed in a transactional way. For example, rewards/recognition for sustained reductions in electricity consumption attributable to desktop computers or certificates for CO_2 or sustainability training. Arguably, policy made by management is transactional, making it a requirement for those subject to policy to enact. However, the change is conceivably rather more than a discrete policy regarding IT equipment and electricity budgets. All of the interventions can meet their objectives without those making corporate policy and those executing it actually understanding the context of the change, namely global climate change. A thread through this text is that of purpose; do firms (and universities) have a purpose beyond the boundaries of the organization? To what extent does the case of 100 idle desktops contribute to fulfilling the purpose of the firm? That purpose, as seen in the work of Mayer (2018), should embrace not only employees and their families (well-being, education, health, participation, retirement) but society more generally. In an age of climate change, that society is global. With that realization, is change directed in a transactional mode sufficient? Is this how we might understand authenticity and authentic leadership? Finding examples of authentic leadership is difficult; few politicians seem to exhibit it, not least because political systems are transactional (vote for me and you get *X*) or coercive. Firms that retain profit as a purpose do so because shareholders are perceived to require growth as a condition of patronage. The need, therefore, for more democratic structures, embracing stakeholders, is a component of authenticity.

Purpose has another dimension. What if the firm produces or handles products that are known to be carbon-intensive or simply indefensible? How do firms in the following industries mitigate: airline, cement, steel, oil extraction, beef, automobiles, space tourism, armaments? Consider international sporting events such as the Olympics or the football World Cup. On the production side, these events require significant investment in infrastructure, often used only for the duration of the event (despite claims to the contrary and so-called legacy objectives). Building stadiums requires huge volumes of concrete and steel, complex global logistics and, often, unregulated labour. The events themselves generate significant demand for air travel, hotels and hospitality more generally. The athletes also have large entourages. The media bring with them mobile studios and large reporting and editorial teams. Sport more generally is a victim of climate change. Many sports, reported by Overend (2021), are affected by water shortages (golf, cricket), extreme heat (athletics) or insufficient snow (winter sports).

Irrespective of styles, all firms will undertake some form of turnaround relating to climate change in the coming years. It is both an opportunity and a threat. The opportunity is to turn a firm or business unit around with sustainability as the driver. Sustainability should be viewed as the new competitive advantage. However, not all firms should be turned around, especially if that means investments in carbon, that is, the firm will be for the long term dependent on carbon-rich fuels or manufacture products that use such fuels. A turnaround company must be sustainable both from a business perspective and the natural environment, which are increasingly synonymous with each other. It is a logic of capitalism that failed firms should be liquidated and their resources and capabilities reconfigured, dispersed and redeployed. The new logic of capitalist managerialism is environmental sustainability.

Summary

This chapter has discussed change management as an integral part of the implementation of strategy and has illustrated strategy being changed in the process. There are styles of change encompassing methods for readying employees for change and achieving high levels of commitment.

Leaders can be transactional or transformational. They can be charismatic and authentic. The transactional leader provides the incentive based on reward; the authentic leader wins on the power of argument and collective growth. The authentic leader needs time; the transactional leader can overcome time constraints with an arm's length approach to decision-making and compliance.

Change has to embrace cultural difference to the extent that diversity actually makes change easier. Diverse organizations have employees who can understand different approaches and incorporate them.

The management focus for change for sustainability, however, should eschew instrumental profit objectives. Not because profit is unimportant, but because climate change requires firms to mitigate and adapt if there is to be a viable future for an enterprise. The change can be incremental, radical or, indeed, involve closure where environmental sustainability cannot be achieved. There is a convergence on the meaning of sustainability in the lexicon of strategy; the economic and environmental have the same meaning.

Business strategy in the future is getting out of unsustainable activities and reducing carbon emissions. Turnaround is to offer cradle-to-cradle products that are serviceable, and when they cease to be so, to take them back for re-use, recycling or disposal. This is the focus of the next chapter.

Questions

1. What is the relationship between Lewin's three-step model and his *field theory, group dynamics* concept and the method of *action research*?
2. In which of Kotter's eight-steps is there likely to be overlap and parallel working?
3. What behaviour is expected of employees when they behave instrumentally? What are they trying to achieve?
4. What is the role of communication in creating "readiness for change"?
5. In what circumstances would you, as a strategic business manager, be transactional in your style? How would the style be practised?
6. In what ways does culture affect or determine approaches to change management?
7. Why do countries with high *Uncertainty Avoidance* scores have more doctors relative to nurses? Why do people in Uncertainty Avoiding societies drive fast on motorways? Would they not be expected to drive slower to avoid accidents?
8. How do firms in the following industries mitigate: airline, cement, steel, oil extraction, beef, automobiles, space tourism?
9. What is a carbon conversion rate and where would you find the current rate?
10. Consider your own consumption of electricity. How would you calculate your own CO_2e score? How would you know if it was high or low?

Chapter 13
Turnaround and monitoring

In the previous chapter, the mechanics of the firms were revealed to be much more human than prescriptive models of strategic analysis portray them. It is human agency, personality, perception and leadership that bring about the change. The further away from the decision the analyst or executive managers get, the more dependent firms become on the people doing the work, such as managers, teams and operatives. Engendering a *belief* in the project and communicating with a compelling narrative the need for change for individuals, their colleagues and their communities is important where change is not coercive. It is this *belief* that is at the heart of successful business turnarounds, and it is human creativity that determines the indicators, measures and targets that not only deliver the turnaround but deliver it on a footing of business and environmental sustainability.

This chapter:

- examines the concept and practice of turnaround
- explores the balanced scorecard as a strategy implementation, monitoring and improvement tool

Turnaround

Consider the following scenario: the post-Covid-19 economy will lead managers to seek to turnaround the fortunes of their firms and adjust to the new reality – for example, ubiquitous home working, online markets, different/less retail, changed personal consumption habits and less travel. Firms have taken on additional debt and restructured in order to stay solvent against the backdrop of considerable uncertainty about when, and if, there will be some return to normal consumption habits, dependent as it is on an unpredictable and uncontrollable virus and its mutations. Post-war strategy thinking has been based on being able to control for environmental factors (increasingly firms react to such factors).

There will be many firms subject to turnaround in the coming years. In retail, for example, pre-Covid-19, there had already been a shift in shopping habits away from physical outlets to online. The lockdowns, reduced mobility imposed by governments because of Covid-19, has made that shift more pronounced and possibly permanent.

Turnaround is a process of stopping and reversing the decline of a firm's financial performance over multiple years. The need for turnaround arises from declining revenues and decreasing competitiveness due to a high cost base and/or products and services whose value propositions diminish; they become less relevant (for example, fashion) or are disrupted. The primary aims are to avoid bankruptcy and to recover. The severity of the decline often determines the speed with which turnaround is enacted.

https://doi.org/10.1515/9783110718430-013

Trahms et al. (2013) detail the turnaround challenges for managers as:
- improvement in performance despite fewer resources
- managing stakeholder challenges, particularly core stakeholders whose interests are most directly threatened
- operating with reduced discretion and more monitoring and scrutiny by boards, creditors, bondholders, banks and suppliers

(p. 1278)

Pearce and Robbins (1993) isolated two phases for turnaround. These are retrenchment and recovery.

Retrenchment

Retrenchment is largely operational where firms (strategic business units/subsidiaries) look to reduce the cost base in the form of competitive sourcing, reduced research and development spend, headcount reduction and asset disposal, among others. All of these options bring their own challenges. Reduced research and development spend can lead to less innovation and less attractive products, services or effective processes. Asset disposal requires very careful evaluation. Portfolio management in good times can lead to inappropriate divestment; for example, a subsidiary or business unit that seemed to be a "dog" on paper actually contributed much more to the rest of the corporate entity than just sales.

Some managers look to delay payments to creditors including suppliers. The ethics of this should be unacceptable to responsible business managers for two reasons: first, late or delayed payment impacts on creditors who may also be suppliers; it is not a cost-free option. Second, late or delayed payment to managers' own firms may be a contributory factor to the need to turnaround in the first place. Firms that have adopted a stakeholder approach to managing would be breaching those principles in doing so. In the longer term, this may be detrimental to a firm that is successfully turned around. This phenomenon, however, can be managed through supply-chain payment intermediaries; though as the Greensill case in the UK illustrates (Leaver 2021), this has the potential for abuse when anticipated receipts (payments) are used to access further borrowing.

Some costs are so-called *low-hanging fruit*, such as employee allowances, company cars, sports facilities, and travel more generally. Some costs, however, are harder to address. They may have legacy causes, such as insufficient investment leading to ageing IT systems, inefficient operations due to antiquated plant or insufficiently integrated supply chains. Many firms have been turned around by outsourcing their non-core activities. For example, in the first half of the twentieth century, automobile manufacturers were vertically integrated, manufacturing and supplying components and materials to themselves. The arrival of Toyota in the post-war period, with its lean manufacturing and tiered approach to supply and suppliers, became the industry model (Womack et al. 1990). Toyota's manufacturing approach was a major shock and challenge to the European and American automobile manufacturers unable to match the cost-base, prices and reliability – a winning trinity.

The boards of declining firms may, additionally, decide that the existing management is a cause. The reasons can be external and/or internal:
- External: the management team fails to anticipate changes to the business environment and hence act to mitigate them in the case of threats or exploit them in the case of opportunities
- Internal: the management fails to update and maintain internal processes, structures and technology

The board of directors may decide that a new management team should be recruited. A new management team may also make it easier to manage core stakeholders whose power base (control of resources) was granted by the existing management. A new management coming into a firm in decline will expect suitable compensation (salary) for reputational damage that might occur if not successful. Moreover, a new management team's compensation and overall pay should be linked to appropriate turnaround indicators. For example, if a rising share price is an indicator of turnaround success, the management team will target the factors that raise share prices but not the prospects for the firm overall: they may initiate share buybacks, asset divestment or removing organizational slack, all of which treat symptoms rather than causes and can be detrimental to any recovery.

Conversely, it may be that the board is the cause. Executive boards can act as an echo chamber where a single perspective is merely reproduced and reinforced. Failures in the banking system leading to the crisis of 2008 in the UK have been linked to poor executive decision-making and governance, though insufficiently to demonstrate negligence in corporate law (Moore 2017). Non-executive board members, with their remit to ask difficult questions, can lead to the external and internal factors being addressed sooner. Ethnic and gender diversity also affects firm performance, resulting from both strategic decision-making and effective oversight (Erhardt et al. 2003).

Recovery

Recovery is a strategic act where firms have undertaken retrenchment to build a future either with existing or new products, processes or markets. Strategic turnaround may result in mergers, acquisitions and alliances (Morrow et al. 2007) as firms seek to access resources and capabilities in preparation for future business growth.

The Lego company diversified beyond its core competence and suffered major losses in the early part of the 2000s. The company diversified through a wholly owned and managed chain of theme parks. The understandable, but ultimately flawed, logic of this venture was exposed when the company realized that the management of theme parks was a capability that a manufacturer of plastic bricks does not have. When the company underwent turnaround under its McKinsey-trained CEO, Jørgen Vig Knudstorp, the theme parks were sold (though retaining a minority stake). Observers indicated that Lego was perhaps unconsciously transforming into a lifestyle company producing watches, clothes and videogames (Schumpeter 2014). Lego had also diversified into feature films. While this was not in itself an incompatible idea, the approach taken was strategically misaligned. Instead of leveraging the company's own intellectual property (IP), it partnered with other IP holders – Star Wars and Harry Potter – who retained much of the value when the revenue was accounted for. In the turnaround, Lego returned to making films under its own brand, Brick Films.

Eventually, Lego diversified into new markets, leveraging the important and founding principle of the company, namely, that the product has educational value. In Asia's developing economies, Lego was seen as an educational toy, one that developed cognitive skills and distracted from video games. This new global approach required major structural changes to the Lego business, with manufacturing shifting to low-cost countries including China, Hungary and Mexico and away from its home base, Billund, Denmark. Half of the workforce in the town lost their jobs as a result (*The Economist* 2006).

More positively, turnaround provides an opportunity for firms to highlight indicators of value for sustainability not just share prices and returns. For example, many of the benefits of strategy based on sustainability are intangible; they relate to brand enhancement, product quality, product reliability, reusability or recyclability and social improvements such as mental or physical health. These are quantifiable but rarely quantified. The opportunity is for firms to detail in their annual and/or sustainability reports the added value these amount to. On the former, measures like net present sustainable value (NPSV) can be used; on the latter, Social Return on Investment (SROI) measures.

The recovery stage may involve trading in unfamiliar territories and require management approaches aligned with entry mode. Whatever mode, managers will be confronted by cultural difference.

Monitoring – the balanced scorecard (BSC) and the sustainability balanced scorecard (SBSC)

The balanced scorecard (Kaplan and Norton 1992) was designed to be an operational monitoring tool, but was quickly taken up by CEOs as a whole strategic management system. As such, it links a firm's long-term strategic objectives with its short-term, operational, actions. Kaplan and Norton found that firms often experienced a gap between a vision – for example, "to be no. 1 in the sector" – and the ability to translate that into action. Moreover, firms measure performance largely through their financial performance with indicators such as profit, turnover, net cash flow, P/E ratios, return on capital and operating costs. These are insufficient for managers' day-to-day decision-making. Managers ask, what factors impact on a daily or weekly basis on financial performance? Is it broader than just making and selling?

The balanced scorecard had the bridging capability when applied strategically. As the name suggests, the tool balances functions within an organization with measures and indicators that can be used to improve performance over the longer term. To implement the balanced scorecard, the firm's vision needs to be expressed and understood by all stakeholders. This requires regular communication and reinforcement. Different managers and personnel make different interpretations that potentially causes inconsistencies in actions across an organization. What is balance? What is a scorecard?

Balance

There are four linked and dynamic perspectives to the balance. To translate the vision into strategy, the management identify and make explicit a firm's (1) objectives, (2) measures. (3) targets and (4) initiatives. This can be summarized as:
- Financial – managers ask how does succeeding financially "appear" to shareholders? What objectives, measures, targets and initiatives give the right appearance or are expected by shareholders?
- Business process – in satisfying the needs of shareholders and customers, what are the business processes necessary and in which the firm should excel?
- Customers – what is the right "appearance" to customers in delivering on the vision and strategy?
- Learning and growth – the vision relies on constant change and improvement. How is that achieved and sustained?

At the time that Kaplan and Norton were writing (1996), the Internet was not a significant operational factor. Many firms scripted company visions around customers and service, for example, "to provide superior service to targeted customers". While this is a simple vision, it defines neither "superior" nor "targeted". It assumes that the current levels of service give, at best, competitive parity and not sustained competitive advantage (using the language of Barney and the VRIO framework).

The word "targeted" can be interpreted in a number of ways. It is helpful to be clear and to share the meaning across the firm. Are some customers more important than others, perhaps because they are long-standing, regular and buy premium products? Is it that the product is niche and sales efforts should be focused on a certain class of customer? Or maybe it is a new product and, in order to develop acceptance and diffusion, innovators or early adopters should be targeted?

Given thought and communication, it is possible to determine the objectives, measures, targets and initiatives for such a vision. Superior, for example, could anticipate guaranteed deliveries, discounts, tailored products, installation, warranties and regular check-ins. In the Internet age, these might be through digital applications. To provide superior service, business processes may need to change or adapt to link the delivery of what is defined as superior service for customers. Internal systems, for example, should identify the targeted customers, enable tailored products, employ installers or manage contractors to do so and enhance product quality in order to issue warranties. These will have cost implications and should be revealed to customers. Equally, employees should be receptive to the behaviour of customers and change accordingly. Change may have implications throughout an organization; this means that change initiatives have to be understood and not impact on other parts of the firm, to the detriment of the firm's performance overall.

In regard to the financial perspective of the balance, these changes will need to show improvement in performance and be reported to the shareholders at meetings or through reporting. Hence, the balance requires careful and thoughtful management. The perspectives are linked and interdependent. Effectively, all employees need to know and understand the corporate or business strategy, the vision that informs it, the indicators, what constitute realistic targets, incentives for meeting them or sanctions for not doing so and initiatives needed to perform sustainably at a higher level.

Scorecards

Scorecards are visual checklists that contain performance data matched against a target. For example, businesses have customer-focused targets such as meeting an on-time delivery commitment (when the customer expects to receive the product) in 95 per cent of cases. Over a week, the scorecard will show all orders, when they were dispatched and confirmed receipt. From those data, it is possible to ascertain whether the target has been met and how often. If it is not met, an initiative to contact customers who will not receive their products on time could be taken or an investigation into the causes with distributors or couriers. These are potentially wholly new business processes.

Other measures might include: reducing customer churn, that is, a one-off purchase vis-à-vis returning customers; recording customer complaints in absolute numbers and in how quickly they are dealt with; and customer satisfaction/needs through an electronic survey.

Some of these indicators and measures are leading: was the delivery on time (yes/no)? Some are lag: was the customer satisfied? Did the product have to be returned? Lag indicators can take some time to be recorded through surveys or physical receipt of the returned product. The design of the scorecard would reflect the temporal element.

Scorecard checklist

- What is being monitored?
- What is the target?
- What is the indicator?
- Is it leading or lag?
- What is the timeframe – daily, weekly, monthly, all?

Linking balance and score

The components of the balance – financial, customers, business processes and learning and growth – can be reported separately. But the enhanced value overall is in comes from synthesis both dynamically and in line with firm strategy. In the case of meeting delivery commitments, this would be recorded in the customer component of the balance. In meeting the target, there would be a positive impact on revenue and cashflow. Not meeting the target would have a negative impact. The scorecard reveals by what margin the target is missed. The solution may require a new business process. If the issue is one of product quality, then rework is undertaken, which is an additional operating cost that managers would seek to eliminate. Having products that are constantly returned because of failure may have an impact on morale, affecting learning and growth, or it may be a source of employee suggestions on how to limit failures such as a revised quality system, initiating a business-process change. For as long as the scorecard delivers data that inform the performance of the firm's strategy or strategies, to meet the vision, a virtuous circle is created: employees are happy as they are rewarded for success, executives can report yearly financial improvements, customers benefit from efforts to exceed targets and the organization itself learns and improves. These links are part of a value system, largely within the firm, but external core stakeholders are captured.

The balanced scorecard: Sustainability and climate

The balanced scorecard is managerialist and transactional in its design and use. Incentives are used to motivate both executives and operatives alike. Its purpose is to marry optimal efficiency and improve margins and/or volumes. It assumes clear cause-and-effect. Climate and sustainability do not ordinarily feature. To address this, so-called sustainability balanced scorecards (SBSCs) have been developed (Hansen and Schaltegger 2016). These SBSCs retain Kaplan and Norton's original architectural framework, while incorporating sustainability goals because, ultimately, they *impact* positively on profit and revenue. There are alternative perspectives whereby sustainability is viewed in terms of ethics and hence impose additional costs on firms without a return, something that Kaplan and Norton's balanced score-card avoided.

One way of reconciling this is for the firm to adopt accounting practices that incorporate six, rather than three, capitals (Gleeson-White 2020). Firms have traditionally reported on three capitals: physical, human and finance. The modern sustainability, climate and global equity agendas have reconfigured these capitals and extended them. These are captured in Table 13.1.

Table 13.1: The six capitals.

Capital	Description
Financial	funds available to the firm/organization to produce goods or provide services
Manufactured	capital products used in manufacture or provision of services, such as plant and equipment, buildings, roads, waste and water treatment plants
Intellectual	intangibles that are knowledge-based, including systems, protocols, patents, copyrights, software and licences – *these belong to the firm*
Human	skills, abilities, intelligence, know-how, health, productivity from an organization's people. Additionally, their support for vision and strategy, leadership and collaboration – *these belong to the individual person*
Relationship	Institutions and relationships within and between communities, stakeholder groups and other networks; additionally, trust, brand, reputation, shared norms, common values and behaviour – *these belong to networks of humans*
Natural	Renewable and non-renewable resources that enable firms to create goods and services. These include the commons of air, water, minerals, forests, biodiversity and ecosystems – *these belong to the planet and its inhabitants*

Source: Author's table, derived from Gleeson-White (2020). The six capitals are drawn from the International Integrated Reporting Council (IIRC).

There are other methods. Many firms advocate the triple-bottom-line (Elkington 1997) as a relatively mature framework. Whichever approach is taken, the importance is in the fact that they:
- allow for sustainability objectives to be pursued while not impacting negatively on the financial perspective
- retain a cause-and-effect link between scorecard indicators and the balance perspectives

Profit maximizers will incorporate sustainability measures only if they impact directly and positively on performance. Under the six capitals approach, profit-maximizers would have to capture all externalities. Puma, a sports apparel firm, has, for example, made these calculations. Not-for-profit organizations, family-owned businesses or cooperatives are likely to take a broader view on performance because they may also have a social purpose.

In retaining the original purpose and integrity, in order for climate to be incorporated, at least three fundamentals need to be in place:

1. Environmental sustainability, mitigation and firm adaptation need to be strategic objectives
2. Sustainability should become a source of competitive advantage in the firm's industry and markets
3. Un-costed externalities need to be subject to fines and penalties that affect negatively on the financial component of the balance

If (3) is absent, the firm could impose one on itself. While that might imply a competitive disadvantage, there is no future for firms that do not mitigate. It is for responsible enterprises to address sustainability challenges. At the very least, the fines would act as an indicator of the extent to which the firm is breaching planetary boundaries.

With regard to using the balanced scorecard, the balance element of the scorecard can remain unmodified if sustainability is a strategic objective; it will then be a factor of all perspectives. Alternatively, a new perspective of sustainability is created alongside the existing four, namely, financial, customers, business processes and learning and growth. Adding sustainability as a perspective is not as effective as it first seems. It is possible to apportion only limited measures to it or even remove it without affecting performance if it proves inconvenient. Integrating sustainability measures across all perspectives is likely to be more effective. Crucially, practitioners must ensure that the measures do not simply justify *business-as-usual*. With this in mind, Table 13.2 shows how a scorecard might be constructed:

Table 13.2: Sustainability scorecard.

Target	Measures	Score	Initiatives
Financial			
	Earnings		
	Net cash flow		
	Operating costs		
	Production costs		
	Costs arising from externalities		Active carbon emissions trading (scope 1)

Table 13.2 (continued)

Target	Measures	Score	Initiatives
	Net mitigation earnings contributing to the country meeting nationally determined Contributions (NDCs under Paris Agreement, 2015)		Photovoltaic cells on roofs Savings on grid purchases Sales into grid Utility costs (scope 2)
	Savings arising from adaptation		Reduced insurance premium; reduced heating and cooling costs
Customer			
Within three days	Delivery time	2 days	Quality partnership with couriers/ distributors
One to five (range)	Customer satisfaction	4	Survey questionnaire to all customers within two days of delivery
80%/20%	Returning/new customers	84%/16%	Check-in trigger for converting new customers to returning customers and returning customers to premium customers
<5pc	Product returns due to quality	4%	Hypothesize cause and test before implementing improvement
Business Process			
90%	Use of recycled materials for manufacture	91%	Source materials from regenerative suppliers
10%	Shorten supply-chain shipping distances	8%	Source materials from suppliers closer to production
30%	Reuse of materials	25%	Repurpose materials from own life-expired products
80%	Successful repairs to product within life cycle	85%	Design to be repaired/upgraded within product life cycle
90%	End-of-life disposal	95%	Safe disposal of end-of-life products returned by customers in line with contract
50%	Percentage of distribution achieved without using liquid carbon fuels	60%	Own fleet of electric vehicles; supply chain leadership in carbon mitigation (scope 3)
<5%	Sick days as a percentage of total employee days lost	4%	Employee welfare scheme

Table 13.2 (continued)

Target	Measures	Score	Initiatives
<4%	Unscheduled down time	5%	Regular maintenance of plant and installation of electronic fault monitoring
85%	Plant utilization (capacity)	96%	Contracting out excess capacity
98%	Supplier reliability – meeting orders within agreed parameters for lean production	93%	Establish cause of delays; work with supplier to improve reliability (stakeholder approach); impose penalty clause (transactional)
Learning and growth			
95%	Employee satisfaction score		Annual survey
15%	Reduced employee churn		"Great place to work" campaign
20%	Fewer days lost to sickness		Healthy working environment and fitness promotion
At least five days per year	Employee training		Individual training contracts
15% per year	Growth in non-meat purchases from restaurants		Vegetarian food promotions
85%	Percentage of coffee purchased in reusable cups		Cup sale/promotion
10% per year	Reduction in paper waste		On-screen working, collaborative software, fewer printers
35% per year	Reductions in plastic waste		Sustainable procurement policy

Source: Author's table, derived from Kaplan and Norton (1992).

Summary

Firms often find themselves needing to enter turnaround arising from a changed industry, environment, market or sustained pressure on business activities due to external factors such as a global pandemic or natural environmental factors in the form of drought or flood. Firm respond through retrenchment actions, including cost control, selling non-core assets and moving out of unprofitable activities, and recovery involving refocusing on brand and products and exploiting core competences. In the age of climate change, turnaround is an opportunity to move away from activities that breach carbon emissions targets and eventually become unjustifiable costs.

Having implemented a turnaround programme, firms are likely to monitor the programme and improve. Tools such as the balanced scorecard are ideal for this as it has both operational and strategic utility. Performance can be developed through both new targets and activities designed to enable them to be met or exceeded. In the context of climate change, the balanced scorecard can be extended to include initiatives to reduce the firm's impact on depletion of natural capital, which, at some point in the future arising from obligations under the Paris Agreement of 2015, will likely be prudent financially.

Questions

1. Using the case of either a firm with which you are familiar, Lego, or an example from the companion resources, describe and justify initiatives that are categorized as retrenchment and recovery. Did they succeed? What were the implications?
2. In cases where turnaround was taken as an opportunity to put the firm on a sustainability footing, which initiatives can inform both retrenchment and recovery? Use a firm with which you are familiar or provide a hypothetical example.
3. Create a scorecard with sustainability measures in each element – financial, customer, business processes and learning and growth – for a firm in one of the following industries: supermarkets, low-cost airlines, fast food, fast fashion, smartphones.

Chapter 14
Scenarios: Do nothing, adapt or build a new vibrant and sustainable economy

Strategy, as understood, is about making a future. In the context of business strategy, it is about making a future for a firm that meets agreed objectives. In whose interests those objectives are set, is a political decision. Shareholders are privileged stakeholders, but increasingly, businesses are having to incorporate a wider stakeholder community because of law or pressure. Firms can do nothing and fail. They can adapt to what is known about doing business on a warming planet, or they can embrace change, decarbonize, innovate and prosper.

Strategy is an opportunity. Undoubtedly there are many variables to manage, and historically, strategists have viewed the discipline as one of controlling the environment in which firms operate and making decisions in conditions of relative predictability. As humanity moves through the first part of the twenty-first century, the world has become less predictable in the strategy sense – though it is safe to predict that the future is different again and possibly more extreme politically, economically, and in terms of climate. Strategists and business leaders have an opportunity to embrace this change or persist with controlling external factors and homogenizing the internal forces – business processes, products, services and people. This book has sought to provide students of strategy with a deeper knowledge of the tools of strategy and how they can be leveraged for a different, unpredictable but fairer future. The tools of strategy, like a good constitution in a successful state, are robust and can be upgraded, augmented and repositioned. The future does not need to be revolutionary, but it does need to be radical.

This chapter considers:
- the shipping container and corporate strategy
- how firms can reposition themselves, not competitively, but by purpose
- the caveats to prescriptive strategic analysis and decision-making: history-culture; culture-chance
- introduces the fork-in-the-road metaphor to illustrate the window of opportunity for sustainability-driven by business strategy
- summarizes how the tools of strategy can be leveraged for sustainability
- revisits the question: what is strategy?

The shipping container – how it changed the twentieth century

The shipping container is strategic analysis, choice and implementation all rolled into one. Its history runs parallel with that of the academic discipline of strategy (business strategy existed prior to academic books on the subject). Some of the most familiar firms in the contemporary economy have succeeded by squeezing costs, managing regulation, lobbying, side-lining labour and avoiding payment of taxes. In doing this, a number of the themes of strategy can be called upon: product and business-model innovation, diversification, managing for stakeholders, emergent and deliberate strategy.

https://doi.org/10.1515/9783110718430-014

Short of the adoption of steam as the motive force for the Industrial Revolution (Malm 2016), the shipping container was arguably the single most transformative innovation for twentieth-century business. Its history is chronicled by Levinson (2016). It was not some immediate lightbulb thought; it came about through a process. It did not come from a shipping business, rather from a trucker named Malcolm Purcell McLean. He was self-made and started out by transporting his own fuel to a filling station he managed in North Carolina, USA. He initially borrowed money from family to increase his fleet and then built a significant relationship with what became Citibank to leverage expansion and takeovers. At that time in the late 1940s, the state regulated transport routes by means of the Interstate Commerce Commission. It was not possible to transport goods in one direction across state boundaries and take another load back. McLean had to buy operators with rights over the routes without falling foul of anti-trust (competition) regulations.

McLean ran a very tight business; he was a cost-leader and his prices reflected that. He provided financial incentives for his truckers to drive carefully to minimize the costs associated with accidents. He facilitated drivers to buy their own trucks and work exclusively for him. He converted trucks from gasoline to diesel. Drivers were given precise route instructions, usually the shortest and most efficient. He made a deal with fuel retailers on the routes to achieve discounts. He streamlined the design of trucks to reduce drag and hence fuel costs.

At that time inter-state highways were limited, and they became too congested for efficient trucking. McLean had the idea to put trailers on ships to move them from North Carolina to New York, avoiding the roads and saving on fuel costs. Coastal shipping, however, was also much cheaper because it was slower. To enter the shipping business, he had to find a way around the law restricting ownership of different modes, in this case road haulage and shipping. He innovated financial tools by leveraging a buyout through a new family-controlled company to take over a shipping company, Sea Land, with operating rights along the East Coast of the USA. On taking control, he sold the non-core assets, including a hotel and a dry dock, among others, to service the debt and to ensure that the diversification was focused, that is, the company did not enter additional markets in which it had neither experience nor synergies.

McLean's original idea to put the trailers on ships was not adopted because, in true cost-leader style, he calculated the waste associated with the wheels. They took up a lot of space and prevented the trailers from being stacked. The solution was a box with dimensions perfectly matching those of the ships. Loading and unloading required innovations around cranes and cooperation with port owners, many of whom were keen to accommodate McLean's inter-modal operation. The operation needed safety clearance – the containers had to be fixed in the ship so as not to destabilize it and to be safe for the men working on the ships. This was 1956. He patented the fixings on the containers. The idea of containers had been around for at least twenty years. However, investment was hard to come by. McLean made the investment – and so, the shipping container revolution started.

In this case, students of strategy can see emergent strategy typical of the entrepreneur: "Let me try this", "Who will lend me money without security?" and "What if trailers go onto ships?" As the business grew in size and volume, more deliberate strategy was adopted in the form of acquisitions and getting around regulations. McLean's mindset was always about beating the competition on cost. To do that, however, he had to engage with a range of stakeholders, most notably regulators and banks. On the former, McLean outflanked them by innovating ahead and at pace. Regulators were always catching up.

Growth was not organic because organic growth did not give access to routes. It was much better to acquire, which is where the banks enter the story. McLean's trucking company was highly in debt. Again, he innovated around a leveraged buyout of a shipping firm having convinced sceptical bank executives that he could service the debt. He also worked closely with suppliers. Crucially he found a container maker willing to design and manufacture for the enterprise. He also engaged port-owners who had seen their volumes decline in the post-war period. Labour costs at ports were in the order of 40 per cent of the overall value of the shipment. The container could reduce that drastically by mechanization (fewer men needed) and turning around ships faster. The first experiments could turn around a ship in a day rather than a week. Every problem solved opened up further opportunities. The McLean approach was disjointed, on the hoof and executed by a man with self-belief. He was transactional, as was his approach to change. McClean delivered a firm-specific containerization. There were no international standards at that time; the standards setting agencies had to catch up.

On the West Coast of the United States was another freight conglomerate with a wholly different approach. The Matson Navigation Company was a family-owned transportation and sugar conglomerate. The family appointed an external president, veteran John E. Cushing, who took a very scientific approach to containerization. Cushing brought in a university professor to consider holistically the business of containers, from the containers themselves, their loading, fitting, hauling, lifting, to the ships that would carry them and the trucks that would haul them. To use Levinson's words, "Matson moved deliberately. Pan Atlantic [Sea Land's original name], under McLean's control, was a scrappy upstart building a brand-new business, and it risked little by acting quickly" (2016, p. 80).

The result was the same, though neither company set the standard; that was a negotiated process with a large number of international stakeholders including: the International Standards Organization (ISO), the American Standards Association (ASA), the National Defense Transportation Association (NDTA) and the United States Maritime Administration (MARAD). These locked horns with the transportation firms and manufacturers of trailers such as Fruehauf – still a familiar European name – Strick Trailers and the National Castings Company. It was not until 1967 that the final global standards were agreed; though two years earlier the stakeholders did agree standards for fittings only to find that their haste omitted necessary real-world testing. A global standard has to work globally and be robust. Haste is often a false economy.

Standards

While the story of the shipping container demonstrates many of the features of deliberate and emergent strategy, it also makes clear that no single actor can dominate, or if such a firm does, then it is a failure of government and regulation/anti-trust. There is a plurality (Dahl 1961).

To be able to control the de facto standard is valuable. The machine on which this manuscript was written relies on a de facto operating system standard that was determined by the market rather than a regulator and is closely linked to the fortunes of the originating firm. However, markets need regulation to stay fair and competitive and for firms within them to innovate. They are not self-correcting or self-regulating. Market failure leads to exclusion, monopoly profits and extraction. Arguably, there is market failure in so-called big tech where a few platforms dominate the information and social media markets. They can influence political debate and impact on democratic decisions (for example, Cambridge Analytica). What to do about such situations is political – the P in PESTEL.

There is a market failure with respect to the climate. While carbon has a price and is tradable, the question remains as to whether the market price is too low to affect the ongoing extraction and burning of carbon fuels and to compensate for the damage caused. The market failure is in the unpriced external costs of carbon emissions. The European Union has a carbon trading system; it sets a cap and emitters unable to meet their obligations buy permits in the market from other actors that are in credit, hence creating a market. Where caps are low, permits are scarce, and therefore the price rises. Emitting without a permit leads to a fine that is higher than the price of a permit. The question as to whether the market sets the correct price – one that reflects the damaged caused by the emissions – is recognized. At the time of writing, the price for 1 tonne of CO_2e is €56.26 (Ember 2021). There is a rough consensus on what the price should be. For example, the World Bank's Carbon Pricing Leadership Coalition "concludes that the explicit carbon-price level consistent with achieving the Paris Agreement temperature target is at least US$40–80/tCO$_2$ by 2020 and US$50–100/tCO2 by 2030, provided a supportive policy environment is in place". Poelhekke (2019) sets the price at US$77 (€63). However, there has been a catch; transportation and utilities have been given free permits. Should these end as proposed, the implications for consumers may be considerable (Inman 2021).

The shipping container plays a significant role in climate change. The box, with its international standardization and diffusion, facilitated a globalized production economy, one in which manufactured goods are manufactured many thousands of kilometres away from where they are consumed. The seeming "costlessness" of container shipping made products affordable to increasing numbers of people at the expense of sustainability. This is an ethical question. Why should the products of modern society not be affordable to the masses? Unfortunately, mass consumption has become unsustainably extractive. Moreover, the emissions from production are accounted for, but those generated by shipping in international waters are not. Container ships using dirty fuels are huge GHG emitters. The EU reports (European Commission 2021) that shipping emits "940 million tonnes of CO_2 annually and is responsible for about 2.5% of global greenhouse gas (GHG) emissions".

Malcolm McLean was clear about the purpose of his firm – to make money. He took on risk and was rewarded financially for doing so. In every sense, he ran a tight ship. His employees were under no illusion about the purpose of the firm and their contribution to meeting that purpose. Levinson (2016) records that some of the younger managers employed by McLean found the pace and pressure exhilarating. The question remains as to whether the purpose of the firm is as McLean defined it.

The purpose of the firm

The de facto purpose of the firm in the Anglo-Saxon world is profit maximization. It has become the widespread belief that this is written into law, and any attempt at adopting strategies that deviates from this sole task is unlawful. This is, however, not the case. Meagher (2020), a former competition lawyer, provides a useful history of the firm and the profit imperative. She argues that it was the depression and oil shocks of the 1970s that elevated and normalized the work and ideas of Milton Friedman and the Chicago School. That period had badly dented the performance of firms, and global competition was also starting to squeeze profit margins. Labour unions (stakeholders) were seen as part of the problem and executives sought to break free of responsibilities beyond making money and profit. With executives as shareholders, the incentive to focus on profit was real – through stock options, bonuses, increasing remuneration, etc.

However, earlier, in 1919, stockholders at the Ford Motor Company had gone to court to test the idea of their primacy and won. Executives and managers can decide how to maximize profit, not whether to. In the UK, this was clarified when, in 1992, a court declared that a board of trustees of a charity set up to enable the Church of England to finance the stipends for clergy must invest to maximize return at the expense of ethical investment. This was enshrined in law in the Companies Act of 2006. However, in section 172, the profit maximization requirement is couched in terms relating to directors "promoting the success of the company . . . for the benefit of its members as a whole". More importantly, directors can "have regard to" factors such as stakeholder interests (employees, suppliers and community) and also the environment, standards of business conduct and fairness (Meagher 2020, p. 102).

The notion of "having regard to" other factors might entail firms amending their legal articles of association as B-Corps have done. In fact, the concept of the B-Corp has changed US corporate law. In order for B-Corps to have legal status it was necessary for US state legislatures to grant them rights to prioritize non-financial capital over others, namely, natural or human. The first states to do this were Maryland and Vermont in 2010. Delaware enacted its law in 2013. This was an important milestone because it is the state of incorporation for US businesses. More broadly, unless firms' articles of association are reconfigured, directors will bias shareholder wealth and value because that is the overriding purpose of the firm as specified. Deviation may still be subject to legal challenge.

The purpose of the firm as currently practised assumes that shareholders are the owners of companies. Meagher (2020, pp. 104–105) challenges this idea. In line with previous thinking about stakeholders, companies may be actors in their own right. A shareholding is not an indicator of ownership (or part-ownership); rather it is merely a legal recognition of a stake, though with limited (liability) legal rights. Companies actually own themselves. Shareholders can sell their shares (stake), but not the company (Stout 2013). Moreover, if they were owners, should the firm fail, shareholders would be liable for more than just the loss of their shares. Because of the invention of the so-called limited liability, they are not. They are protected from the full impact of the firm's failure. Stout argues that even where executives have duties to meet profit targets, they can satisfice; that is

> [w]hen managers are allowed to satisfice, they can retain earnings to invest in safety procedures, marketing, and research and development that contribute to future growth. They can eschew leverage that threatens the firm's stability. They can keep commitments that build customer and employee loyalty. They can protect their shareholders' interests as employees, taxpayers and consumers by declining to outsource jobs, lobby for tax loopholes, or produce dangerous products. Finally, they can respect the desires of their prosocial shareholders by trying to run the firm in a socially and environmentally responsible fashion.

The concept of satisficing is drawn from the work of Simon (1996), where a satisficer is "a person who accepts a 'good enough' alternative, not because less is preferred to more but because there is no choice" (p. 29). By this he means that even processes that seem straightforward are in actual fact complex. There are "unknowables", and human decision-making is beyond optimization, even if we knew what that meant. Though against the backdrop of a complex and unknowable system of climate change, satisficing may be the best that society has as a guiding principle.

In discussing prescriptive methods of strategy development, it appears that there is a formula for successful – even optimal – strategy making. There are a series of steps and analyses to be performed. Do so with rigour and application, goes the argument, and success will follow. Stakeholder management concepts have revealed a wide range of stakeholders holding or acquiring resources and power. This power can effectively derail the most carefully planned and executed business strategy and stakeholder management approaches.

There are caveats to prescriptive strategy development. Three mutually exclusive caveats are worthy of note: history-culture, culture-chance.

History-culture

Probably everyone knows someone who owns a Samsung smartphone. It may – or may not – be known that Samsung is a Korean firm. It may be a revelation that Samsung started as a vegetable shop supplying the Chinese region of Manchuria, then (1937) the focus of the Japanese war effort. Some may know that Samsung translates as *three stars* "symbolizing the big, the many and the strong" (Samsung founder, B. C. Lee, quoted in Cain 2020, p. 34).

What is probably not known is that Samsung is not a conglomerate, despite its many subsidiaries; it was modelled on the Japanese pre-war family Zaibatsu, translated in modern Korean as Chaebol. The company's patriarch, B. C. Lee, made many compromises with a succession of military leaders (post-Korean war) to develop the company in the country's rapid industrialization. Samsung is part of the DNA of the Korean state. Its success is not explicable by some prescriptive strategy. Diversification into computer micro-chips in 1983 is unlikely to have passed any prescriptive strategy test; it would fail when opened to scrutiny. Cain (2020) reveals how Samsung entered licensing negotiations with the US chip maker, Micron. As a starting point, Samsung employees were shown technical diagrams – in essence the intellectual property of Micron. However, the Samsung people had photographic memories and later faithfully reproduced the diagrams they had seen.

Samsung Semiconductor corporation lost a lot of money in its first years. It was supported by state aid and transfers from profitable parts of Samsung – two things that were not possible in Western economies at that time. Cain (2020, p. 56) sums up viz:

> Samsung's success wasn't about sales, operations, economic policies, and bottom lines. It was a story of patriotism and spirit. Samsung tapped into the feelings, emotion and sense of belonging that South Koreans experienced. It understood the human need to be part of something great, something bigger than oneself; it offered Koreans the promise of glory.

Culture-chance

Honda is a household name. It has a core competence in engines. Its engines are found in cars, motorbikes, boats and lawnmowers. Honda had an international strategy for its motorbikes; accessing the US market was prioritized. Mintzberg et al. (2009)

describe how the Honda strategy was export-led. It was *deliberate*, defined from the top and resources allocated to its execution (Mintzberg and Waters 1985) In executing that strategy, the company sent across to Los Angeles, California, a consignment of high-end motorbikes and a small team to do the selling. Dominant in the US market was Harley-Davidson, and Honda's 125/250 and 305cc capacity motorbikes proved to be no match for Harley-Davidson. Loyalty to the brand was high, and the Honda product proved to be unreliable. The motorbikes leaked oil and experienced clutch failure. This was later understood by the fact that Americans would ride their motorbikes much farther and harder than Asian and European counterparts (c/f Porter's diamond). Ultimately, Honda was selling the wrong product into the wrong market.

The application of the tools of strategic analysis would, conceivably, have picked this up and advised the management at Honda against entering the US market with this particular product. However, there was success to be celebrated out of the venture. Not by design; rather by chance. Those salespeople trying to sell high-end motorbikes to Harley-Davidson users were given 50cc Honda Supercubs to get around the city. Californians had seen nothing like those previously. In Japan, they were ubiquitous because it is a country with limited street space. The demand was for the Honda Supercubs, not for motorbikes. They even had their own pop song, "Little Honda" (YouTube 1964). A market was created – existing product, new market. It also disrupted the power relations between dealers and manufacturers (in favour of the latter). All by chance and the good fortune that for unforeseen reasons the larger motorbikes failed. Strategy became *emergent* rather than deliberate.

That is not quite the whole story. In strategy, there is always another story. This alternative story, told by Pascale (1984), revolves around a now celebrated report written by the Boston Consulting Group (BCG) – the people behind the matrix with cash cows and problem children. The BCG was commissioned by the British government, which was concerned about the steep decline of the British motorcycle industry (49 to 9 per cent global share in the period 1959–1973). The BCG set about applying the tools of strategic analysis; highly prescriptive with a plausible series of causal links, the explanation was clear. A rational and largely micro-economic approach to entering new markets had been deployed – existing product, new market, by design. Honda had been meticulous in its analysis and decision-making.

It was not quite like that in reality. Strategists using the wrong lens can misread situations, such as markets, trends, culture and perspectives. The world is interpreted differently often by virtue of where one sits as an employee, manager, executive, regulator, legislator or user. Chance has a role. One never knows who is watching and looking at a disruptive 50cc moped.

Degrowth

It seems self-evident that growth is an inherent good. Firms that grow, contribute to GDP as a measure of economic welfare. Governments want domiciled firms to grow. GDP is, however, partial in what it measures. Many economic activities that are detrimental to society, such as deforestation, count towards growth (Coyle 2015). Protecting habitats does not qualify as positive economic activity; indeed, quite the contrary, as such activities are often seen as costs. Likewise, work within the home, looking after children and the elderly, does not contribute to GDP. There is a gender issue here, too. These activities are normally done by women. The same is true, therefore, of business growth. Firms will increase activity in areas where revenue and rents can be extracted, irrespective of the damage that such activities might cause to the environment, society or individuals more generally. Firms may also increase their scope and enter these markets should their analysis indicate that an industry is attractive, that is, that there is profit to be extracted in doing so.

Business strategy retains its managerialism; managers have checklists and make decisions on the basis of ticks and crosses, industries and markets. The twenty-first century, however, is not quite so simple. Climate change – mitigation and adaptation – challenges managerialism in fundamental ways. Mitigation and adaptation are two new imperatives for firms. Those firms that do not act risk being regulated out of business for not mitigating or collapsing under the pressure of severe environmental conditions for not adapting. The example of the failure of the Texas power grid in the winter of 2020/2021 (Holden et al. 2021) is a case in point. Any partnership may need to add mitigation and adaptation to the checklist. It may also be necessary for partners to check one another's "social rating" before proceeding (Varoufakis 2020). This is a system rather like venue and holiday reviews that reveal an un-advertised reality.

A question remains: can firms operate in a system of degrowth? Degrowth has its origins in the early 1970s – the era of the Club of Rome's report, *The Limits to Growth* (Meadows et al. 1972) and the work of Gorz (1980). It was a largely a French intellectual debate until its re-emergence in the 2000s, very much as a response to the neoliberal economics that used consumption as a measure of well-being, wealth and status in the 1980s.

Degrowth has two flavours:

1. Substitute products; for example, from air travel to train travel; from meat products to substitutes (meat-like but plant-based or lab grown)
2. Less monetized consumption – more sharing, volunteering and learning

The former of these sees degrowth in terms of sustainability; it is the recognition that change is necessary, but a change in forms of consumption is sufficient rather than radically curtailing consumption itself (Roulet and Bothello 2020). The second flavour is a broader political project. Its foundational idea is that once human beings have satisfied their needs for food, shelter and warmth, further individual consumption does not increase welfare. Buying things and being acquisitive only fuels all of the activities that make acquisition possible: work and increasing remuneration.

If degrowth is a manifesto (Kallis et al. 2015), these are the aspirations (pp. 3–15):

- sharing, simplicity, conviviality and care; care under managerialism subsidizes financial capital
- ending GDP as a measure of social welfare because it distorts value; replace with the Genuine Progress Index (GPI) or Index of Sustainable Economic Welfare (ISEW)
- ending the commodification of materials, food and labour because it is inherently exploitative and extractive
- reconstructing the commons, namely, space, resources such as water, and ideas
- wealth re-distribution, for example, universal basic incomes and fairness with less-developed nations and people
- job guarantees, work sharing, shorter working weeks
- re-politicization – a move away from "communities of experts" to "expert communities"
- elevation of cooperatives, community currencies and banks, and volunteering

While this list may seem undesirable, unrealistic or utopian, it is a plausible outcome (scenario) that has to be considered by businesses. It is possible for firms, however, to incorporate a number of these ideas into their systems and routines. For example, by introducing a four-day week, a shift that has been shown to improve productivity by improving work – life balance (Laker and Roulet 2019), firms have benefited from reduced sickness absence, improved motivation and therefore savings arising from improved productivity. There are also demographic differences. Laker and Roulet's study reveals that Generation Zs and Xs use their additional "leisure time" to upskill, volunteer and "side hustle" by which they mean establish their own micro-enterprises or participate in the so-called gig economy. There are benefits here to society through volunteering, but also boosts in economic activity, potentially in a non-extractive sense (that is, sustainably). This demographic – or at least those with the requisite skills – select employers on the basis of their human resource policies, of which the four-day week is a factor. The multinational company Unilever is trialling the four-day week with its eighty-one employees in New Zealand in a research collaboration with University of Technology Business School in Sydney with a view to extending it to its 155,000 global employees (Elegant 2020). Microsoft's experiment in Japan reported a productivity increase of 40 per cent and a 23 per cent reduction in electricity consumption (Chappell 2019).

Detractors – both firms and employees – argue that, managerially, it is difficult to implement and sustain, and among peers, the four-day week is viewed as a mark of laziness rather than productivity. In terms of the UN's Sustainability Development

Goals (SDGs), the four-day week, however, has the potential to contribute to achieving ten of the seventeen goals.

Strategic degrowth partnerships share strategic intent with traditional growth approaches. The intent is to operate within planetary boundaries and develop circular- or butterfly-economy products and services (Raworth 2017). This intent is likely to involve mitigation and/or adaptation as a minimum. Importantly, SDG 17 is partnerships; there are eight factors (UN n.d.):

1. Capacity development (of states and societies "to design and implement strategies that minimize the negative impacts of current social, economic and environmental crises and emerging challenges")
2. Finance (mobilizing finance to facilitate developing countries' initiatives on sustainability)
3. Financial inclusion (reducing barriers to accessing investment funds for sustainability)
4. Multi-stakeholder partnerships and community commitments (pooling financial resources, knowledge and expertise/know-how)
5. Science (as a public good, to be generated, shared and acted upon)
6. Technology (access to, and diffusion of, affordable and appropriate technologies)
7. Trade (liberalization, environmentally sustainable, debt management, macroeconomic policy development)
8. National sustainable development strategies (defined as "a cyclical and interactive process of planning, participation and action in which the emphasis is on managing progress towards sustainability goals rather than producing a 'plan' as an end product")

The change comes about when firms re-evaluate the purpose of the firm (Mayer 2018) as some multinationals are doing; for example, Unilever. The company's own website (Unilever n.d.) states the following: "Our Corporate Purpose states that to succeed requires 'the highest standards of corporate behaviour towards everyone we work with, the communities we touch, and the environment on which we have an impact.'" Caution is needed, however. The public statements need to match those of the legal incorporation documents that specify the legal purpose of the firm and not the interpretation for marketing purposes.

Scenarios and the fork-in-the-road

One of the twenty-first century's most prolific commentators on the world economy has been Yanis Varoufakis, an economics professor in Athens and one-time Finance Minister in the government of Alexis Tsipras in Greece. In a recent book, Varoufakis (2020) used the medium of the science-fiction novel to map out what a future world economy could look like and the firms that comprise it. Essentially, Varoufakis presents readers with a scenario, a plausible future. It is a future that humanity can aspire to and implement policies to achieve, or accept business-as-usual in full knowledge of the implications of that course of action.

One of Varoufakis's characters, Costa, is an IT expert. He's liberated from daily work by having anticipated the financial crisis of 2008 and bet against it (or for it, whichever way one thinks). Costa then dedicated himself to working on an alternate reality in which one can choose to enter but never return. Having created this alternate reality in a game called *Freedom*, he finds that holed up in it is another being, Kosti, who shares Costa's DNA and past. Kosti inhabits a world known as the *Other Now*, in contrast to that which Costa inhabits, namely, *Our Now*. Importantly for strategy and the scenario method, the revelations that Kosti presents must be thoroughly tested with sceptics – or challenging stakeholders – before they can be accepted and acted upon. Costa calls on two friends to help with this. Iris is an elderly socialist; Eve is a young libertarian who was there when the investment bank, Lehman Brothers, collapsed in 2008. Together, they test the ideas. With such disparate experiences and worldviews, could the alternate reality of *Other Now* supplant *Our Now* and be sustained?

Core to *Other Now* are the following:
1. Elimination of retail and investment banks
2. Universal basic income (UBI)
3. Employee ownership of firms and the elimination of hierarchies
4. Nationalization of land

The elimination of retail banks (1), for Varoufakis, is linked to the form and function of the UBI (2). UBI is paid to every citizen, regardless of status. In Varoufakis's alternate world, it has three components in a Personal Capital (PerCap) account. These are captured in Table 14.1.

Table 14.1: Components of a Personal Capital (PerCap) account.

Component	Rationale
Accumulation	Made up of basic pay and democratically allocated work bonuses
Legacy	Paid on birth, but not redeemable until adulthood and a plan for using it!
Dividend	UBI element funded by a tax on corporations at 5 per cent of gross revenues. The payments are stored in an electronic wallet and transfers can be made independent of retail banks

Source: Author's table, derived from Varoufakis (2020).

Furthermore, Varoufakis advocates bank lending being replaced by a peer-to-peer scheme. Investment banks will disappear because they will no longer be able to trade their complex derivatives and create money. They will be reduced to mere lenders and have no advantage over peer-lending mechanisms.

Regarding (3), each employee is given one share of equal value to all other shares in the company on Day 1 of joining the new firm. All employees engaged in adding value in a collective manner will have the share entitlement. The stock market will have been dispensed with by the radical activists who bring about the change. Firms will become democratic with no senior managers telling others what to do. The surpluses created by firms will be allocated by peer assessment on a points system. Those who are particularly creative and/or productive will be recognized by their peers and given credit points that equate with a portion of the excess. These points can also be used by future employers to assess the suitability of a candidate.

For Varoufakis (4), landlords have ordinarily received inflated unearned income. The nationalization of land in *Other Now* resulted in new global commons being created (gComms). Under this system, all freehold land passes to the gComms. Leases are awarded to landlords and democratic businesses are also privileged. The two zones – one for commercial housing, the other for commercial businesses – enables communities to extract maximum rents in these areas to pay for social housing.

A number of these ideas form the basis of recommendations offered by Meagher (2020), whose epiphany came when she was charged with making the case for two soft-drinks companies to merge on the basis of efficiency and, hence, reduced product prices. She was doing this against the backdrop of the textile factory collapse in Dhaka, Bangladesh, on 24 April 2013.

Varoufakis's *Other Now* is a parallel world created by the *fork-in-the-road* after the financial crisis of 2008. The question for Costa and the characters of Varoufakis's *Our Now*, is should they take the opportunity to transfer through a wormhole to the *Other Now*, while they can? It is science-fiction, after all. The characters spend much time discussing the merits of the *Other Now*, and the different perspectives give all readers food-for-thought. Why did humanity not choose to take the fork-in-the-road after 2008?

There is a similar fork-in-the-road now in regard to climate change, which opened up after the Paris Agreement of 2015. There were not too many takers, but they are inviting us to join them now. Should we go? While there is a voluntary dimension to the current invitation to a sustainable *Other Now*, there are some sticks being wielded, pushing some corporations in directions that they have resisted. For example, the oil industry is finding business-as-usual challenged in the courts and boardrooms. In separate cases clustered around one day in late May (26th) 2021, a court in the Dutch capital, The Hague, ruled that Royal Dutch Shell should achieve a much higher rate of GHG emission reductions than its current plan. The court ruled that the company has to reduce emissions by 40 per cent by 2030. The case was brought by climate campaigners using UN human rights law to force Royal Dutch Shell drastically to reduce emissions (Ambrose 2021; Pratley 2021).

Meanwhile, in the USA, activist shareholders have found themselves disproportionately affecting the climate policy of two oil majors, ExxonMobil and Chevron. In the ExxonMobil case, an activist hedge fund going under the name of Engine No. 1 (named after a Californian fire station) won the backing of BlackRock, Vanguard, California Public Employees' Retirement System and the New York State Common Retirement Fund to remove three incumbents and replace them with climate-focused board members. They did this with only 0.02 per cent shareholding, but in true stakeholder style, they mobilized other stakeholders (shareholders with significant shareholdings) to achieve power disproportionate to their stake. While they do not have a majority on the board, their influence in the future is likely to be significant.

BlackRock and Vanguard are leading global investment funds, while institutional investors like pension funds are expressing their concern about their members' and their families' futures. There is also a case that in a more regulated decarbonizing economy, the existing assets of oil companies can become stranded and increasingly worthless. In the Chevron case, 60 per cent of shareholders voted in favour of a resolution to impose cuts to GHG emissions. Why? Investors share a view that corporate action to mitigate and adapt is needed to protect shareholder value (DesJardine and Bansal 2021; Nauman et al. 2021; *Economist* 2021d).

Arising from Engine No. 1's success and the court ruling in The Hague, Moody's rating agency warned that the credit risk of oil companies has now increased. The investment companies, by contrast, view decarbonization as essential to maintaining long-term shareholder value, hence their backing for activist shareholders and a change to the board membership at ExxonMobil. This only works, however, in the case of public companies in functioning democracies. Other major oil company GHG emitters are out of reach of activist shareholders, but maybe a change in these companies can come by means of procurement decisions, investment (banks funding carbon projects are now being exposed) and even sanctions by international governments? Royal Dutch Shell will appeal against the decision in the court. The company's executive seemingly chooses to stay in the world of *Our Now*. Will ExxonMobil and Chevron choose *Other Now*?

Getting more from the tools of strategy

Strategic analysis is, for analysts and some practitioners, exciting because of the uncertainty around outcomes and its potential regarding competitive advantage and potential riches. This has been seen in the Big-Tech world and previously by those behind the shipping container, automobiles and aviation, among others. Business strategy can be viewed as a game (in the sense of game theory) – a set of manoeuvres to outsmart competition and even stakeholders. The game is, however, changing. While climate change is a great unknown, for strategists, it introduces some degree of certainty. Climate change is happening, which means firms have to adapt to that future. Good strategists realize this and build adaptation into analysis, choice and implementation. Moreover, because climate change is happening arising from human activity, often by the activities of firms, the extent of the adaptation needed depends on the extent of the warming. If global temperatures are kept within the 1.5–2.0 degrees Celsius, the extent of adaptation is knowable and manageable. If temperatures go above 2 degrees Celsius, the effects are much more unpredictable. It is in the interests of all firms and stakeholders to contribute to keeping global temperature rises well below 2 degrees Celsius. That means that firms *have* to mitigate. They have to cut carbon emissions. All firm objectives have to incorporate mitigation (to keep temperatures down) and adaptation (to adapt to changes that are known or knowable). The strategies that meet objectives will include decarbonization measures and business culture change.

The tools of strategic analysis used are largely managerialist. They help decision-makers to survive and prosper in a world of infinite resources, acceptable externalization (of waste) and competition. The world is now in a period where this is no longer the case. The tools of strategic analysis, choice and implementation are versatile and foster critiques that enable them to be reconfigured. In Chapter 2, Porter's five-forces model was introduced, which demonstrates the mechanics of industry analysis. Those mechanics, once exposed, become open to scrutiny. In doing so, a different application is possible. It was always true that firms operating in industries are not always as economically rational as the model suggests, though many are. A future in which firms share resources (equipment, know-how), form regenerative networks (as in the butterfly/circular economy), partner with public bodies (as in the case of vaccine development, or in the roll-out of electric vehicles (EV) charging infrastructure) and shorten supply chains, is possible.

In Chapter 3, Jay Barney's VRIO framework was presented. Firms use the model as a tool for micro-level resource and capability auditing. It tells analysts which resources are strategic and provide long-term competitive advantage. Resources and capabilities that are useful in the future are those that provide for economic sustainability, which is itself dependent on environmental sustainability, hence what is important to a customer and to a firm mirror each other. Rarity has never been about uniqueness. Rare resources can be leveraged positively. Moreover, causal ambiguity renders most internal processes and unique combinations of skills, resources, know-how and culture inimitable. What changes is the meaning of sustained competitive advantage.

In Chapter 4, stakeholder theory augmented and challenged the dominant business strategy mindset that firms should deliver primarily – or even only – for shareholders. If shareholders are looked after, the welfare of all other stakeholders is taken care of in that such firms provide jobs with salaries and pay taxes. Recent history has shown this welfare argument to be increasingly challengeable. The advocates of managing for stakeholders, however, argued that the returns from firms that were managed in this way were as good as, if not better than, those that profit-maximized through cost control and overtly transactional relationships. However, for as long as the planet as the source of all value and wealth is excluded from having a voice (from being a stakeholder), the balance of decisions will remain skewed towards the short-term economic thinking. The voice is being heard, however. The International Court in The Hague has spoken for the planet in its decision to require Royal Dutch Shell to reduce its emissions in line with the Paris Agreement by 2030. However, in many boardrooms and at government policy tables, the voice is not there or represented. All firms should look to incorporate the planet into their decision-making structures.

Chapter 5 emphasized the potential for cooperative strategy vis-à-vis competitive strategy. Cooperative strategies, such as joint ventures or strategic alliances, have always been part of the competitive landscape. However, in the future, such cooperative strategies may have a different purpose. At a very simple level, firms can cooperate over carbon emissions. Equally, they could cooperate in reducing the length of supply chains, or in distribution. For example, even on the shortest of walks in any UK city, one is likely to see a food retailer's home delivery service. They are uncoordinated and wasteful. Perhaps the supermarkets will, in future, co-operate over this? Maybe they could work particular territories? The products are generic; it does not really matter who delivers them. Moreover, managerialism has always sought to be efficient. Applying that logic to distribution would reduce waste, emissions and even traffic congestion. Porter's value chain, on this logic, comes into its own if the planet has a voice.

At the heart of Chapters 6–8 is the concept of growth. Firms look to grow out of an expectation from shareholders. Growth is problematic. Growth has limits. In the past, firms have sought to overcome those limits by incorporating absent resources and capabilities through partnership, acquisition or other market-entry modes. However, economic growth – as measured by gross domestic product (GDP) – breaches planetary boundaries. The $200 burger is a clear illustration of this. The task of firms is to work within those boundaries and help other firms to do so, for example, those in the supply chain. Clearly, firms in some sectors will grow because their products or services are new, increasingly important and contribute to human welfare. Other sectors will decline. Firms in some sectors that are carbon-intensive will need to close and their resources be reconfigured and redeployed. While this is easy to say for a writer whose livelihood is not affected by such decisions, critics miss two essential points. The first point is that in a cooperative world, the role of the state changes. It becomes more interventionist (and this power has been demonstrated through the pandemic with financial support for firms unable to trade because of lockdowns). Where industries close, states and the governments that control them can support people who are affected, direct investment to particular areas and retrain others. Not to do so is a political decision, not an economic one. The second point is that to have environmental sustainability or not is a choice to be made. Without it, the future is uncertain, unpredictable and dangerous.

Chapter 9 conceptualized innovation through time and into the present. Societal innovation (firms and governance) is an increasingly valuable capability. Innovation requires thought and co-ordination in commercial products and processes. In a decarbonized world, innovation will deliver products and services that will help to maintain economic activities within planetary boundaries. Historical innovation models have conceptualized the innovation process from early linear to later coupled and parallel/decentralized/global working. Future innovation models will factor in planetary boundaries that will change the nature of innovation and the products and services that result from it. The rate of innovation is crucial to meeting carbon emission targets.

Chapter 10 detailed how strategists can broaden their investment criteria and use evaluation tools that capture the value of longer-term investments, particularly those relating to mitigation and adaptation. The dominant investment indicators have been short-term and simple measures, easy to interpret, but with damaging effects. For example, discounted cash flow biases projects that have a shorter duration enabling investors to re-use their funds elsewhere more quickly. The deployment of more complex, but environmentally complementary, indicators such as those found in NPSV and SROI help in better informing decision-makers and also in audit reporting. The latter is a capability that will grow as global carbon budgets are exhausted.

The puzzle of creating the perfect organizational structure was the focus of Chapter 11. The challenge for small firms with discrete products and services is straightforward. For firms that are complex and often constituted as conglomerates, the challenge is greater. This is made more difficult because, in some cases, structures were designed for the extraction and exploitation of resources in global networks, externalizing the costs in the process. The modern multinational will need to reconfigure itself to bring in-house these costs and manage them. Firms will be accounting for scope 3 emissions across the whole of the supply chain, and will need to reconfigure structures to limit liabilities.

Finally, Chapters 12 and 13 examined what firms really are, namely, collections of individuals bound together by a mixture of cultures – the firm, the community and the ethnic. Managerialist firms use transactional techniques to get compliance from employees and stakeholders more generally. Change, however, is a social process. Compliance is not enough in a world of rising global temperatures. It is important for governments and all firms to communicate what is happening in the world. It is important to promote engagement with the science among employees, and the scientific, political and economic bodies and structures defining global affairs. Transactional approaches may not be fit-for-purpose. Authentic leadership is called for that aligns with sustainable management for stakeholders. With all of these observations, it is necessary to return to the question of definitions.

What is strategy?

In Chapter 1, definitions of strategy from its leading thinkers such as Michael Porter, Alfred Chandler and Henry Mintzberg were presented. All capture something in what is a dynamic subject and discipline. Strategy as an economic science lets down future generations. There are no irrefutable laws. However, the dominant tools of strategic analysis are locked into this idea. Causality can be established. Mintzberg, by contrast, is not overly enamoured by prescriptive economic approaches, and views strategy as a process of learning, trial-and-error and almost as an art. That is not to say the art of strategy is without foundation and that strategic analysis has no value. Far from it. However, business strategy is subject to human whim, vision, often flawed, misinterpretation and environmental shocks or a combination of these things.

This text distilled the definitions and arrived at the following:

> Strategy is something to do with setting and meeting organizational goals, courses of action (long-, medium- and short-term), and the allocation of sufficient and correctly configured resources appropriate for those courses of action. There is usually some element of competition involved, and winning is about being different and creating value. It is always about change and the tools of change derived from analysis, choice and implementation. It can be prescribed and deliberate composed by those in positions of power, or it can emerge from below, rise to the top, gain legitimacy and diffuse as though it was deliberate.

Does this sense of strategy hold up to this book's aspirations for change?

Where it does

The courses of action for organizations remain long-, medium- and short-term, though the short-term must not act against the medium and long-term objectives. They must not be "decoupled" from the longer-term objectives. There is a correlation between Anglo-Saxon world business models and timeframes for meeting objectives. Moreover, the long-term objectives are often defined imprecisely, especially as climate objectives projected into the future (2050, for example) still seem not to have the urgency needed to meet emission targets. At the very least, a short-term objective should involve installing the necessary equipment to mitigate emissions, such as photovoltaic cells. The medium-term objectives should be simply to achieve the emission cuts to 2030 and the longer-term to be carbon negative by 2050 and being fully adapted to the anticipated changes associated with global temperature increases from 1.5 to 2.0 degrees Celsius.

The resources necessary to deliver on these goals have to be provided. These are derived from investment decisions informed by analysis and the application of tools that capture natural capital as well as financial, human and manufacturing. Strategy is always about change in whichever era because nothing stands still.

Where it does not

Competition and winning need to be rethought. Winning has to be a collective effort to reconfigure the world economy and the firms that create products that add value. The reconfiguration has to be more participative at firm, governmental and societal levels. Consumers also need to change preferences. In the developed world, they need to consume and want/desire less. Consumers need to create demand for products that are high-quality, reliable, re-useable, recyclable and/or returnable at the end of the product's useful life. Firms need to reconfigure their business models to deliver on the circularity of products such that it becomes the value proposition. Competition often just wastes resources and leads to homogenization in products and services (dominant design). It promotes downward pressure on costs, leading to exploitation of resources, extended supply chains and unfavourable labour conditions. Markets may be efficient at distributing resources, but they do not allocate resources sustainably.

Monopolies are not, however, the solution.

Business strategy is not just about the business. It arguably never has been if the capitalist managerialist power structures, access to authority and influence are examined closely. Those very factors, however, have enabled firms to externalize costs (pollution) and piggy-back on publicly-funded infrastructure, often without contributing through taxation. Many multi- and trans-national corporations extract and exploit resources in developing countries, again externalizing costs. Business, by definition, is a partnership between public and private entities and society. Moreover, it is not just about infrastructure. As Mazzucato (2018a, 2018b) notes, many technologies that consumers take for granted have their roots in publicly-funded research in universities. The people behind the technologies are educated in public institutions – schools, colleges and universities. The benefits of this research are often privatized and patented. There are lessons from the Covid-19 pandemic. Governments from rich countries collectively invested substantial sums in the development of vaccines and purchased them before regulatory approval (UK Department for Business 2020). The UK government, for example, in addition to an initial £200m in vaccine development, invested a further £100m in a Cell and Gene Therapy Catapult Manufacturing Innovation Centre to accelerate production and roll-out (Partridge 2020). The private sector cannot deliver and roll-out such products at pace without state funding. The current debates about unlocking the intellectual property behind the vaccines to allow the benefits to flow to middle- and low-income countries illustrate again that benefits are often privatized (Adler and Anyona 2021).

What is needed for a new definition

Natural resources are the basis of all products and services. They are finite. Existing definitions do not capture this bald fact; the idea of operating within planetary boundaries is absent. There is also an absence relating to the purpose of the firm. There is room for little discussion – though it is still being had – for profit maximizing and welfare being best delivered by firms pursuing it. Such an approach will externalize costs at the expense of the commons, that is, Earth's life support systems such as the air, oceans and soils. Moreover, firms are social phenomena as much as economic ones. This needs to be recognized in the context of ownership and participation. Work provides meaning and dignity to those employed or engaged. Business strategy has to support the social and economic purpose of firms in pursuit of human advancement through innovation, sustainability and partnership. However, in the interests of brevity, references to the legally binding international treaty, the Paris Agreement of 2015, are a proxy for maximizing welfare, a purpose beyond profit, and the dignity of the act of work itself.

The journey leads to the following definition of *sustainable* business strategy:

> Strategy is the execution of agreed courses of action for the long-, medium- and short-term, and the allocation of resources appropriate for those courses of action to meet the goals defined by the organization. The goals and courses of action should not *knowingly* and/or *wilfully* lead to the breach of planetary boundaries or international treaties when aggregated to goals, activities and courses of action employed by other organizations, whether business competitors or stakeholders more broadly.

Summary

This text has been a journey through history and related business strategy tools that have come to define strategy as a discipline and a practice. As such, strategic analysis and implementation has largely taken a managerialist form, aimed at achieving competitive advantage and rewarding shareholders through dividends and share price premiums. The share prices, however, seem negatively related to the health of the natural environment that supplies all of the resources that firms use for their products and services. The fork-in-the-road scenario, presented to the world after the Paris Agreement of 2015, seemed not to have attracted too many drivers, but as carbon budgets get smaller and the consequences of business-as-usual become starker, a wormhole has emerged allowing businesses belatedly to change direction and mitigate and adapt to a sustainable future. Adaptation is an exciting proposition for those strategists who thrive on opportunity. Decarbonizing products, services and supply chains is a big task, but it is necessary not just because humans like trees, flowers, birds and animals. Rather, it is because humans love life, society and the prospect of a better future for their children and grandchildren.

This text is no panacea. It was written as a starting point for students and practitioners who have familiarity with the tools of strategic analysis, choice and implementation, but struggle to see how to transform businesses incrementally and to take stakeholders through the transition. Business management students will notice that all of their disciplines make guest appearances – economics, marketing, human resource management, finance and law and operations management. There is much room, however, for the humanities – languages, history, literature and education to be incorporated. The change is something that everyone can be suitably motivated by and work towards achieving. We are all stakeholders as we try to sustain the global commons – the air, the soil, the oceans. The business of business has transformed the lives and fortunes of millions of people throughout history, particularly through the twentieth century, despite that century's terrible strife in war and disease. The driver of the transformation was the burning of carbon in the form of a store of concentrated energy that has changed the global climate. Fortunately, humanity has the technology and the know-how to decarbonize and, with it, to transform the meaning ascribed to work, business and consumption. Time is short. Let the world's businesses create the future.

Bibliography

Adler, David and Mamka Anyona (2021). "It's good Biden wants to suspend vaccine patents. But the whole rotten system needs overhaul". *The Guardian*. https://tinyurl.com/28j2bmb8. Accessed: 5 September 2021.

Agence France-Presse (2021). "Michelin awards star to vegan restaurant for the first time in France". *The Guardian*. 19 January. https://tinyurl.com/btux8h8d. Accessed: 27 July 2021.

Albers, Sascha, Franz Wohlgezogen and Edward J. Zajac (2016). "Strategic alliance structures: An organization design perspective". *Journal of Management* 42(3): 582–614.

Ambrose, Jillian (2021). "'Black Wednesday' for big oil as courtrooms and boardrooms turn on industry". *The Guardian*. 29 May. https://tinyurl.com/5nr5j5pt. Accessed: 25 July 2021.

Andrews, Kenneth R. (1971). *The Concept of Corporate Strategy*, Homewood, IL: Dow Jones-Irwin.

Ansoff, H. Igor (1957). "Strategies for diversification". *Harvard Business Review* 35(5): 113–124.

Armenakis, Achilles A., Stanley G. Harris and Kevin W. Mossholder (1993). "Creating readiness for organizational change". *Human Relations (New York)* 46(6): 681–703.

Atrill, Peter and E. J. McLaney (2019). *Accounting and Finance for Non-specialists*, Harlow: Pearson.

Bachrach, P. and M. S. Baratz (1970). *Power and Poverty: Theory and practice*, New York, NJ: Oxford University Press.

Bachrach, Peter and Morton S. Baratz (1963). "Decisions and nondecisions: An analytical framework". *The American Political Science Review* 57(3): 632–642.

Bailey, Andrew, Mark Carney, François Villeroy de Galhau and Frank Elderson (2020). "The world must seize this opportunity to meet the climate challenge". *The Guardian*. 5 June. https://tinyurl.com/2tk8yukj. Accessed: 12 June 2021.

Bakari, Haroon, Ahmed Imran Hunjra and Ghulam Shabbir Khan Niazi (2017). "How does authentic leadership influence planned organizational change? The role of employees' perceptions: Integration of theory of planned behavior and Lewin's three step model". *Journal of Change Management* 17(2): 155–187.

Balconi, Margherita, Stefano Brusoni and Luigi Orsenigo (2010). "In defence of the linear model: An essay". *Research Policy* 39(1): 1–13.

Bansal, Pratima (2005). "Evolving sustainably: A longitudinal study of corporate sustainable development". *Strategic Management Journal* 26(3): 197–218.

Bansal, Pratima and Mark R. DesJardine (2014). "Business sustainability: It is about time". *Strategic Organization* 12(1): 70–78.

Barnard, Catherine, Sam Lowe, David Henig and Lisa O'Carroll (2020). "Committees, visas and climate change: Brexit experts' verdicts on the deal details". *The Guardian*. 29 December. https://tinyurl.com/57s7t222. Accessed: 5 September 2021.

Barney, Jay (1991). "Firm resources and sustained competitive advantage". *Journal of Management* 17(1): 99–120.

Baron, David P. (2013). *Business and its Environment*, Upper Saddle River, NJ: Pearson.

Barsky, Noah P., Mohamed E. Hussein and Stephen F. Jablonsky (1999). "Shareholder and stakeholder value in corporate downsizing – The case of United Technologies Corporation". *Accounting, Auditing & Accountability Journal* 12(5): 583–604.

Bartlett, Christopher A. and Sumantra Ghoshal (1987). "Managing across borders: New organizational responses". *Sloan Management Review* 29(1): 43.

Bass, Bernard M. and Ronald E. Riggio (2006). *Transformational Leadership*, Mahwah, NJ: L. Erlbaum Associates.

Bateson, Lynne (2012). "Why Tesco's Fresh & Easy turned Americans off". *The Guardian*. 5 December. https://tinyurl.com/rd8tn2dm. Accessed: 21 July 2021.

https://doi.org/10.1515/9783110718430-015

British Broadcasting Corporation (BBC) (2014). "Pfizer drops AstraZeneca takeover bid". BBC. 26 May. https://www.bbc.com/news/business-27572986. Accessed: 10 August 2021.

British Broadcasting Corporation (BBC) (2019). "Climategate: Science of a scandal". BBC. Broadcast date: 14 November. https://www.bbc.co.uk/mediacentre/proginfo/2019/46/climategate-science-of-a-scandal. Accessed: 8 November 2021.

British Broadcasting Corporation (BBC) (2020). "Green originals". *Joe Farman*. BBC. Broadcast date: 7 January 2020. https://www.bbc.co.uk/programmes/m000cz17. Accessed: 8 November 2021.

British Broadcasting Corporation (BBC) (2021). "39 ways to save the planet". *The Chill Hunters*. T. Heap. Broadcast date: 19 April 2021. https://www.bbc.co.uk/programmes/m000v89m. Accessed: 13 June 2021.

Becker, Markus C., Nathalie Lazaric, Richard R. Nelson and Sidney G. Winter (2005). "Applying organizational routines in understanding organizational change". *Industrial and Corporate Change* 14(5): 775–791.

Bell, Alice (2021). *Our Biggest Experiment: A history of the climate crisis*, London: Bloomsbury UK.

Beloev, Ivan, Katerina Gabrovska-Evstatieva and Boris Evstatiev (2017). "Compensation of CO_2 emissions from petrol stations with photovoltaic parks: Cost-benefit and risk analysis". *Acta Technologica Agriculturae* 20(4): 85.

Berners-Lee, Mike (2019). *There is No Planet B: A handbook for the make or break years*, Cambridge: Cambridge University Press.

Berners-Lee, Mike (2020). *How Bad are Bananas?: The carbon footprint of everything*, London: Profile.

Bessant, John R. (2015). "Case study – Espresso Mushroom Company". 15 July. http://www.innovation-portal.info/resources/case-study-espresso-mushroom-company/. Accessed: 30 August 2021.

Bessant, John R. (2021). "Building an open innovation ecosystem – interview with Christoph Krois, Siemens". 29 January. https://www.youtube.com/watch?v=H2cDoyos9Zc. Accessed: 27 July 2021.

BHP (2001). BHP Billiton Merger Complete. Press release. 29 June. https://tinyurl.com/yhf93ydt. Accessed: 23 July 2021.

Blanchard, Tamsin (2020). "'Put Earth first': Can a greener, fairer fashion industry emerge from crisis?" *The Guardian*. 27 March. https://tinyurl.com/bc7mtxur. Accessed: 6 July 2020.

Boden, Anne (2020). *Banking on It: How I disrupted an industry*, London: Penguin Books Limited.

Boffey, Daniel (2020). "Dutch city redraws its layout to prepare for global heating effects". *The Guardian*. 29 July.

Bogers, Marcel and Joel West (2012). "Managing distributed innovation: Strategic utilization of open and user innovation". *Creativity and Innovation Management* 21(1): 61–75.

Bowers, Simon and Jill Treanor (2011). "RBS 'gamble' on ABN Amro deal: FSA". *The Guardian*. 12 December. https://tinyurl.com/2az78jsf. Accessed: 21 July 2021.

Bregman, R. (2020). *Humankind: A hopeful history*, London: Bloomsbury Publishing.

Brook, Jacques W. and Fabrizio Pagnanelli (2014). "Integrating sustainability into innovation project portfolio management – A strategic perspective". *Journal of Engineering and Technology Management* 34: 46–62.

Buchanan, Richard (1992). "Wicked problems in design thinking". *Design Issues* 8(2): 5–21.

Burnes, Bernard (2015). "Understanding resistance to change – building on Coch and French". *Journal of Change Management* 15(2): 92–116.

Burnes, Bernard and David Bargal (2017). "Kurt Lewin: 70 years on". *Journal of Change Management* 17(2): 91–100.

Burnes, Bernard, Mark Hughes and Rune T. By (2018). "Reimagining organisational change leadership". *Leadership (London, England)* 14(2): 141–158.

Bushby, Mattha (2019). "Record number of UK workers paid below minimum wage – report". *The Guardian*. 26 April. https://tinyurl.com/uk8u86r5. Accessed: 22 July 2020.

Butler, S. (2021). "Asda buyers aim to spin off petrol forecourts in £750m deal". *The Guardian*. 3 February. https://tinyurl.com/3stkdx6f. Accessed: 23 July 2021.

Butler, Sarah (2013). "Tesco pays out to rid itself of US chain Fresh & Easy". *The Guardian*. 10 September. https://tinyurl.com/2st2pxcj. Accessed: 21 July 2021.

Butler, Sarah and Sean Farrell (2014). "Price war fears wipe £2bn off value of UK supermarkets". *The Guardian*. 13 March. https://tinyurl.com/yx86ncx7. Accessed: 19 July 2021.

Byrnes, William, Nima Khodakarami and Carlos Perez (2016). *The Value Chain: A study of the coffee industry*, preprint researchgate.net. 24 April 2020. https://www.researchgate.net/publication/326786435_The_value_chain_A_study_of_the_coffee_industry. Accessed: 8 November 2021.

Cabinet Office – Office of the Third Sector (2009). "A guide to Social Return on Investment". https://tinyurl.com/yeere3h6. Accessed: 10 November.

Cain, Geoffrey (2020). *Samsung Rising: Inside the secretive company conquering Tech*, London: Ebury Publishing.

Campbell, Andrew, Michael Goold, Marcus Alexander and Jo Whitehead (2014). *Strategy for the Corporate Level: Where to invest, what to cut back and how to grow organisations with multiple divisions*, Chichester: Wiley.

Caracostas, Parakevas (2007). "The policy-shaper anxiety at the innovation kick: How far do innovation theories really help in the world of policy". In F. Malerba, and S. Brusoni, *Perspectives on Innovation*, Cambridge: Cambridge University Press. 464–489

Carroll, Archie B. (1979). "A three-dimensional conceptual model of corporate performance". *Academy of Management Review* 4(4): 497–505.

Carroll, Archie B. (1998). "The four faces of corporate citizenship". *Business & Society Review 99* (100/101): 1–7.

Casadesus-Masanell, Ramon and David B. Yoffie (2007). "Wintel: Cooperation and conflict". *Management Science* 53(4): 584–598.

Castells, M. (2000). *The Rise of the Network Society: The information age: Economy, society, and culture*, Oxford: Blackwell.

Cavalieri, Paulo and Peter Singer (1996). *The Great Ape Project: Equality beyond humanity*, New York, NY: St. Martin's Press.

Cecere, Grazia, Nicoletta Corrocher and Riccardo David Battaglia (2015). "Innovation and competition in the smartphone industry: Is there a dominant design?" *Telecommunications Policy* 39(3): 162–175.

Chandler, Alfred D. (1962). *Strategy and Structure: Chapters in the history of the industrial enterprise*, London and Cambridge, MA: MIT Press.

Chappell, Bill (2019). "4-day workweek boosted workers' productivity by 40%, Microsoft Japan says". *NPR (National Public Radio)*. 4 November. https://tinyurl.com/ufh4x3mb. Accessed: 7 November 2021.

Chesbrough, Henry W. (2003). *Open Innovation. The new imperative for creating and profiting from technology*, Boston, MA: Harvard Business School Press.

Christensen, Clayton M. (1997). *The Innovator's Dilemma: When new technologies cause great firms to fail*, Boston, MA: Harvard Business School Press.

Christian, Jose (2015). *The User Organisation: Structure and governance in an open source project*, PhD thesis, University of Brighton. October. https://tinyurl.com/sy5uyaup. Accessed: 7 November 2021.

Christian, Jose and Anh N. Vu (2021). "Task-based structures in open source software: Revisiting the onion model". *R&D Management* 51(1): 87–100.

Christopher, M. (1992). "Logistics and supply chain management: Strategies for reducing costs and improving services". London: Financial Times.

Ciszek, Erica and Nneka Logan (2018). "Challenging the dialogic promise: How Ben & Jerry's support for Black Lives Matter fosters dissensus on social media". *Journal of Public Relations Research* 30(3): 115–127.

Clark, Duncan (2011). "A complete guide to carbon offsetting". *The Guardian*. 16 September. https://tinyurl.com/55y2m5k2. Accessed: 5 September 2021.

Clark, Duncan (2018). *Alibaba: The house that Jack Ma built*, New York, NY: HarperCollins.

Clegg, Stuart R. (1989). *Frameworks of Power*, London: SAGE Publications.

Cobb, Anthony T. (2011). *Leading Project Teams: The basics of project management and team leadership*, Thousand Oaks: SAGE Publications.

Cohen, Wesley M. and Daniel A. Levinthal (1990). "Absorptive capacity: A new perspective on learning and innovation". *Administrative Science Quarterly* **35**(1):128.

Collins, Lauren (2011). "House perfect: Is the IKEA ethos comfy or creepy?" *The New Yorker*. 26 September. https://www.newyorker.com/magazine/2011/10/03/house-perfect. Accessed: 5 September 2021.

Collis, David, David Young and Michael Goold (2007). "The size, structure, and performance of corporate headquarters". *Strategic Management Journal* 28(4): 383–405.

Commerzbank (2009). "Dresdner Bank merged into Commerzbank". Press release. 11 May. https://tinyurl.com/2krjctpj. Accessed: 23 July 2021

Coyle, Diane (2015). *GDP: A brief but affectionate history – Revised and expanded edition*, Princeton: Princeton University Press.

Coyne, Kevin P. and Somu Subramaniam (1996). "Bringing discipline to strategy". *McKinsey Quarterly* 14.

Crane, Andrew, Guido Palazzo, Laura J. Spence and Dirk Matten (2014). "Contesting the value of 'creating shared value'". *California Management Review* 56(2): 130–153.

Cumming, Douglas and Lars Hornuf (2018). *The Economics of Crowdfunding: Startups, portals and investor behavior*, Basingstoke: Palgrave Macmillan.

Daft, Richard L. (1983). *Organization Theory and Design*, St. Paul: West Publishing Company.

Dahl, Robert A. (1961). *Who Governs?: Democracy and power in an American city*, Yale University Press.

Dasgupta, Partha (2021). *The Economics of Biodiversity: The Dasgupta Review*. London, HM Treasury. https://tinyurl.com/u9kxpuw.

Davies, Rob (2019). "Why the heatwave is disrupting the UK railways". *The Guardian*. 25 July. https://tinyurl.com/rf6j828k. Accessed: 5 September 2021.

Davies, Rob (2020) "Arm Holdings: what is it and does its sale to Nvidia matter?". The Guardian. 15 September. https://tinyurl.com/pvbcp45x. Accessed: 6 November 2021.

Davies, Serena (2017). "Climate change – The facts". BBC. https://www.bbc.co.uk/programmes/m00049b1.

Davis, Nicola (2020). "How has a Covid vaccine been developed so quickly?" *The Guardian*. 8 December. https://tinyurl.com/39934rbn. Accessed: 5 September 2021.

Davis, Stanley M. and Paul R. Lawrence (1977). *Matrix*, Addison-Wesley Publishing.

Day, Peter (2000). "Global Business – the Bluetooth revolution". BBC. Broadcast date: 24 November. https://www.bbc.co.uk/sounds/play/p03jrnhh. Accessed: 24 November2020.

Doughnut Economics Action Lab (DEAL). (2021). "Doughnut Economics Action Lab." Accessed: 26 July 2021.

DeHoratius, Nicole (2020). "How will COVID-19 change the supply chain?" 7 May. 7 https://www.youtube.com/watch?v=nBQ3lOkaAI8. Accessed: 29 December 2020.

Department for Business, Energy & Industrial Strategy (2020). Press Release "UK government secures new COVID-19 vaccines and backs global clinical trial". 14 August. https://tinyurl.com/3v5zmdhy. London. Accessed: 8 November 2021.

DesJardine, Mark and Tima Bansal (2021). "Engine No. 1's big win over Exxon shows activist hedge funds joining fight against climate change". *The Conversation: Economy + Business*. 26 May. https://tinyurl.com/vt3pmpaz. Accessed: 5 September 2021.

Deutsche Welle (2019). "Making cheese in the Alps – a story of integration". 8 March. https://www.youtube.com/watch?v=CF0nQXrEJ30. Accessed: 8 November 2021.

Dicken, Peter (2014). *Global Shift: Mapping the changing contours of the world economy*. Los Angeles: SAGE.

DiMaggio, Paul J. and Walter W. Powell (1983). "The Iron Cage revisited: Institutional isomorphism and collective rationality in organizational fields". *American Sociological Review* 48(2): 147–160.

Doz, Yves L. (1996). "The evolution of cooperation in strategic alliances: Initial conditions or learning processes?" *Strategic Management Journal* 17(S1): 55–83.

Driscoll, Cathy and Mark Starik (2004). "The primordial stakeholder: Advancing the conceptual consideration of stakeholder status for the natural environment". *Journal of Business Ethics* 49(1): 55.

Drucker, Peter F. (1994). "The theory of the business (cover story)". *Harvard Business Review* 72(5): 95–104.

Drzensky, Frank, Nikolai Egold and Rolf van Dick (2012). "Ready for a change? A longitudinal study of antecedents, consequences and contingencies of readiness for change". *Journal of Change Management* 12(1): 95–111.

Dunphy, Dexter and Doug Stace (1993). "The strategic management of corporate change". *Human Relations* 46(8): 905.

Dyson, Robert G. and Fernando S. Oliveira (2007). "Flexibility, robustness and real options". In F. O'brien and R. G. Dyson, *Supporting Strategy: Frameworks, methods, models*. Chichester: John Wiley & Sons: 343–366.

The Economist (2006). "Lego's turnaround: Picking up the pieces". *The Economist*. 26 October.

The Economist (2012). "The last Kodak moment?" *The Economist*. 14 January.

The Economist (2013). "The rise of the sharing economy". *The Economist*. 9 March.

The Economist (2015a). "What's in a name?" *The Economist*. 11 August.

The Economist (2015b). "Spelling it out". *The Economist*. 15 August.

The Economist (2016). "Alphabet's Google is searching for its next hit". *The Economist*. 15 December.

The Economist (2017). "A deal sparks talk of car-industry mega-mergers". *The Economist*. 11 March.

The Economist (2020a). "Untangling Warren Buffett's unique firm". *The Economist*. 27 February.

The Economist (2020b). "The expansion of Heathrow airport is scotched on climate grounds". *The Economist*. 29 February.

The Economist (2020c). A grim outlook: How worse weather will disrupt businesses and their supply chains. *The Economist*. 19 September.

The Economist (2021a). "Searching for the next big thing". *The Economist*. 20 March.

The Economist (2021b) "It is not easy being green". *The Economist*. 27 March 2021

The Economist (2021c). "Governments have identified commodities essential to economic and military security". *The Economist*. 31 March.

The Economist (2021d). "The future of big oil: The little engine that could". *The Economist*. 29 May.

Editorial (2016). "What's the carbon footprint of your computer?" 23 May. https://tinyurl.com/77afkcu8. Accessed: 2 August 2021.

Elan, Priya (2021). "Renting clothes is 'less green than throwing them away'". *The Guardian*. 6 July. https://tinyurl.com/kseydbbw. Accessed: 7 July 2021.

Elegant, Naomi Xu (2020). "The old ways of working are outdated: Unilever is experimenting with a 4-day work week". *Fortune*. https://fortune.com/2020/12/01/unilever-four-day-work-week. Accessed: 5 September 2021.

Elkington, J. (1997). *Cannibals with Forks: The triple bottom line of 21st century business*, Oxford: Capstone.

Ember. (2021). "Daily carbon prices". https://ember-climate.org/data/carbon-price-viewer/.

Erhardt, Niclas L., James D. Werbel and Charles B. Shrader (2003). "Board of director diversity and firm financial performance". *Corporate Governance: An international review* 11(2): 102–111.

European Commission (2020). "Trade and Cooperation Agreement between the European Union and the European Atomic Energy Community, of the One Part, and The United Kingdom of Great Britain and Northern Ireland, of the Other Part". Brussels. 26 December. https://ec.europa.eu/transparency/regdoc/rep/1/2020/EN/COM-2020-857-F1-EN-ANNEX-1-PART-1.PDF Accessed: 7 November 2021.

European Commission (2021). "Reducing emissions from the shipping sector". https://ec.europa.eu/clima/policies/transport/shipping_en. Accessed: 15 May 2021.

European Union (2011). "Directive 2011/61/EU of the European Parliament and of The Council". https://tinyurl.com/5katdw37 Accessed: 23 July 2021.

Eurostat (2021). " Foreign Direct Investment stocks at the end of 2019 ". https://tinyurl.com/fw9unp9s.

Farrell, Sean (2016). "Three's takeover of O2 blocked by Brussels on competition concerns". *The Guardian*. 11 May. https://tinyurl.com/54ntz7xv. 11 May. Accessed: 16 August 2021.

Faulkner, D. and C. Bowman (1995). *The Essence of Competitive Strategy*, Hemel Hempstead: Prentice Hall.

Finch, Julia (2018). "What's the controversy over Melrose's hostile takeover of GKN?" *The Guardian*. 29 March. https://tinyurl.com/kfx39t79. Accessed: 23 July 2021.

Fiol, C. Marlene (1991). "Seeing the empty spaces: Towards a more complex understanding of the meaning of power in organizations". *Organization Studies* 12(4): 547–566.

Folke, Carl, Henrik Österblom, Jean-Baptiste Jouffray, Eric F. Lambin, W. Neil Adger, Marten Scheffer, Beatrice I. Crona, Magnus Nyström, Simon A. Levin, Stephen R. Carpenter, John M. Anderies, Stuart Chapin, Anne-Sophie Crépin, Alice Dauriach, Victor Galaz, Line J. Gordon, Nils Kautsky, Brian H. Walker, James R. Watson, James Wilen and Aart de Zeeuw (2019). "Transnational corporations and the challenge of biosphere stewardship". ORE Open Research Exeter. http://hdl.handle.net/10871/39158.

Forsgren, Mats (2002). "The concept of learning in the Uppsala internationalization process model: A critical review." *International Business Review* 11(3): 257–277.

Francis, David L. (2020). *Exploiting Agility for Advantage*, Berlin/Boston: De Gruyter.

Frankel, Todd C. (2016) "The cobalt pipeline: Tracing the path from deadly hand-dug mines in Congo to consumers' phones and laptops". *The Washington Post*. 30 September. https://tinyurl.com/6xmh7xrp. Accessed: 21 July 2021.

Freeman, Alex (2015). "Climate change by numbers". 2 March. London: BBC. https://www.bbc.co.uk/programmes/p02jsdrk

Freeman, R. Edward (1984). *Strategic Management: A stakeholder approach*, Pitman.

Freeman, R. Edward (2009). "What is stakeholder theory. Business roundtable: Institute for Corporate Ethics". 1 October. https://www.youtube.com/watch?v=bIRUaLcvPe8

Freeman, R. Edward (2010). *Strategic Management: A stakeholder approach*, Cambridge: Cambridge University Press.

Friedman, Milton and Rose D. Friedman (1962). *Capitalism and Freedom*, Chicago: University of Chicago Press.

Fryer, Peter (2018). *Staying Power: The history of black people in Britain*, London: Pluto Press.

Furr, Nathan (2018). "What happens to firms that don't adopt dominant technologies?" Insead. 27 August. https://knowledge.insead.edu/node/9971/pdf. Accessed: 24 January 2021.

Furrer, Bettina, Jens Hamprecht and Volker H. Hoffmann (2012). "Much ado about nothing? How banks respond to climate change". *Business & Society* 51(1): 62–88.

Gardner, William L., Claudia C. Cogliser, Kelly M. Davis and Matthew P. Dickens (2011). "Authentic leadership: A review of the literature and research agenda". *The Leadership Quarterly* 22(6): 1120–1145.

Geringer, J. Michael (1991). "Strategic determinants of partner selection criteria in international joint ventures". *Journal of International Business Studies* 22(1): 41–62.

Gleeson-White, Jane (2020). *Six Capitals Updated Edition: Capitalism, climate change and the accounting revolution that can save the planet*, Crows Nest, NSW: Allen & Unwin.

Goodall, Chris (2016). *The Switch: How solar, storage and new tech means cheap power for all*, London: Profile Books.

Goodley, Simon (2015). "Revealed: How Sports Direct stripped USC assets before it collapsed". *The Guardian*. 11 December. https://tinyurl.com/y2e6sncz. Accessed: 31 July 2021.

Google. (n.d.) "Mission statement". https://about.google/. Accessed: 27 June 2021.

Gorz, A. (1980). *Ecology as Politics*, Montréal: Black Rose Press.

Gow, David (2008). "German government seeks power to veto takeovers by sovereign wealth funds". 21 August. *The Guardian*. https://tinyurl.com/6jabwxs. Accessed: 22 July 2021.

Grantham, Andrew (1998). Privatisation and reorganisation: case studies in rail policy implementation. PhD thesis, University of East Anglia.

Grantham, Andrew (2001). "How Networks Explain Unintended Policy Implementation Outcomes: The Case of UK Rail Privatization." *Public Administration* 79(4): 851–870.

Grey, Chris (2021). "Britain – the neighbour from hell". 9 July. https://tinyurl.com/2vftrz97. Accessed: 20 July 2021.

Hansen, Erik G. and Stefan Schaltegger (2016). "The sustainability balanced scorecard: A systematic review of architecture". *Journal of Business Ethics* 133(2): 193–221.

Harper, Keith (2000). "Stagecoach takes a wrong turn". *The Guardian*. 13 April. https://www.theguardian.com/business/2000/apr/13/2. Accessed: 21 July 2021.

Harrison, Jeffrey S., Douglas A. Bosse and Robert A. Phillips (2010). "Managing for stakeholders, stakeholder utility functions, and competitive advantage". *Strategic Management Journal* 31(1): 58–74.

Harvey, Fiona (2020). "Covid-19 relief for fossil fuel industries risks green recovery plans". *The Guardian*. 6 June. https://tinyurl.com/tprp2pma. Accessed: 16 August 2021.

Harvey, Fiona (2021). "A million young people urge governments to prioritise climate crisis". *The Guardian*. 22 January. https://tinyurl.com/ay9hbj6f. Accessed: 12 June 2021.

Hax, Arnoldo C. and Nicolas C. Majluf (1995a). "The use of the growth-share matrix in strategic planning". In R. G. Dyson, *Strategic Planning: Models and analytical techniques*. Chichester: Wiley: 73–92.

Hax, Arnoldo C. and Nicolas C. Majluf (1995b). "The use of industry attractiveness – Business strength matrix in strategic planning". In R. G. Dyson, *Strategic Planning: Models and analytical techniques*. Chichester: Wiley: 51–71.

HBR (n.d.). "The value chain". https://www.isc.hbs.edu/strategy/business-strategy/Pages/the-value-chain.aspx. Accessed: 17 July 2021.

Henderson, Bruce D. (1979). *Henderson on Corporate Strategy*, Cambridge, MA: Abt Books.

Herscovitch, Lynne and John P. Meyer (2002). "Commitment to organizational change: Extension of a three-component model". *Journal of Applied Psychology* 87(3): 474–487.

Hirst, Paul, Grahame Thompson and Simon Bromley (2009). *Globalization in Question*, Cambridge: Polity.

HM Government (2020). The GB/EU border case studies: The border with the European Union. London: Border Protocol and Delivery Group. https://assets.publishing.service.gov.uk/govern ment/uploads/system/uploads/attachment_data/file/949044/BordersOpModel_Case_Stud ies.pdf. Accessed: 5 September 2021.

Hofstede, Geert (2014a). "10 minutes with Geert Hofstede . . . on power distance". 18 November. https://www.youtube.com/watch?v=DqAJclwfyCw&t=3sAccess. Accessed: 7 November 2021.

Hofstede, Geert (2014b). "10 minutes with Geert Hofstede on uncertainty avoidance". 7 March. https://www.youtube.com/watch?v=fZF6LyGne7Q. Accessed: 7 November 2021.

Hofstede, Geert (2015b). "10 minutes with Geert Hofstede on individualisme versus collectivisme. 18 November. https://www.youtube.com/watch?v=zQj1VPNPHlI&list=PL6gSiOFcJsJGwmD6bA-CySCg51qlc-TrP&index=55. Accessed: 7 November 2021.

Hofstede, Geert (2015c). "10 minutes with . . . Geert Hofstede on masculinity versus femininity". 18 November. https://www.youtube.com/watch?v=Pyr-XKQG2CM. Accessed: 7 November 2021.

Hofstede, Geert (2015d). "10 minutes with Geert Hofstede on long versus short term orientation". 7 March. https://www.youtube.com/watch?v=H8ygYlGslQ4&t=320s. Accessed: 7 November 2021.

Hofstede, Geert (2015e). "10 minutes with Geert Hofstede on indulgence versus restraint". 7 March. https://www.youtube.com/watch?v=V0YgGdzmFtA. Accessed: 7 November 2021

Hofstede, Geert H. (2001). *Culture's Consequences: Comparing values, behaviors, institutions, and organizations across nations*, Thousand Oaks, CA and London: Sage Publications.

Holden, Emily, Amal Ahmed and Brendon Gibbons (2021). "A Texas city had a bold new climate plan – until a gas company got involved". *The Guardian*. 1 March. https://tinyurl.com/ymtbtpcb. Accessed: 5 September 2021.

Hood, Neil, Stephen Young and David Lal (1994). "Strategic evolution within Japanese manufacturing plants in Europe: UK evidence". *International Business Review* 3(2): 97–122.

Hörisch, Jacob and Stefan Schaltegger (2018). "Business, the natural environment and sustainability". In J. S. Harrison, J. B. Barney, R. E. Freeman and R. A. Phillips, *The Cambridge Handbook of Stakeholder Theory*. Cambridge: Cambridge University Press: 132–146.

Hotez, Peter (2021). "The New Abnormal". The Daily Beast. 2 April. https://tinyurl.com/3nju7sw6. Accessed: 7 November 2021.

House, Robert, J, Paul Hanges, J, Mansour Javidan, Peter Dorfman, W and Vipin Gupta, Eds. (2004). *Culture, Leadership, and Organizations: The GLOBE Study of 62 Societies*, Thousand Oaks: Sage Publications.

Howard, Emma, Andrew Wasley and Alexandra Heal (2020). "Revealed: UK banks and investors' $2bn backing of meat firms linked to Amazon deforestation". *The Guardian*. 4 June. https://tinyurl.com/zeae2jp3. Accessed: 5 September 2021.

Huber, Florian (2015). "Duell auf hoher See – Der Kampf um die Brent Spar, WDR". 5 December. https://www.youtube.com/watch?v=KlrXevmfwHM. Accessed: 7 August 2021.

Hunt, Vivian, Dennis Layton and Sara Prince (2014). "Diversity matters, McKinsey & Company". 2 February. https://www.insurance.ca.gov/diversity/41-ISDGBD/GBDExternal/upload/McKin seyDivmatters-201501.pdf Accessed: 7 November 2021

Hunter, Floyd (1953). *Community Power Structure: A study of decision makers*, Chapel Hill, NC: University of North Carolina Press.

Inman, Phillip (2021) "Pressure on UK as Germany backs ending free carbon permits for airlines". *The Guardian*. 6 June. https://tinyurl.com/yu47xv66. Accessed: 7 June 2021.

Intergovernmental Panel on Climate Change (IPCC) (2021). "Climate change 2021: The physical science basis". UNEP/WMO. 7 August. https://tinyurl.com/y5akvyr4. Accessed: 14 August 2021.

Jackson, Terence (2020). "The legacy of Geert Hofstede". *International Journal of Cross Cultural Management: CCM* 20(1): 3–6.

Jacobides, Michael G. (2019). "In the ecosystem economy what's your strategy". *Harvard Business Review* 97(5): 128–137.

Jessop, Bob (2002). *The Future of the Capitalist State*, Oxford: Polity.

Johanson, Jan and Jan-Erik Vahlne (1977). "The internationalization process of the firm – A model of knowledge development and increasing foreign market commitments". *Journal of International Business Studies* 8(1): 23–32.

Jolly, Jasper (2020). "Boeing's 737 Max flies again: But orders are needed to get it off the ground". *The Guardian*. 20 December. https://tinyurl.com/yvmthtfw. Accessed: 7 November 2021.

Judson, Arnold S. (1991). "Invest in a high-yield strategic plan". *The Journal of Business Strategy* 12(4): 34–39.

Kallis, Giorgos, Federico Demaria and Giacomo D'Alisa (2015). "Introduction – Degrowth". In G. Kallis, F. Demaria and G. D'Alisa, *Degrowth: A vocabulary for a new era*. London: Routledge: 1–17.

Kaplan, R. S and D. P Norton (1992). "The balanced socrecard – measures that drive performance". *Harvard Business Review* (January–February): 71–79.

Karlsson, Svenolof and Anders Lugn (n.d.). "Three big decisions". https://tinyurl.com/wxt3hdz8. Accessed: 20 February 2021.

Kelly, Annie (2020). "Garment workers face destitution as Covid-19 closes factories". *The Guardian*. 19 March. https://tinyurl.com/svuckfs8. Accessed: 21 July 2021.

Kelton, Stephanie (2020). *The Deficit Myth: Modern monetary theory and how to build a better economy*, London: John Murray Press.

Kemfert, Claudia (2017). *Das fossile Imperium schlägt zurück: Warum wir die Energiewende jetzt verteidigen müssen*, Hamburg: Murmann Publishers GmbH.

Khan, Mozaffar, George Serafeim and Aaron Yoon (2016). "Corporate sustainability: First evidence on materiality". *The Accounting Review* 91(6): 1697–1724.

Klein, Richard J. T., E. Lisa, F. Schipper and Suraje Dessai (2005). "Integrating mitigation and adaptation into climate and development policy: Three research questions". *Environmental Science & Policy* 8(6): 579–588.

Kollewe, Julia (2011). "Japan earthquake and tsunami forces Toyota to cut production at UK plant". *The Guardian*. 20 April. https://tinyurl.com/yktk7289. Accessed: 21 July 2021.

Kollewe, Julia and Jasper Jolly (2019). "Fiat Chrysler and Peugeot owner PSA agree £35bn merger". 31 October. https://tinyurl.com/32nvbhdk. Accessed: 23 July 2021.

Koperniak, Stefanie (2015). "MIT Climate CoLab, in collaboration with Nike, launches new materials competition". 29 October. https://tinyurl.com/xrwdy5xc. Accessed: 15 August 2021.

Kotter, John (1996). "Transforming organizations". *Executive Excellence* 13(9): 13.

Kratena, Kurt (2004). "'Ecological value added' in an integrated ecosystem–economy model – an indicator for sustainability". *Ecological Economics* 48(2): 189–200.

Kudina, Alina, George S. Yip and Harry G. Barkema (2008). "Born global". *Business Strategy Review* 19(4): 38–44.

Kwahk, Kee-Young and Jae-Nam Lee (2008). "The role of readiness for change in ERP Implementation: Theoretical bases and empirical validation". *Information & Management* 45(7): 474–481.

Laasch, O. and R. Conaway (2017). *Responsible Business: The textbook for management learning, competence and innovation*, Abingdon: Taylor & Francis.

Laker, Ben and Thomas Roulet (2019). "Will the 4-day workweek take hold in Europe?" August. Researchgate.net. https://tinyurl.com/rpfjwhce. Accessed: 5 September 2021.

Lang, Tim (2020). *Feeding Britain: Our food problems and how to fix them*, London: Penguin Books Limited.

Latour, Bruno (2018). *Down to Earth: Politics in the new climatic regime*, Cambridge: Polity Press.

Leahy, Terry (2012). *Management in 10 Words*, London: Random House Business.

Leaver, Adam (2021) "What did Greensill Capital actually do?" *The Guardian*. 15 April. https://tinyurl.com/sdpn9hz6. Accessed: 3 July 2021.

Lee, I-Min, Ralph S. Paffenbarger and Charles H. Hennekens (1997). "Physical activity, physical fitness and longevity". *Aging: Clinical and experimental research* 9(1–2): 2–11.

Lehne, Johanna and Felix Preston (2018). *Making Concrete Change Innovation in Low-carbon Cement and Concrete*. London: Chatham House. 13 June. https://tinyurl.com/jvhd32df. Accessed: 25 July 2021.

Leonard-Barton, Dorothy (1992). "Core capabilities and core rigidities: A paradox in managing new product development". *Strategic Management Journal* 13(S1): 111–125.

Leswing, Kif (2021). "Companies have bid $81 billion for the airwaves to build 5G, and winners will be revealed soon". CNBC. 31 January. https://tinyurl.com/cy3nx69d. Accessed: 23 July 2021.

Levinson, Marc (2016). *The Box: How the shipping container made the world smaller and the world economy bigger – Second edition with a new chapter by the author*, Princeton, NJ: Princeton University Press.

Liesen, Andrea, Frank Figge and Tobias Hahn (2013). "Net present sustainable value: A new approach to sustainable investment appraisal". *Strategic Change* 22(3–4): 175–189.

Llavador, Humberto (2015). *Sustainability for a Warming Planet*, Cambridge, MA: Harvard University Press.

Luehrman, Timothy A. (1998a). "Investment opportunities as real options: Getting started on the numbers". *Harvard Business Review* 76(4): 51–67.

Luehrman, Timothy A. (1998b). "Strategy as a portfolio of real options". *Harvard Business Review* 76(5): 89–99.

Lukes, Steven (2005). *Power: A radical view*, Basingstoke: Palgrave Macmillan.

Luthans, Fred and Bruce J. Avolio (2003). "Authentic leadership development". In K. S. Cameron, J. E. Dutton and R. E. Quinn, *Positive Organizational Scholarship: Foundations of a new discipline*. San Francisco: Barrett-Koehler: 241–261.

Mahdawi, Arwa (2019). "Meet the 'cleanfluencers', the online gurus who like things nice and tidy". *The Guardian*. 29 January. https://tinyurl.com/3es6pecf. Accessed: 16 August 2021.

Malm, Andreas (2016). *Fossil Capital: The rise of steam-power and the roots of global warming*, London: Verso.

Mansfield, Edwin (1985). "How rapidly does new industrial technology leak out?" *The Journal of Industrial Economics* 34(2): 217–223.

Massiot, Aude (2020). "Climate action: The latest target of Europe's fossil fuel lobbyists". *The Guardian*. 4 March. https://tinyurl.com/4h8z3j3r. Accessed: 5 September 2021.

Mattingly, James E., Steven A. Harrast and Lori Olsen (2009). "Governance implications of the effects of stakeholder management on financial reporting". *Corporate Governance: The international journal of business in society* 9(3): 271–282.

Mayer, Colin (2018). *Prosperity: Better business makes the greater good*, Oxford: Oxford University Press.

Mazzucato, Mariana (2018a). *The Entrepreneurial State: Debunking public vs. private sector myths*, London: Penguin Books Limited.

Mazzucato, Mariana (2018b). *The Value of Everything: Making and taking in the global economy*, London: Penguin Books Limited.

McGahan, Anita M. and Michael E. Porter (1997). "How much does industry matter, really?" *Strategic Management Journal* 18: 15–30.

McGreal, Chris (2021). "Big oil and gas kept a dirty secret for decades. Now they may pay the price". *The Guardian*. 30 June. https://tinyurl.com/8yudrtad. Accessed: 30 June 2021.

McSweeney, Ella (2021) "Cows might fly: Ireland to jet calves to Europe to cut travel time". *The Guardian*. 6 March. https://tinyurl.com/7zc7w7s. Accessed: 21 July 2021.

Meadows, Donella H., Dennis L. Meadows, Jørgen Randers and William W Behrens III (1972). *The Limits to Growth: A report for the Club of Rome's project on the predicament of mankind*, New York, NY: Universe Books.

Meagher, Michelle (2020). *Competition is Killing Us: How big business is harming our society and planet – and what to do about it*, London: Penguin Books Limited.

Meer, David (2005). "Enter the 'chief growth officer': Searching for organic growth". *Journal of Business Strategy* 26(1): 13–17.

Meins, Erika, Holger Wallbaum, Regina Hardziewski and Annika Feige (2010). "Sustainability and property valuation: A risk-based approach". *Building Research & Information* 38(3): 280–300.

Mellor, Maria (2020). "Biofuels are meant to clean up flying's carbon crisis. They won't". *Wired*. 12 February. https://www.wired.co.uk/article/biofuels-aviation-carbon-emissions. Accessed 25 July 2021.

Mentzer, John T., William DeWitt, James S. Keebler, Soonhong Min, Nancy W. Nix, Carlo D. Smith and Zach G. Zacharia (2001). "Defining supply chain management". *Journal of Business Logistics* 22(2): 1–25.

Meyer, John W. and Brian Rowan (1977). "Institutionalized organizations: Formal structure as myth and ceremony". *American Journal of Sociology* 83(2): 340–363.

Miles, Samantha (2019). "Stakeholder theory and accounting". In J. S. Harrison, J. B. Barney, R. E. Freeman and R. A. Phillips, *The Cambridge Handbook of Stakeholder Theory*. Cambridge: Cambridge University Press: 173–188.

Mintzberg, Henry (1980). "Structure in 5's: A synthesis of research on organization design". *Management Science* 26(3): 322–341.

Mintzberg, Henry (2015). *Rebalancing Society: Radical renewal beyond left, right, and center*, Oakland, CA: Berrett-Koehler Publishers.

Mintzberg, Henry, Bruce Ahlstrand and Joseph Lampel (2009). *Strategy Safari: Your complete guide through the worlds of strategic management*, Harlow: FT Prentice Hall.

Mintzberg, Henry and James A. Waters (1985). "Of strategies, deliberate and emergent". *Strategic Management Journal* 6(3): 257–272.

Mitchell, Robert K. and Jae Hwan Lee (2018). "Stakeholder identification and its importance in the value creating system of stakeholder work". In J. S. Harrison, J. B. Barney, R. E. Freeman and R. A. Phillips, *The Cambridge Handbook of Stakeholder Theory*. Cambridge: Cambridge University Press: 53–76.

Mitchell, Ronald K., Harry J. Van Buren III, Michelle Greenwood and R. Edward Freeman (2015). "Stakeholder inclusion and accounting for stakeholders". *Journal of Management Studies* 52(7):851–877:53–76.

Moore, Marc T (2017). "Redressing risk oversight failure in UK and US listed companies: Lessons from the RBS and Citigroup litigation". *European Business Organization Law Review* 18(4): 733–759.

Morrow, J. L., David G. Sirmon, Michael A. Hitt and Tim R. Holcomb (2007). "Creating value in the face of declining performance: Firm strategies and organizational recovery". *Strategic Management Journal* 28(3): 271–283.

Moyer, Kathy (1996). "Scenario planning at British Airways – A case study". *Long Range Planning* 29(2): 172–181.

Mylonopoulos, Nikolaos A. and Georgios I. Doukidis (2003). "Introduction to the special issue: Mobile business: Technological pluralism, social assimilation, and growth". *International Journal of Electronic Commerce* 8(1): 5–22.

Naughton, John (2021a). "Apple comes out swinging in the duel of the data titans". *The Guardian*. 1 May. https://tinyurl.com/v2fsap8s. Accessed: 21 August 2021.

Naughton, John (2021b). "Welcome to DarkSide – and the inexorable rise of ransomware". *The Guardian*. 15 May 2021. https://tinyurl.com/y5whjfua. Accessed: 5 July 2021.

Nauman, Billy, Patrick Temple-West and Kristen Talman (2021). "Exxon shareholder victory charts new course for ESG advocates". *Financial Times*. 28 May.

Ndubisi, N. O. and Sumesh R. Nair (2009). "Green entrepreneurship (GE) and green value added (GVA): A conceptual framework". *International Journal of Entrepreneurship* 13(1): 21–34.

New Economics Foundation (2009). *Measuring Value: A guide to Social Return on Investment (SROI)*. 11 May. https://neweconomics.org/2009/05/guide-social-return-investment. Accessed: 7 November 2021.

Newcombe, Robert (2003). "From client to project stakeholders: A stakeholder mapping approach". *Construction Management and Economics* 21(8): 841–848.

Nicholas, John M. and Herman Steyn (2017). *Project Management for Engineering, Business and Technology*, London: Routledge.

Nicholson, Rebecca (2019). "Jean Paul Gaultier, challenging those who churn out fast fashion". *The Guardian*. 6 July. https://tinyurl.com/udtcnxtf. Accessed: 20 July 2021.

Nordhaus, William D. (2013). *The Climate Casino: Risk, uncertainty, and economics for a warming world*, New Haven, CT: Yale University Press.

Norton-Griffiths, Michael and Clive Southey (1995). "The opportunity costs of biodiversity conservation in Kenya". *Ecological Economics* 12(2): 125–139.

O'Carroll, Lisa (2021). "Sussex medicines firm takes production line abroad in white van to beat Brexit ban". *The Guardian*. 21 February. https://tinyurl.com/3km6c97w. Accessed: 21 July 2021.

O'Dea, S. (2020). *Smartphone Market Share Worldwide by Vendor 2009–2020, Statista*. 11 August. https://tinyurl.com/hjzuase9. Accessed: 7 November 2021.

O'Neill, Daniel W., Andrew L. Fanning, William F. Lamb and Julia K. Steinberger (2018). "A good life for all within planetary boundaries". *Nature Sustainability* 1(2): 88–95.

Obersteiner, M., Azar Ch, P. Kauppi, K. Möllersten, J. Moreira, S. Nilsson, P. Read, K. Riahi, B. Schlamadinger, Y. Yamagata, J. Yan and J. P. van Ypersele (2001). "Managing climate risk". *Science* 294(5543): 786–787.

Office for National Statistics (ONS) (2020). "Ethnicity pay gaps: 2019". London: Office for National Statistics. https://file:///C:/Users/ag155/Downloads/Ethnicity%20pay%20gaps%202019.pdf Access.

Oreg, Shaul, Maria Vakola and Achilles Armenakis (2011). "Change recipients' reactions to organizational change: A 60-year review of quantitative studies". *The Journal of Applied Behavioral Science* 47(4): 461–524.

Orlikowski, Wanda J. (1996). "Improvising organizational transformation over time: A situated change perspective". *Information Systems Research* 7(1): 63–92.

Overend, Jonathan (2021). "Emergency on Planet Sport". NinetyFour19 Productions, 22 January. https://emergency-on-planet-sport.simplecast.com/. Accessed: 7 November 2021.

Özel, T., P. J. Bártolo, E. Ceretti, J. De Ciurana Gay, C. A. Rodriguez and J. V. L. Da Silva (2016). *Biomedical Devices: Design, prototyping, and manufacturing*, Hoboken, NJ: Wiley.

Özkan, Gülsel and Ludger Pfanz (2010). "Brent Spar Greenpeace vs. Shell". https://www.youtube.com/watch?v=KToV-c8uvPc. Accessed: 7 August 2021

Parida, Bhubaneswari, S. Iniyan and Ranko Goic (2011). "A review of solar photovoltaic technologies". *Renewable and Sustainable Energy Reviews* 15(3): 1625–1636.

Parker, Martin (2018). *Shut Down the Business School: What's wrong with management education*, London: Pluto Press.

Partridge, Joanna (2020). "Government to develop £100m Covid-19 vaccine manufacturing centre". *The Guardian*. 23 July. https://tinyurl.com/pn9467fc. Accessed: 5 September 2021

Pascale, Richard T. (1984). "Perspectives on strategy: The real story behind Honda's success". *California Management Review* 26(3): 47–72.

Pearce, John A. and Keith Robbins (1993). "Toward Improved theory and research on business turnaround". *Journal of Management* 19(3): 613–636.

Penrose, Edith T. (1959). *The Theory of the Growth of the Firm*, Oxford: Basil Blackwell.

Perez-Solero, Ricardo (2020). "Can Spain fix its worst ecological crisis by making a lagoon a legal person?" *The Guardian*. 18 November. https://tinyurl.com/t5t9z9u6. Accessed: 27 June 2021.

Perraudin, Frances (2019). "Low pay in the garment industry still a reality despite pledges – study". *The Guardian*. 30 May. https://tinyurl.com/3usuuukd. Accessed: 22 July 2021.

Peteraf, Margaret A. and Jay B. Barney (2003). "Unraveling the resource-based tangle". *Managerial and Decision Economics* 24(4): 309–323.

Phillips, Robert A. and Joel Reichart (2000). "The environment as a stakeholder? A fairness-based approach". *Journal of Business Ethics* 23(2): 185–197.

Pinkse, Jonatan and Ans Kolk (2012). "Addressing the climate change – Sustainable development nexus: The role of multistakeholder partnerships". *Business & Society* 51(1): 176–210.

Poelhekke, Steven (2019). "How expensive should CO2 be? Fuel for the political debate on optimal climate policy". *Heliyon* 5(11): e02936–e02936.

Porter, Lyman W., Richard M. Steers, Richard T. Mowday and Paul V. Boulian (1974). "Organizational commitment, job satisfaction, and turnover among psychiatric technicians". *Journal of Applied Psychology* 59(5): 603–609.

Porter, Michael E. (1980). *Competitive Strategy: Techniques for analyzing industries and competitors*, New York, NY: Free Press.

Porter, Michael E. (1990). The Competitive Advantage of Nations, Basingstoke: The Macmillan Press

Porter, Michael E. (1998). On Competition. Boston, MA: A Harvard Business Review Book

Porter, Michael E. (2008). "The five competitive forces that shape strategy". *Harvard Business Review* 86(1): 78–93.

Porter, Michael E. and Mark R. Kramer (2011). "Creating shared value: How to reinvent capitalism – and unleash a wave of innovation and growth". *Harvard Business Review* 89(1/2) (January–February): 63–77.

Prahalad, C. K. and Gary Hamel (1990). "The core competence of the corporation". *Harvard Business Review* 68(3): 79–91.

Prahalad, Combatore K. and Harvey C. Fruehauf (2005). *The Fortune at the Bottom of the Pyramid*, Philadelphia, PA: Wharton School Publishing.

Pratley, Nils (2019). "Cobham's demise could herald a flood of private equity takeovers". *The Guardian*. 25 July. https://tinyurl.com/2yh99pzu. Accessed: 27 June 2021.

Pratley, Nils (2020a). "Grounded easyJet faces further turbulence with Stelios negotiations". *The Guardian*. 30 March. https://tinyurl.com/xhme2mxc. Accessed: 27 June 2021.

Pratley, Nils (2020b). "AstraZeneca success should prompt review of takeover rules". *The Guardian*. 29 April. https://tinyurl.com/9a8kavah. Accessed: 27 June 2021.

Pratley, Nils (2021). "How did a green, newbie hedge fund out-play Exxon so comprehensively?" *The Guardian*. 27 May. https://tinyurl.com/2m8xps77. Accessed: 27 June 2021.

Pulkkinen, Levi (2021). "'We thought it wouldn't affect us': Heatwave forces climate reckoning in Pacific north-west". *The Observer*. 3 July. https://tinyurl.com/3uzjz6jr. Accessed: 3 July 2021.

Rachinger, Michael, Romana Rauter, Christiana Müller, Wolfgang Vorraber and Eva Schirgi (2019). "Digitalization and its influence on business model innovation". *Journal of Manufacturing Technology Management* 30(8): 1143–1160.

Rawls, John (1999). *A Theory of Justice*, Oxford: Oxford University Press.

Raworth, Kate (2017). *Doughnut Economics: Seven ways to think like a 21st-century economist / Kate Raworth*, London: Random House Business Books.

Reid, Carlton (2021). "Brexit halts home sales of made-in-England brooks bicycle saddles". Forbes. 2 January. https://tinyurl.com/cjwc2s2d. Accessed: 22 July 2021.

Reuters (2018). "Pfizer bets on biotech flu vaccine in $425 million BioNTech alliance". Reuters. 16 August. https://tinyurl.com/5ckwk2hz. Accessed: 23 July 2021.

Reuters (2020). "Germany tightens rules on foreign takeovers". Reuters. 8 April. https://tinyurl.com/5e2e8u4s. Accessed: 22 July 2020.

Reuters (2021). "Boeing says it will make planes able to fly on 100% biofuel by 2030". *The Guardian*. 23 January. https://tinyurl.com/272uvszd. Accessed: 24 July 2021.

Rodrik, Dani (2007). "The inescapable trilemma of the world economy". *Dani Rodrik's Weblog: Unconventional thoughts on economic development and globalization*. 27 June. https://rodrik.typepad.com/dani_rodriks_weblog/2007/06/the-inescapable.html. Accessed: 22 July 2021.

Rodrik, Dani (2012). *The Globalization Paradox: Why global markets, states, and democracy can't coexist*, Oxford: Oxford University Press.

Rodrik, Dani (2015). "Dani Rodrik: Globalisation – the trade-offs". YouTube. 21 July 2021. https://www.youtube.com/watch?v=LRDIejhdtYk.

Rodrik, Dani (2016). "Brexit and the globalization trilemma". *Dani Rodrik's weblog*. https://rodrik.typepad.com/dani_rodriks_weblog/2016/06/brexit-and-the-globalization-trilemma.html.

Rogers, Everett M. (1995). *Diffusion of Innovations*, New York, NY: The Free Press.

Rosenberg, Mike (2016). *Strategy and Sustainability: A hardnosed and clear-eyed approach to environmental sustainability for business*, UK: Palgrave Macmillan UK.

Rothwell, Roy (1994). "Towards the fifth-generation innovation process". *International Marketing Review* 11(1): 7–31.

Roulet, Thomas and Joel Bothello (2020). "Why 'de-growth' shouldn't scare businesses". 14 February. https://hbr.org/2020/02/why-de-growth-shouldnt-scare-businesses. Accessed: 5 February 2021.

Roy, Tirthankar (2016). *The East India Company: The world's most powerful corporation*, Penguin Books Limited.

Ruddick, Graham (2017) "Peugeot owner PSA close to deal to buy Vauxhall and Opel". *The Guardian*. 4 March. https://tinyurl.com/2eyzukcu. Accessed: 5 August 2021.

Rugman, Alan M., Simon Collinson and Richard M. Hodgetts (2006). *International Business*, Harlow: Financial Times Prentice Hall.

Rumelt, Richard P. (1991). "How much does industry matter?" *Strategic Management Journal* 12(3): 167–185.

Sainato, Michael (2020). "'I can't get above water': How America's chicken giant Perdue controls farmers". *The Guardian*. 14 March. https://tinyurl.com/7dhjvvs8. Accessed: 6 July 2021.

Salam, Erum (2021). "Millions without power and 21 dead as ferocious winter weather sweeps US". *The Guardian*. 17 February. https://tinyurl.com/y6ppsntv. Accessed: 12 June 2021.

Samadi, Sascha (2018). "The experience curve theory and its application in the field of electricity generation technologies – A literature review". *Renewable and Sustainable Energy Reviews* 82: 2346–2364.

Sarwary, Zahida (2019). "Capital budgeting techniques in SMEs: A literature review". *Journal of Accounting and Finance* 19(3): 97–114.

Schattschneider, E. E (1975). *The Semisovereign People: A realist's view of democracy in America*, Hinsdale, IL: Dryden Press.

Schmid, Stefan (2013). *Strategien der Internationalisierung*, München: Oldenbourg Wissenschaftsverlag.

Schoenmaker, Dirk and Willem Schramade (2018). *Principles of Sustainable Finance*, Oxford: Oxford University Press.

Schumpeter (2014). "Unpacking Lego: How the Danish firm became the world's hottest toy company". *The Economist*. 8 March.

Schumpeter (2018) "What Natarajan Chandrasekaran must do next at Tata". *The Economist*. 10 February.

Segrestin, Blanche (2005). "Partnering to explore: The Renault–Nissan alliance as a forerunner of new cooperative patterns". *Research Policy* 34(5): 657–672.

Shaxson, Nicholas (2018). *The Finance Curse: How global finance is making us all poorer*, London: Bodley Head.

Shell (2010). "Shell energy scenarios to 2050". 16 February. https://www.youtube.com/watch?v=jQ2uIPeiEYQ&t=96sAccess. Accessed: 5 July 2021.

Simon, Herbert A. (1996). *The Sciences of the Artificial*, Cambridge, MA: The MIT Press.

Stationery Office (2006). Companies Act 2006. Chapter 46. London. UK. https://www.legislation.gov.uk/ukpga/2006/46/pdfs/ukpga_20060046_en.pdf Accessed: 7 November 2021.

Stead, W. Edward and Jean Stead Garner (1992). *Management for a Small Planet: Strategic decision making and the environment*, Newbury Park, CA.

Stern, Carl W. and Michael S. Deimler (2012). *The Boston Consulting Group on Strategy: Classic concepts and new perspectives*, Hoboken, NJ: Wiley.

Stern, Nicholas H. (2006). *Stern Review: The economics of climate change*, London: The Stationery Office.

Stopford, John M. and Louis T. Wells (1972). *Managing the Multinational Enterprise: Organization of the firm and ownership of the subsidiaries*, New York, NY: Basic Books.

Stout, Lynn A. (2013). "The shareholder value myth". *European Financial Review*. https://www.europeanfinancialreview.com/the-shareholder-value-myth-2/. 30 April. Accessed: 30 April 2013.

Sundin, Heidi, Markus Granlund and David A. Brown (2010). "Balancing multiple competing objectives with a balanced scorecard". *European Accounting Review* 19(2): 203–246.

S.P.R.U., Science Policy Research Unit, University of Sussex, H.S.D. Cole, Christopher Freeman, Marie Jahoda and K. L. R. Pavitt (1974). *Thinking about the Future: A critique of the limits to growth*, London: Chatto & Windus for Sussex University Press.

Taleb, Nassim (2007). *The Black Swan: The impact of the highly improbable*, London: Penguin.

Tatoglu, Ekrem, Jedrzej George Frynas, Erkan Bayraktar, Mehmet Demirbag, Sunil Sahadev, Jonathan Doh and S. C. Lenny Koh (2020). "Why do emerging market firms engage in voluntary environmental management practices? A strategic choice perspective". *British Journal of Management* 31(1): 80–100.

Tayeb, Monir (1994). "Japanese managers and British culture: A comparative case study". *International Journal of Human Resource Management* 5(1): 145–166.

Teece, David J. (2018). "Business models and dynamic capabilities". *Long Range Planning* 51(1): 40–49.

Teece, David J. (2019). "A capability theory of the firm: An economics and (strategic) management perspective". *New Zealand Economic Papers* 53(1): 1–43.

Teece, David, Gary J. Pisano and Amy Shuen (1997). "Dynamic capabilities and strategic management". *Strategic Management Journal* 18(7): 509–533.

Teske, Sven (2019). *Achieving the Paris Climate Agreement Goals: Global and regional 100% renewable energy scenarios with non-energy GHG pathways for +1.5°C and +2°C*, Cham: Springer.

Thomson, Lydia (1993). "Reporting changes in the electricity supply industry and privatisation". *Financial Accountability & Management* 9(2): 131–157.

Tidd, Joseph and John R. Bessant (2009). *Managing Innovation: Integrating technological, market and organizational change*, Chichester: John Wiley.

Topham, Gwyn (2019a). "FirstGroup confirms sale of UK bus division to focus on US business". *The Guardian*. 30 May. https://tinyurl.com/344z9pw9. Accessed: 5 September 2021

Topham, Gwyn (2019b) "Uber loses London licence after TfL finds drivers faked identity ". The Guardian. 25 November. https://tinyurl.com/e9emacrp. Accessed: 31 July 2021.

Topham, Gwyn and Mark Sweney (2017). "EasyJet to set up Austrian HQ to operate EU flights after Brexit". *The Guardian*. 14 July. https://tinyurl.com/muvttkwh. Accessed: 22 July 2021.

Trahms, Cheryl A., Hermann Achidi Ndofor and David G. Sirmon (2013). "Organizational decline and turnaround: A review and agenda for future research". *Journal of Management* 39(5): 1277–1307.

Treanor, Jill (2017). "Lloyds shareholders 'mugged' by 2008 HBOS takeover, high court told". *The Guardian*. 18 October. https://tinyurl.com/djk778fu. Accessed: 23 July 2021.

Treasury (2018). *The Green Book: Central government guidance on appraisal and evaluation*, London: H. Treasury.

Tsang, Eric W. K. and Shaker A. Zahra (2008). "Organizational unlearning". *Human Relations* 61(10): 1435–1462.

Tucker, Robert C. (1968). "The theory of charismatic leadership". *Daedalus* 97(3): 731–756.

United Nations (UN) (2010). "Gro Harlem Brundtland – The Environment and the United Nations". *United Nations History*. 14 December 2010. https://vimeo.com/17820951. Accessed: 27 June 2021.

United Nations (UN) (2015). "Paris Agreement". UN. https://unfccc.int/files/essential_background/convention/application/pdf/english_paris_agreement.pdf Accessed: 7 November 2021.

United Nations (UN) (n.d.). "17: Strengthen the means of implementation and revitalize the global partnership for sustainable development". https://sdgs.un.org/goals/goal17. Accessed: 24 July 2021.

United Nations Environment Programme (UNEP) (1987). "Montreal Protocol on Substances that Deplete the Ozone Layer". 16 September 1987. https://treaties.un.org/Pages/ViewDetails.aspx?src=TREATY&mtdsg_no=XXVII-2-a&chapter=27&clang=_en Accessed: 5 September 2021.

Unilever (n.d.). "Purpose, values & principles". https://www.unilever.co.uk/about/who-we-are/purpose-and-principles/. Accessed: 24 July 2021.

Untiedt, Robert, Michael Nippa and Ulrich Pidun (2011). "Corporate Portfolio Analysis Tools Revisited: Assessing Causes that May Explain Their Scholarly Disdain: Corporate Portfolio Analysis Tools." *International journal of management reviews: IJMR* 14(3): 263–279

Utterback, James M. and William J. Abernathy (1975). "A dynamic model of process and product innovation". *Omega* 3(6): 639–656.

Varoufakis, Yanis (2020). *Another Now: Dispatches from an alternative present*, London: Bodley Head.

ViacomCBS (2019). "ViacomCBS announces completion of the merger of CBS and Viacom". 4 December. https://tinyurl.com/tuvs3fzz. Accessed: 23 July 2021.

von Hippel, Erik (2005). *Democratizing Innovation*, MIT Press.

Waddock, Sandra and Andreas Rasche (2012). *Building the Responsible Enterprise: Where vision and values add value*, Stanford, CA: Stanford University Press.

Wall, Tom (2020). "'We won't be cash cows': UK students plan the largest rent strike in 40 years". *The Guardian*. 6 December. https://tinyurl.com/nr6m95bp. Accessed: 16 August 2021.

Wallace-Wells, David (2019). *The Uninhabitable Earth: A story of the future*, UK: Allen Lane.

Walsh, Philip R. (2005). "Dealing with the uncertainties of environmental change by adding scenario planning to the strategy reformulation equation". *Management Decision* 43(1): 113–122.

Wasley, Andrew and Alexandra Heal (2020). "Revealed: Development banks funding industrial livestock farms around the world". *The Guardian*. 22 July. https://tinyurl.com/3pc9u5nv. Accessed: 12 June 2021.

World Commission on Environment and Development (WCED) (1987). *Our Common Future*, Oxford: Oxford University Press.

Weihrich, Heinz (1982). "The TOWS matrix – A tool for situational analysis". *Long Range Planning* 15(2): 54–66.

Wenger, E. (1998). *Communities of Practice: Learning, meaning, and identity*, Cambridge: Cambridge University Press.

Wernerfelt, Birger (1984). "A resource-based view of the firm". *Strategic Management Journal* 5(2): 171–180.

West, Joel and Marcel Bogers (2014). "Leveraging external sources of innovation: A review of research on open innovation". *The Journal of Product Innovation Management* 31(4): 814–831.

Wheelwright, Steven C. and Kim B. Clark (1992). *Revolutionizing Product Development*, New York, NY: Free Press.

Wind, Yoram, Vijay Mahajan and Donald J. Swire (1983). "An empirical comparison of standardized portfolio models". *Journal of Marketing* 47(2): 89–99.

Womack, James P., Daniel T. Jones and Daniel Roos (1990). *The Machine that Changed the World*, New York, NY: Rawson Associates.

Wood, Zoe (2019). "Sainsbury's-Asda merger blocked by competition watchdog". *The Guardian*. 25 April. https://tinyurl.com/4d8n6tdz. Accessed: 16 August 2021.

Wooldridge, Frank (2011). "Dual board system under German law". *Amicus curiae (Bicester, England)* 2005(60): 31–32.

World Business Council for Sustainable Development and World Resources Institute (2015). "The Greenhouse Gas Protocol, revised edition". https://ghgprotocol.org/sites/default/files/stand ards/ghg-protocol-revised.pdf. Accessed: 10 November 2021.

World Resources Institute (2015). "GHG Protocol Scope 2 guidance". https://ghgprotocol.org/ scope_2_guidance. 26 September. Accessed: 7 November 2021.

World Resources Institute and World Business Council for Sustainable Development (2011). "Corporate value chain (scope 3) accounting and reporting standard". September. https:// ghgprotocol.org/standards/scope-3-standard. Accessed: 5 September 2021.

WRAP (2012). "Valuing our clothes, the true cost of UK fashion retail". https://tinyurl.com/ 5y6bwryn. Accessed: 5 September 2021.

Wright-Mills, Charles (1959). *The Power Elite*, London: Oxford University Press.

Young, Paul J., Anna B. Harper, Chris Huntingford, Nigel D. Paul, Olaf Morgenstern, Paul A. Newman, Luke A. Oman, Sasha D. Madronich and Rolando R. Garcia (2021). "The Montreal Protocol protects the terrestrial carbon sink". *Nature* 596(7872): 384–388.

YouTube (1964). "The Hondells – little Honda". https://www.youtube.com/watch?v=WwWa POlzWnI. 15 Jun 2010. Accessed: 22 July 2021.

Yukl, Gary (1999). "An evaluation of conceptual weaknesses in transformational and charismatic leadership theories". *The Leadership Quarterly* 10(2): 285–305.

Zorzut, Adrian (2020). "Spanish foreign minister praised for explanation of deadlock in Brexit trade talks Author Picture Icon". *The New European*. 14 December. https://tinyurl.com/sjbaazhp. Accessed: 5 September 2021.

List of abbreviations

3PL	third-party logistics
AI	artificial intelligence
ASA	American Standards Association
B2B	business-to-business
BCG	Boston Consulting Group
BECCS	bioenergy with carbon capture and storage
BSC	balanced scorecard
CEO	chief executive officer
CFC	chlorofluorocarbons
COP	Conference of the Parties (United Nations)
CR	contingent reward
CSF	critical success factor
CSI	cement sustainability initiative
CSR	corporate social responsibility
DCF	discounted cash flow
ECB	European Central Bank
EE	emerging economy
ERP	enterprise resource planning
ESG	environmental, social and governance
ETC	Energy Transitions Commission
EU	European Union
EV	electric vehicles
FDI	foreign direct investment
GATT	General Agreement on Tariffs and Trade
gComms	global commons
GDP	gross domestic product
GFANZ Alliance	Glasgow Financial Alliance
GHG	greenhouse gases
GLOBE	Global Leadership and Organizational Behavior Effectiveness
GMO	genetically modified organism
GNU	GNU's Not Unix! (completely free software operating system)
GPI	genuine progress indicator
GRI	Global Reporting Initiative
GUI	graphical user interface
HBR	*Harvard Business Review*
HBS	Harvard Business School
HCFCs	hydrochlorofluorocarbons
HRM	human resource management
ICC	International Criminal Court
ICTs	information and communication technologies
IDV	Individualism versus Collectivism
IEA	International Energy Agency
IFC	International Finance Corporation
IIRC	International Integrated Reporting Council
IMF	International Monetary Fund
IoT	Internet of Things
IP	intellectual property

https://doi.org/10.1515/9783110718430-016

IPCC	United Nations' Intergovernmental Panel on Climate Change
ISEW	Index of Sustainable Economic Welfare
ISIC	International Standard Industrial Classification of All Economic Activities
ISO	International Organization for Standardization
IVR	indulgence versus restraint
JV	joint venture
KPI	Key Performance Indicator
LTO	Long Term Orientation versus Short Term Normative Orientation
MARAD	United States Maritime Administration
MAS	Masculinity versus Femininity
MBE	management by exception
MIT	Massachusetts Institute of Technology
NACE	Statistical Classification of Economic Activities in the European Community
NDC	nationally determined contribution
NDTA	National Defense Transportation Association
NGFS	Network for Greening the Financial System
NGOs	non-governmental organizations
NIP	Northern Ireland Protocol
NPSV	net present sustainable value
NPV	net present value
OD	organization development
OECD	Organisation for Economic Co-operation and Development
OPEC	Organization of the Petroleum Exporting Countries
OS	operating system
PDI	power distance index
PerCap	Personal Capital
PESTEL	Political, Economic, Social, Technological, Environmental, and Legal
PPE	personal protective equipment
PUV	perceived use value
RBV	resource-based view (of the firm)
RoI	Return on Investment
SA	strategic alliance
SASB	Sustainability Accounting Standards Board
SBSC	sustainability balanced scorecard
SBU	strategic business unit
SDGs	United Nations' Sustainable Development Goals
SIC	Standard Industrial Classification
SIG	special interest group
SME	small medium-sized enterprise
SPRU	Science Policy Research Unit (University of Sussex)
SROI	Social Return on Investment
STEM	science, technology, engineering and maths
SWOT	strengths, weaknesses, opportunities, and threats
TOWS	threats, opportunities, weaknesses, and strengths
TQM	total quality management
Uac	Uncertainty acceptance
UAI	Uncertainty Avoidance Index
Uav	Uncertainty avoidance
UBI	universal basic income

UK	United Kingdom
UN	United Nations
UNEP	United Nations Environment Programme
UNCC	United Nations Climate Change
UNFCCC	United Nations Framework Convention on Climate Change
VAT	value-added tax
VC	venture capital
VEM	voluntary environmental management
VRIN	valuable, rare, inimitable, and non-substitutable
VRIO	valuable, rare, inimitable resources, and organization
WCED	World Commission on Environment and Development
WEF	World Economic Forum
WHO	World Health Organization
WMO	World Meteorological Organization
WRAP	Waste & Resources Action Programme
WTO	World Trade Organization
WWII	World War II

List of figures

https://doi.org/10.1515/9783110718430-017

List of tables

https://doi.org/10.1515/9783110718430-018

Index

https://doi.org/10.1515/9783110718430-019